P9-CFO-080

More Praise for
Imagine It Forward

"*Imagine It Forward* offers an experienced look at how nonlinear, ever evolving change saved one of America's oldest, most traditional companies and brought it into the digital, socially conscious, irreverent era we now live in. Beth Comstock's account of her unconventional career at a very conventional corporation, General Electric, is frank, funny, and spot-on about the need to abandon the top-down methods of the past in favor of greater collaboration, disruption, and prioritizing the needs and wants of customers and consumers over profit."
>—Joi Ito, director, MIT Media Lab, and author of *Whiplash*

"Beth is a true force—smart, practical, and most of all, she inspires executions in the new business world. There are few people who I think 'get it', and she's at the top of that list."
>—Gary Vaynerchuk, entrepreneur and author of *Crushing It!*

"*Imagine It Forward* offers good examples of teaching bravery not perfection—in education and work. Beth offers valuable lessons that should help readers challenge themselves to risk more in pursuit of a better future for themselves and their organizations."
>—Reshma Saujani, founder and CEO of Girls Who Code

"Beth Comstock has a track record of innovating, leading, and being an agent of change. In *Imagine It Forward,* she proposes thought provoking ways to envision your future and build strategy around it."
>—Sophia Amoruso, *New York Times* bestselling author
>of *#GIRLBOSS* and founder of Nasty Gal

Imagine It Forward

Imagine It Forward

Courage, Creativity, and the Power of Change

Beth Comstock

with Tahl Raz

CURRENCY
NEW YORK

Copyright © 2018 by BeeCom Media LLC

All rights reserved.
Published in the United States by Currency, an imprint of the Crown
Publishing Group, a division of Penguin Random House LLC, New York.
crownpublishing.com

CURRENCY and its colophon are trademarks of
Penguin Random House LLC.

Currency books are available at special discounts for bulk purchases for sales
promotions or corporate use. Special editions, including personalized covers,
excerpts of existing books, or books with corporate logos, can be created in
large quantities for special needs. For more information, contact Premium
Sales at (212) 572-2232 or e-mail specialmarkets@penguinrandomhouse.com.

Library of Congress Cataloging-in-Publication Data
Names: Comstock, Beth, author. | Raz, Tahl, author.
Title: Imagine it forward : courage, creativity, and the power of change /
  Beth Comstock, Tahl Raz.
Description: 1 Edition. | New York : Currency, 2018. | Includes index.
Identifiers: LCCN 2018001839| ISBN 9780451498298 (hardback) | ISBN
  9780451498304 (eISBN)
Subjects: LCSH: Organizational change. | Decision making. | Management. |
Success in business. | BISAC: BUSINESS & ECONOMICS / Management.
  | BUSINESS & ECONOMICS / Entrepreneurship. | BIOGRAPHY &
  AUTOBIOGRAPHY / Business.
Classification: LCC HD58.8 .C6486 2018 | DDC 658.4/06—dc23
  LC record available at https://lccn.loc.gov/2018001839

ISBN 978-0-451-49829-8
Ebook ISBN 978-0-451-49830-4
International edition 978-1-9848-2242-0

Printed in the United States of America

Jacket design and art by Rodrigo Corral Studio

10 9 8 7 6 5 4 3 2

First Edition

To Katie and Meredith
Your imagination and courage inspire me

CONTENTS

*The future is not in our stars but in our
imaginations, and our actions.*

SECTION III
Agitated Inquiry

*Innovation is the result of seeking out tension, not avoiding it.
It's not about reassurance or consensus—it often encourages
confrontation.*

SECTION IV
Storycraft

*You have to adapt your narrative to help the people in an
organization understand their world. That, in turn, will change
how they act in order to create a different, better future.*

SECTION V

Creating a New OS

Share a new mind-set, spreading ideas bottom-up and outside-in,
finding dedicated agents of change within the company to make the
story their own.

If you see a better way, you have an obligation to
pursue it. That's the change-maker's rallying cry.

CLOSING THE IMAGINATION GAP

I was able to see the sunset fade from red to purple as the plane began to descend over the rolling hills of Northern Virginia. A few moments later we were down, puttering to a stop in a small airstrip carved into rural Virginia farmland barely 40 miles from where I'd grown up.

A man in a blue jumpsuit waved me over after the pilot had helped me down the plane's narrow stairs to the grass. As I walked toward him, carrying my overstuffed tote bag, notes hastily crammed in the side pocket, I heard the plane's engine fire back up. Soon it was riding up over the trees, and banking into the purple sky.

"Anything I need to know?" I asked.

"Sorry, ma'am. They just pay me to bring the planes in and then guide them back out," he said.

I didn't know exactly who was going to pick me up, and I had no number to call. All I knew was that the CIA wanted my advice. I closed my eyes and inhaled the autumn air. Wild grasses, oak and pine trees. The smell of home.

Soon a black SUV with tinted windows pulled up in front of me. Three men get out, each in a dark jacket and, of course, aviator-style glasses. "Beth? Come with us."

We talked a bit about the weather, about my hometown (where one of them lived), before I turned my mind to the notes I'd scribbled down after a brief talk with the CIA deputy director a few days before:

> We're siloed. We need to collaborate more with each other and across the agency.
>
> It's hard to keep up with the pace of change. We're in the business of secrets and yet we need to continually open up to new perspectives, to taking risks, and being ready when change shows up.
>
> We need to continually reinvent ourselves.

Although it would be my first time lecturing our nation's spymasters, the worries they expressed were the same urgent concerns I have been hearing from organizations and businesses around the world: How do we navigate the relentless pace of change? How can we open up our culture and innovate more quickly? How do we stay relevant in a world that is being constantly disrupted?

Inside a CIA training center, about thirty-five regional leaders were having predinner cocktails. I've been brought into this kind of gathering on hundreds of occasions. Sometimes I play the spark, an instigator to seed new ideas and directions for change. Sometimes I'm brought in to play the explorer, teaching others the process I use to truffle-hunt for new ideas. Other times I'm the champion, preaching the need for leaders to support the lonely voices at the edge that are calling on their organizations to change. And sometimes my role is to coach a team to create the prototypes that will serve as the "proof points" that justify a leap into the new.

As we chatted, they didn't talk about what they did, which I understood, of course. But I found it telling how eager they were to steer the conversation away from the work I did—spreading change. It's not polite dinner conversation. It's easier to keep your nose to the grindstone, do what you are doing and do it well, than it is to lift your head up and figure out where you or your organization is going and what the future may bring. It's usually not until an organization is engulfed by chaos or, more simply, wakes up to a stark reality that it has been left behind, that it begins to seek a new way forward. And by that point it lacks either the energy or the time to make it through to the other side. Fifty years ago, the life expectancy of a Fortune 500 firm was around seventy-five years; now it's less than fifteen. And the sobering reality is that the world is never going to be slower in terms of change than it is today. Futurist Ray Kurzweil predicts that "we won't experience 100 years of progress in the 21st century—it will be more like 20,000 years of progress." What we are witnessing is the battle for the future of many of our businesses.

One of the defining characteristics of our new age of rapid-fire change is that leaders, managers, and employees have to be able to move forward without having all the answers. They have to feel their way in the dark. It is very disconcerting, particularly when you have to do it at full speed. They know they need to be more inventive to succeed, but they admit to being uncomfortable with creative people and their rule-breaking ways. They realize they need to partner more with other companies, but are afraid of reaching beyond their own insular communities. They know they need to make changes, but want proof of success before doing so.

I've been courting change my whole career. It has taken me from media manager to Business Innovations leader and vice chair for GE, a company that lived through 125 years of change and adaption. I'm known as a change wrangler, the person who chases tornados

What we are witnessing
is the battle for
the future of our
businesses.

of disruption, driving full speed into the funnel clouds. Not a week goes by when I don't hear from some leader or practitioner seeking advice on how to reinvent their way forward. An Australian official asks me to be part of a working group to outline a vision for Australia 2030; they want to know how to "surf the crest of the wave of change." A team manager asks me how to convince her boss to pursue a big idea—the customer needs it desperately. An executive at a major broadcast network calls me to brainstorm how to help her people spot disrupters before the competition does. An energy executive corners me after the Saudis initiated a major OPEC price cut and caused a collapse in oil prices. "How the hell did I miss that?" he wondered.

I've learned that you have to pay close attention to what's emerging before it turns into a crisis or an emergency for your company or industry. Things are good until they aren't. The question about how to respond to the uncertainty and the chaos is coming from many quarters now: the taxi industry, the media world, big box and one-store retail, the post office, the school board. "How do I get a handle on change? How do we adapt, evolve, thrive?"

As the CIA dinner came to dessert, I walked to a lectern at the front of the room. I smiled at their skeptical expressions and said hello. I was about to tell them the message of this book in front of you. But first I was going to have to answer two questions that you probably have as well:

Why are so many of our organizations shortsighted—unable to see around corners and unable to move forward in the face of accelerating change?

And, why do people think I have some of the answers that will lead them to the way forward?

About three years after the September 11 attacks, an independent commission issued a report that cited "deep institutional failings" at the CIA leading up to the attacks. The most important failure, it said, was "one of imagination."

What started out as seemingly isolated, episodic incidents has come to resemble an epidemic. We are failing in government, failing in education, and, too often, failing in business. Thrust into an unpredictable and profoundly complex world, the nature of today's challenges cannot be solved by yesteryear's tried-and-true expertise. Instead of investing more resources in understanding the art and science of innovating our way forward, we've doubled down on the diminishing returns of financial engineering.

That is why we are now confronting such a huge gap between the knowledge, critical thinking, problem-solving, and creativity needed to survive the challenges and exploit new opportunities, and our dogged insistence on doing things as they've always been done. I call this *the imagination gap*, where possibility and options for the future go to die. But I refuse to give up on possibility. We have to narrow the gap—that is why I had to write this book.

We must become "change ready"—that is, fearless, perpetually ready to reenvision, rethink, and redesign, whatever we do and wherever we are. We must constantly adapt, discover, think ahead, and iterate. We must meet change early and continually adapt to it. Yes, we must focus on the scaled-operations part of work—we must deliver for our customers and shareowners; but we also need to liberate the forward-thinking parts of business—our ability to evolve, to defy convention, to embrace emerging change. And to do that requires imagination: infusing our work with a disciplined capacity to go beyond what we know and can conceive is possible. And that starts with a shift in mind-set. You must give yourself permission to imagine a new future and act on it.

We've been taught to believe that our capacity for imagination is reserved for artists and inventors. The science on this is clear, however: imaginative thinking is a *universal* human talent, an evolutionary gift handed down to us that has made us who we are, the undisputed champions of adaptation. But with the rise of the Industrial Revolution and the corporation, we lost some of our ability to adapt.

We designed our institutions and our people to function as machines, a reflection of the machine-driven industrial revolution. We've optimized ourselves to maximize standardization, specialization, predictability, productivity, and control. We have tried to take the variability, the improvisation—the human—out of the workplace.

It has made our organizations efficient and predictable. But it has excised the imagination part. We stopped telling stories. We stopped pushing discovery. Our institutions became less imaginative and, in so doing, increasingly lost their ability to collaborate, improvise, and respond to change. That is, to adapt. For over a century, that worked because organizations flourished on repeatability at scale. But recently—say, over the last twenty or thirty years—the pace of change accelerated. Things moved much faster, fueled by advances in technology and digital networks and data that have radically altered the way we—and our colleagues, partners, and customers— behave, live, and work. The nature of change has changed. With more intersections of technology and global humanity, there are exponentially more places for change and chaos to emerge. And also for ingenuity and opportunity.

"It is not the strongest of the species that survives, nor the most intelligent . . ." Charles Darwin wrote. "It is the one that is most adaptable to change. Those who have learned to collaborate and improvise most effectively have prevailed."

Well, Darwin's theories are now having their way with our institutions and businesses. The cogs of those machines—you and me—have been stripped of our unique evolutionary advantage, of our power to create. The research says 75 percent of people in advanced economies feel that they are not meeting their creative potential. We've created legions of managers afraid to absorb new perspectives, unable to work without a script or respond quickly by letting go of strategies that no longer work and embracing new ones that do.

Marry that with the coming onslaught of even more digitization, and automation and artificial intelligence—it means virtually every industry is coming to its point of reckoning. What's more, we face massive and massively complex problems—climate change, economic inequality, global trade—that will require an extraordinary degree of imaginative problem-solving, collaboration, and forward-driven leadership. It will require our most powerful institutions to adopt a more adaptive operating system, one that can unlock the creative potential of all of our people.

We can no longer afford to fail to imagine.

In many ways, I am an unlikely change-maker. I'm fundamentally shy. I didn't go to business school, and I had no formal training when I was tapped by CEO Jeff Immelt to lead marketing and innovation at GE. I lived in the small town of Winchester, Virginia, until I was ready for college. I went to the College of William and Mary in my home state. I liked the comfort of my world; I knew my way around.

It wasn't until my midtwenties that I had to face a big, disruptive life change. A divorced single mother of a three-year-old daughter, I was working in Washington, DC, doing public relations at NBC—then a GE division—when my department was moved to New York. I grabbed the opportunity, even as I was uncertain about what kind of my life my daughter and I would find in an unfamiliar city where I had no family. But in that period, I taught myself the skill that has fueled my career ever since: how to imagine, and then make real, a future I couldn't yet see. I've done it my entire life—from succeeding in roles in which few others saw value to putting crazy ideas out there to embracing change before its time, in clean energy and digital technology. And I've done it wherever I have worked, from CNN to CBS, NBC to GE.

I've had to work hard to excel at reinvention and disruption. But what it instilled in me is an absolute conviction that *anyone* can master the process.

In the seventeen years since Jeff Immelt tapped me in 2001 to lead change at GE, we reimagined, then reengineered the company into the world's first "digital industrial."

We went from seeing 70 percent of our revenue coming from the United States to having 70 percent of it coming from our global operations. We launched the clean-tech initiative Ecomagination, which has generated $270 billion in revenue from clean-tech products, the most of any company in the world. The new GE is developing the Industrial Internet, embedding the company's big machines—everything from MRIs and LED lighting systems to wind turbines and jet engines—software and analytics that make them, and the industries they serve, more predictive and productive.

The GE of today would be barely recognizable to its founder and inventor, Thomas Edison. It is barely recognizable to those of us who were there when the story of *Imagine It Forward* begins. We took a 130-year-old corporation, with more than 300,000 employees, and transformed it from a risk-averse, perfection-seeking organization to one that increasingly encouraged speed, adaptability, iteration, and discovery.

What emerged from my decades as a dedicated change-maker on the front lines of the reinvention of American business is a systematic approach to reinventing business that can be applied to virtually any company in any industry. It can be applied to change how your business grows or learn how to launch a new business line or perform as a more innovative team. I call this approach *imagining it forward*. At heart, it's an orientation to the world based on adaptive problem-solving that makes real a future few can see.

But to be clear: change starts, first, with you. As an individual, as an employee, as a leader. Coming up with new ideas is rarely the problem. What holds all of us back, really, is fear: the attachment to the old, to What We Know. It's the paralysis engendered by resistance from our institutions when we invoke change, from our local middle school to our government to the companies we work for—to, often, everyone around us.

No one is immune to this fear, I discovered, as I pushed for change in myself and across GE.

As I finished this book, GE was undergoing yet another major transformation. I left at the end of 2017, following the departure of Jeff Immelt. The transition to new CEO John Flannery came amidst investor activism and dramatic changes in the energy industry GE serves, reminding us that uncertainty and disruption always lurk.

My goal was never to write a book about best practices at GE, but to write a book about the challenges of change we face in every company, large and small. GE is merely the backdrop, the testing ground for many of these ideas. As it turns out, GE's story, I believe, serves as both an example of success and a cautionary tale—a reminder that change is a never-ending journey. It doesn't stop at the end of a quarter, or a fiscal year. And it is filled with hard work, triumph, surprise, struggle, and heartbreak.

So don't look for a simple victory here; when it comes to transforming a culture, everything does not get neatly wrapped in a bow. Many things worked, and others didn't. Some things won't play out for years, if indeed they are even given the chance to take root. But as time will surely tell, I believe we imagined forward one of the largest, oldest companies in the world, ushering it into a brave new digital process. If no one pushes for it then an organization has no chance to transform itself.

Imagine It Forward tells the story of my multidecade quest to infuse GE, and the broader business world, with this vitally necessary, change-making practice.

I intend to be candid about what has worked and what hasn't, and what it takes to harness the courage, discipline, and skills to keep trying. Throughout the book, I tell my story as a way to offer valuable lessons, as well as simple tools that convert theory to action—what I call challenges—to push yourself further. I've organized the book into five sections that make up the *imagining it forward* approach:

Section I: Self-Permission. Every change-maker is forced to learn to give herself permission to push outside expectations and limitations. I was no exception.

Section II: Discovery. This is the change-making step that makes all the other steps possible. Discovery is about exploring—infusing yourself and your culture with a spirit of inquiry and curiosity, turning the world into a classroom for learning and for unearthing ideas that can make change possible.

Section III: Agitated Inquiry. Innovation is the result of seeking out tension, not avoiding it. Innovation is not about reassurance or consensus; in fact, it often encourages confrontation.

Section IV: Storycraft. Strategy is a story well told. To innovate successfully, you have to adapt your narrative to help the people in an organization understand their world. That, in turn, will change how they act in order to create a different, better future.

Section V: Creating a New OS. Changing an organization's operating system requires adopting a new mind-set—often in an uncertain or difficult environment. That means spreading ideas bottom-up and outside-in, finding dedicated agents of change within the company to make the story their own. It means developing emergent leaders who embrace and inspire a better, more adaptable way of working.

Change is a messy, collaborative, inspiring, difficult, and ongoing process—like everything meaningful that leads to human progress.

Imagine It Forward is the book I wish I'd had before starting my journey. I want to use the stories of change that I instigated and led to inspire others to explore and rethink their own path. I want to put flesh and blood on the ideas and concepts, advocating for a new way of doing things. I know how difficult change is. And how necessary. We can't go on doing things the way we used to—the very ground is shifting daily under our feet. Change is a messy, collaborative, inspiring, difficult, and ongoing process, like everything meaningful that leads to human progress.

My hope is that this book will help everyone, everywhere to learn and master the change-maker's craft. To believe, as I have, that the future is not in our stars but in our imaginations, and our actions.

Self-Permission

CHAPTER 1

REINVENTION

Taking Ownership of My Life

I was leading East Coast entertainment publicity at CBS—the "Tiffany Network"—when I got the call offering me the job as vice president of NBC News Media Relations.

People's resistance to me taking the job—to even considering it—started immediately after I got the call. Totally crazy! Career suicide!

It was late at night as I considered the job, and the resistance from colleagues and friends to my taking it. I know it was late because that's always the time when I try to create the logical rationale for a decision I've already made on instinct. The pros, the cons, every possible scenario. Morning came and the only clarity I had was emotional. I felt it in an almost spiritual way. *I'm taking the job.* I'm going back to NBC, where my career had started.

Only this time, in the fall of 1993, the network was a national disgrace.

We are hardwired to flee ambiguity, chaos, and the unknown.

And yet here I was, running toward a disaster, embracing it. My colleagues and friends were sure it was professional ruin.

Not long before, the NBC news division's *Dateline* program had aired "Waiting to Explode," an investigative report that showed a sedan T-boning a Chevy pickup truck, with the truck erupting in a fiery explosion.

The problem was, the whole thing was a fake. An investigation revealed that NBC News had duct-taped model rocket engines to the truck's frame and initiated the blast with a remote-control device. It took anchors Jane Pauley and Stone Phillips three and a half minutes to issue a full on-air apology—an eternity in TV time— and promise that "unscientific demonstrations" would never again be conducted by NBC.

But the *Dateline* crisis was just the latest in a string of NBC failures that included the highly public and embarrassing departure of David Letterman for CBS, and a ratings dive to third place among the networks. "Morale is in the toilet," a veteran NBC producer told *Entertainment Weekly* at the time, in what became a months-long public flaying. "There's nobody at the rudder."

CBS was the ratings leader. Friends and colleagues thought I was crazy to leave. "I'm worried about you," someone confided. A reporter from the *Wall Street Journal* was even more blunt: "NBC News is washed up." Why would I leave the "Tiffany Network" for a demoralized number three?

And yet, in my gut, I knew this was the job I was meant to take.

Well-meaning colleagues will try to stop you from making these bravely instinctive choices. That's just how it is. Change-making creates resistance. It is against the rules. Change is seen as loss. It is scary.

But you have to learn not to stop yourself. You have to learn to give yourself permission to imagine a better way, to envision opportunity where others see only risk.

It's something I had to learn for myself.

Who are you waiting for to tell you it's okay? Your boss? Your mother? Yoda? Grab your own permission. No one is going to give it to you.

Perhaps the best way to explain why I took the NBC job is to take you back to 1985, to tell you the kind of deeply personal story that doesn't often appear in business books. In this story, I'm hiding behind a closed bedroom door, listening as my husband conveyed my first truly life-changing decision to my mother.

At the time I was in my midtwenties. I'd always followed the rules in my life, kept to the straight and narrow. I did very well in school, got involved in all kinds of clubs and community activities, and I astutely protected my "good girl" reputation. But I'd been beset by the growing realization that, like so many people, I had been keeping myself "small" by pleasing others and fitting in, by looking to see what everyone else was doing before acting, by making sure all I attempted was sanctioned, what nice girls do.

Conformity had created in me an insurmountable fear of being different, of putting myself out there. Every day I was killing off my true self with compromises.

The door was cold against my ear. My mother, at our house for the weekend to visit and care for our daughter, Katie, was sitting in the kitchen with my husband, Dave, as he told her something that I knew wouldn't register: Dave and I were getting divorced. I had decided I needed to leave—without being able to say exactly why.

I was the woman who seemed to have it all at the time: a fancy new home near DC, a seemingly happy marriage to a handsome man of means, a new job as the NBC publicity coordinator, and a beautiful baby daughter. By every normal measure of success, I'd made it. Underneath that success, however, I was filled with despair.

Up to that moment, I'd lived my life more or less by someone else's narrative. A simple story, with defined roles, that led to a simple happy ending. Elegant, without complications. But with every day that passed, I realized just how large the gap was between the story I was expected to follow and the life I actually wanted to live. While I had ideas—I wanted to be a television reporter, specifically a science reporter—mostly, I dreamed of setting out in the world.

Once my father, who was a dentist then, convinced a patient, a news producer who commuted to DC, to have me shadow a reporter. (My dad, a big supporter of my future career, was not afraid to use his unique advantage of extracting promises for his kid while extracting a patient's back molar.) As it turns out, I spent two hours with Diane Sawyer, then a young State Department reporter for CBS, just back from Chad. A few years later, sitting in the auditorium at my sister's high school graduation soon after I graduated from college, I day-dreamed of the career I'd surely have by the time she graduated from college. In my mind's eye, I had the sophisticated worldliness of Diane Sawyer. What big city would I be living in? Would it be New York, where Diane had recently moved? What travel would I be returning from? Keep in mind that at this point I was working two jobs in Richmond—one as a Mexican-restaurant waitress to pay for my second, barely paying job as Jackie of all trades (and on-camera reporter) in a small news service covering the Virginia House of Delegates, which I had landed via a friend of a friend's friend.

I was the daughter of a small-town dentist and a schoolteacher, and while my parents did well and afforded my sister, brother, and me opportunities, we were not wealthy, and certainly not well-connected. My father's other aching-molar patients didn't work in media. I jokingly call my mother "the mayor," because she knows and talks to everyone; our town was our world. While working in the news service, I continued to seek out bigger jobs, perusing the want ads of *Broadcasting* magazine. That's how I came to apply for TV meteorologist in Salisbury, Maryland, where I horribly mis-pronounced the name of the town as I did the on-set interview. In Richmond, I hounded a local TV station's news director with my videotapes, calling him so relentlessly that he lost control. "You look like you're twelve," Mr. Rant barked. "Why would I put anyone like you on camera?" My confidence was shaken, and my fear of striking out into the unknown had held me back. I was happy to say yes to getting married. I was in love and lacked the maturity to ask what that meant beyond saying no to pushing for jobs that would jump-start my career—jobs in TV markets beyond Richmond or Salisbury or locations as exotic as, well, Tulsa, where I had in fact been offered a job.

Dave's outlook didn't change as much as mine did after Katie was born. He still went out, had fun with his friends. I was the earnest wife, and now mother. In fairness to him, I had never declared that I wanted to be otherwise. In fact, I may not have known, or at least been able to articulate it. That was the worst part, being slowly caged by my own passivity. I had a growing, painful sense that another side of me needed to be released, and the only person standing in my way was me.

I don't even remember the conversation we had in which Dave and I decided on a divorce. I initiated the process, but I don't remember the words. I just knew: I. Can't. Be. *This*. Until that moment, my fear had held me in place. I was worried about what my family would think, what my friends would think, what my colleagues would think. I was terrified of traumatizing my daughter. And I was deeply afraid of going against convention.

My mother, knowing me to be shy, had pushed me to be a joiner in my small town, where the ethos was to always say the "right thing." That mentality followed me at school, with friends and teachers who encouraged me to do what I was told, do well, look good, and obey the rules. My school, like most, was pervaded by the myth that rewards are reserved for those who say "I know," instead of reveling in "I don't know" and learning to ask the probing questions.

Wading into the unknown just wasn't a skill I had acquired yet as an ambitious but aimless twenty-three-year-old trying to shake off my limited perspective. So I gravitated to "what was done": I got married to my college boyfriend, Dave. And then not long after, without planning it, I was pregnant. Everything was happening too fast. It was as if someone else was narrating my life.

The moment Katie was born, she created a love in me so strong that it yanked a fierce clarity from my depths. My vague despair morphed to a clear-eyed vision of a future that I knew had little to do with my present. I knew I had to chart my own course, be the captain of my soul. What was clear was that I had to go; what was less clear was where. I had fantasies of fleeing back to Richmond, Katie and me rooming with a high school friend. I was going to start over and this time get that job at the local TV station. When fantasies weren't enough, I'd tell the babysitter that I was going out. I'd drive to the movie theater at the local mall and buy a ticket to an emotional movie like *Terms of Endearment*. And cry in the dark. Alone in every sense.

I came to see that—while incredibly hard—there was nothing shameful about endings or mistakes. It can be a wise decision to leave one path and choose another. Scary, yes, but it can be the first step to something better. And that itself was a massive insight for me: *something better* was a deliberate choice. Already I had a different perspective on reality.

Once I'd spoken the word *divorce* aloud, it didn't feel like as much of a failure to me. I felt free, in a slightly terrified way. Finding the optimism to imagine a better future allowed me the courage I so desperately needed to move forward, as me.

Of course, my new life was no *Eat Pray Love* romantic journey, where I could shrug off my responsibilities in the quest for a sexy guru and the perfect cup of chai. I was *choosing* life as a single mom and just starting out in a career. I rented a little place of our own in Alexandria. I loved every square inch of that tiny house, even with all the pressures of motherhood and work and change. I had bills to pay. (I even had to take out a loan to hire a lawyer to "petition the court" to get *my* surname back.) I was alone. My baby, Katie, was crying. *I* was crying. It was scary. But it was also exhilarating. The thing I'd only imagined was now happening, and I was frozen in disbelief. Now what?

My future was now blank. I would have to write my own narrative. From now on, my story wouldn't be so traditional, or perhaps so elegant, or simple. But that was the point. It was becoming clearer to me that the fullest lives were lived by people not afraid of complication, mistakes, or imperfection.

I threw myself into my work. Basking in my recently acquired publicity job at NBC's Washington news bureau, I began to assert my ambition and test my boundaries.

GE bought NBC the month I started working there. I was hired as a publicity coordinator—a far cry from the globe-trotting television journalist I had wanted to be, but at least I was in the newsroom. (Way in the back, in a micro-cubicle near the filing room, where few people journeyed, but it was just perfect to me.) I had found my way there after a series of jobs, as administrative assistant in a cable television association and as a programming coordinator for cable access community television, like Mike Myers's *Wayne's World* but even wackier. With GE at the helm, things changed quickly. NBC started to employ GE efficiency, and there was a rash of layoffs. Before long I was in charge of the publicity department—actually, I *was* the department. My bosses recognized me as a quick learner, efficient and willing to take on and manage many projects at once, and someone with a growing portfolio of small accomplishments on which to stand. I put out a behind-the-scenes newsletter to share updates across the bureau; I organized new photos so that the journalists looked more contemporary; and after attending the morning editorial meetings, I pitched ideas to the few reporters in DC who covered media, building relationships that NBC hadn't had earlier. For all my shyness, pitching reporters was now my job. That, and the fact that I could do it over the phone, gave me a much-needed dose of courage.

I began traveling to the New York NBC headquarters once a

month. After spending time in New York, all I could think about was how much I wanted to work there.

In early 1988, I got a new boss, an ambitious former lobbyist named J.R. He had landed in the New York mothership, handling corporate communications. He knew that I wanted to be on a bigger stage as well and started to prepare me for the jump. Then, in December 1988, after the first of what would be many annoying negotiations with J.R., I was officially offered the job.

I suppose the decision to move to New York should have terrified me. I was leaving a place I knew, two hours from my parents' house, for one of the largest cities in the world, where I had few friends, no family—and no increased salary to pay for my new life. I would have to get permission from Dave to move our daughter out of state. I was racked with guilt that would shadow me for years. But determined to look forward, I leapt off that cliff.

I've since come to understand that charging into the unknown, optimistically and courageously, with all flags flying, is a *skill*, one that needs to be developed and nurtured, rather than quashed.

By the time I left for New York, I had learned to listen to that inner voice that encouraged me to imagine the future that I could create. The price was to uproot my daughter and start a new life— our life, but also for once, my life.

Ignore the Gatekeepers

A few years ago, I heard the fashion designer Marc Eckō give an amazing talk in which he distinguished between the Gatekeepers in his life—the "thought leaders," the press, the critics—and what he calls the Goalkeepers, the ones who actually matter.

Gatekeepers are those looking to keep hold of the little power they have. They see divergent thinking and action as threatening. They bank on our desire for approval. The worst thing they do is to

Bias for Action

Most people have the notion that only people with real power, those who don't need permission from others, have the ability to act. It's natural to think, "That's the work of 'leaders,' and I'm not that." But once you accept that you're a change-maker, you give yourself the right to confront the unasked questions about whatever work you do—even PR kits. Embracing such a mentality is crucial for anyone who wants to effect change: a parent intervening in her child's school, a mother who demands clean water, an office worker who questions the point of doing reports . . . any one person who steps forward to make a difference on the path to *better*.

My own success is a testament not to an improbable succession of good decisions—I've had plenty of failures—but to a *bias for action*. Steven Pressfield, the author of *The War of Art*, once said that our enemy is not a lack of preparation or the difficulty of a project. "The enemy is our chattering brain," he wrote, "which, if we give it so much as a nanosecond, will start producing excuses, alibis, transparent self-justifications and a million reasons why we can't/shouldn't/won't do what we know we need to do."

I've realized you can't worry so much about making the right decision. What is more important is to develop a habit of acting decisively. It's not that I have less doubt—as with most people, my insecurities run deep—but that I act in spite of it.

create and police the standards that the rest of us accept and internalize. You will find gatekeepers everywhere, in every job, in every classroom, in every family. And sometimes, I discovered, we invite them inside our own minds. When I moved to New York with NBC, I got a PhD in Gatekeepers.

I was still working my way up at NBC, and the opportunities were proving plentiful. The work was intense in the years after GE bought it. Jack Welch had promoted Bob Wright, a GE plastics and finance veteran, to be NBC's president. Bob was a slight man, with nervous energy. Educated as a lawyer, he peppered everyone with a string of questions. I even got a few. As a corporate communications manager, I was now dealing with upper-level NBC executives—and was making small creative moves. One of my "big" ideas was getting varsity sports letters to glue onto the covers of press books as part of a campaign to attract media to a briefing about how great NBC was at reaching college students. It wasn't much, but it was just a little different, and a little edgy and creative in its own small way. I purchased the materials, including fabric peacock icons, with my own money, afraid to ask if it was okay. It was an example of giving myself permission, of not waiting for the office gatekeepers to tell me I could or couldn't do it. But fear meant that I paid for the items myself, as if to inoculate me from potential failure.

At last my life was palpably moving forward. Katie was doing well with the change. We moved to a suburban New Jersey neighborhood with four girls her age on our block. We drove back to DC regularly for her to see Dave. I was in a good relationship with a man who I really cared about, an Australian journalist named Chris. I had a good job in media. And I now worked in New York City. Yet, riding the 5:45 p.m. DeCamp bus home to Bloomfield, New Jersey, through the Lincoln Tunnel, always in a mad dash to retrieve Katie from daycare before they closed, I was often dissatisfied, and sometimes miserable. And the reason was J.R.

I'd begun to hate working for J.R. An odd character who always dressed in brown, paneled three-piece suits that might have been hip today if worn with irony, J.R. was a bureaucratic custodian for the Way Things Were Done, a hall monitor who made everyone stay in line.

J.R. had his human side, of course—he loved his wife and their daughter, who was going blind. But he somehow managed to make all of us hate him. He kept his door shut at all times, squirreling himself away, barking out orders through his assistant and enforcing the small rules of the office with oversized demands.

With J.R., I was never insubordinate—I was quiet. At most, I rolled my eyes, a mildly disrespectful display of body language. To let off steam, I'd gossip about J.R. to a few colleagues. Our commiseration provided a release valve for my sanity, but it didn't really make things better. We could gossip all day, but that didn't change anything. He was still there, still our boss.

And then, a year into my new job, Betty Hudson—the head of the department whom I likened to a movie star (the rumor was she had appeared as an Amazonian beauty in a sci-fi thriller once)—called J.R. and me down to her office on the sixth floor, where the senior executives sat. I remember it was a slice of corporate heaven, beset with orderly desks, marbled shelves adorned with brass tchotchkes that never tarnished, and gloved waiters serving steaming hot coffee from silver trays. J.R. didn't let me in on what was coming, but he knew.

I had been quoted on the front page of the *New York Times*, where I'd given our standard statement on a piece of media industry regulation. But we hadn't cleared it with Betty first. When Betty came to J.R. angry about the quote, he sold me out.

As Betty started to lecture me, walking me through NBC's procedures, J.R. gave me an enigmatic smile. "We don't do that here," he echoed. "What were you thinking?"

I stared daggers at J.R. It was my job to talk to reporters, and the statement had been approved. And then I thought, "I'm not going to take it!" I don't need to listen to the hall monitors anymore. I'm not going to give myself an alibi for not standing up and making things change.

Betty had hired a management consultant, a smooth-talking southern guy named Jimmy. I marched into Jimmy's office to lay out J.R.'s management failings. After talking with our team—Bonnie, me, and a few others—Jimmy made the ultimate bureaucratic suggestion: "Why don't you write up a report, make some recommendations?"

Fine, I thought. So I threw myself into the "report," and in October 1989, I presented J.R. with an "NBC According to Me" dossier: eight pages on the disappointments of working in our department—including a lack of creative thinking and aversion to new ideas at the top, and an unwillingness to let employees stretch.

While not in so many words, I essentially said J.R. was a jerk and accused him of not knowing how to write. (He had an annoying habit of elongating words to make himself sound more corporate and sophisticated—"cross-pollinate" became "cross-pollinizationalize.") Reading the report, J.R. got very defensive. "What do you mean? What did *I* do?" he said, as if we had really surprised him.

And then nothing happened.

That was when I decided that I had to leave NBC. I was never going to get ahead as long as J.R. was in place. I didn't have a voice and never would. Hall monitors attack any attempt to weaken their power. My letter hadn't loosened J.R.'s grip. If anything, it turned down the volume of my voice even more.

Ignoring the gatekeepers and giving yourself permission to advance your ideas is almost more frightening than the path-clearing that follows. To tell yourself, "Permission granted!" you have to find the strength to deny the voice inside your head screaming, "No, it's too dangerous!" And you have to be prepared to face the "Are you crazy?" you'll hear from peers or friends or family.

One of the things I've discovered over the course of my career is that people who effect radical change have to exhibit an uncompromising faith in experimentation, a radical impatience with the default, a bias for novelty and action, and a sense that disruption is something you *engage*, not observe. We have to give ourselves permission at times to embrace work as a kind of joyful insurrection. Giving ourselves permission allows us to hack rules that don't make sense rather than follow them; to take ideas and stories apart that aren't working; to go around the gatekeepers, bullies, and bureaucratic bottlenecks that would stifle change. Developing a habit of self-permission will instill in you the belief that you are in control of your career and your life, regardless of what is going on around you.

In the wake of my meeting with J.R., I reminded myself that I was the boss of my story—and *I* had to chart *my* own course. I gave myself permission to ignore the gatekeeper and find a different route. Late in 1989, I took a job at a pirate ship, a place whose raison d'être was to banish the old corporate hall monitors. The ship was CNN, the pirate Ted Turner.

Ted Turner's Wet Hands

From my school days, people often didn't know how to take me.

I can come across as aloof, although I certainly don't feel that way on the inside. I am a natural introvert, and I struggle to this day with my habit of at first keeping people at bay. With my reserved nature, combined, in the early years of my career especially, with a relative lack of confidence, I could be hard to get to know.

I remember in college someone saying to me, as we were rounding a path on tricycles we had "borrowed" and were riding with wild abandon, "Wow, I had no idea you could be fun."

Over the years, I've come to realize that my innate curiosity and something I call *social courage* can help me compensate for the confidence and extroversion that are not part of my nature. The best I could find was a work-around. The issue came to a head while I was at CNN. Oddly, it had much to do with Ted Turner's wet hands.

I arrived at Turner Broadcasting just before CNN became famous with the first Gulf War in 1991. The network was a little down-market from NBC (Turner owned a wrestling league) but fascinating, giddy, and unstructured.

I was leading PR for those pirates of TV news, overseeing people—my first time in management—and running Turner's New York PR machine. At NBC, I had built good working relationships with the largely New York–based reporters who covered the media, due to my just-the-facts manner. They took my calls; they counted on me for fast answers. Now it was my job to pitch reporters to write stories about the Turner machine—getting people to tune in and become familiar with the various Turner branded channels.

While I was working as CNN's liaison to the public, the Gulf War turned CNN reporters into stars. As I was walking in Times Square with "the Boys of Baghdad," Peter Arnett and Bernard Shaw, people erupted with spontaneous applause, giving them high fives and calling out their names. They basked in the adulation and attention; I was happy to be on the sidelines.

Part of my job was handling PR for Ted Turner when he came to New York, which he did frequently to accept awards or make a speech. Ted was a superstar, a swashbuckling media darling. He had created the first "Superstation" in the 1970s and by the early 1990s had launched CNN as the first all-news cable network. It was a huge success. And of course there was Ted's famous wife, Jane Fonda.

When I wasn't pitching stories about him, my role was to accompany Ted to his endless stream of speeches and media appearances. But did I take advantage of this incredible opportunity for exposure and advancement? No, I receded. Sure, I managed the schedule with professional zeal and competence, but then I made myself disappear into the background once the public-facing part began. I intentionally went out of my way to be invisible. I don't think Ted even learned my name.

The turning point came at the United Nations. Ted was getting an award, and I was there to run point. It was one of those moments when I thought to myself, "I work with this powerful guy, and he doesn't know who I am." I needed to do something. So when I saw him burst out of the men's room, I stuck out my hand and said, "Hi Ted, I want to formally introduce myself, I'm . . ."

At least I tried to say it. I barely whispered. After saying, "Oh, hi," in his country baritone and giving my outstretched hand a quick shake—his hand was still wet—Ted paused to see if I had anything to add. I looked down. Ted then casually walked away, zipping his fly.

I slunk off, kicking myself.

When I got home at the end of the day, I was furious at how I let my timidity take over. Why are you letting this opportunity pass you by? I chastized myself. What do you want? Spending time with Captain Outrageous, as the media called Ted Turner, had forced me to look for "Beth Courageous." I realized I would have to start dealing with my lack of social presence.

As a vast array of research has shown, success correlates as closely with confidence as it does competence. This is particularly true for someone who intends to be a change agent. So I made a plan. I would push myself outside of my comfort zone and do what scared me most: connect with other people. With my introvert personality, introducing myself to someone new was awkward, even painful. Every day, I vowed, I would make one new connection: I would engage with a colleague or someone in my industry, at the coffee machine or over lunch. My strategy would be to ask him or her a question—about their work or what interested them—to get a conversation going.

I would use the strength of my natural curiosity as a tool to open doors.

Genuine change first starts with a mind-set. I needed to psych myself up, the way an athlete does before a big game. Before an event, I would map out what I was going to do, what I was going to say. I became just raw energy. I would introduce myself by saying, "Hi I'm Beth Comstock. I thought the speaker was excellent. I particularly liked her point about teaching more art in schools. What did you think?" Or whatever. The point, I realized, was just to get out of my own head, out of my own way, and engage.

While you're freaking out worrying what the other person thinks about you, they're often doing the same thing. And so we're stuck in our own heads, trying to come across as smart or clever, rather than revealing ourselves to be the awkward, insecure beings we are. We miss our moment to connect.

I realized I had to make the encounter about them, not about me. I knew I had to turn off that internal critic. I had to act more like an anthropologist: "Tell me what makes you tick." I would ask myself, "Is there something new I can learn from you?"

Even today, I find it takes an extra boost of energy to go up to someone new. It's far easier to say, "Next time," and quietly exit the room. But what a missed opportunity to connect and learn.

Once I began to force myself to interact with the world, I began to gain more faith and confidence in myself. I believed that there was always a "better way" to do things. And that became my mantra, my mission: the quest for *better*. It gave me the courage to act in spite of my awkwardness and fear.

At heart, I'm an explorer. So I've learned to use my natural curiosity as my guide. It's the camouflage that covers the insecurity of not knowing. It means constantly looking outward, constantly pushing myself to ask the next question.

What I was learning was the skill called *social courage*, a concept that originated in the literature of "Positive Psychology," which studies the strengths that allow individuals and groups to thrive. *New York Times* columnist David Brooks offered a memorable take on the

People who effect
radical change
have to exhibit an
uncompromising faith
in experimentation,
a bias for novelty and
action, and a sense that
disruption is something
you *cause*, not observe.

idea a few years ago: "In today's loosely networked world, people with social courage have amazing value," he wrote. "Everyone goes to conferences and meets people, but some people invite six people to lunch afterward and follow up with four carefully tended friendships forevermore. Then they spend their lives connecting people across networks. People with social courage are extroverted in issuing invitations, but introverted in conversation—willing to listen 70% of the time."

The idea has an almost religious sensibility to me. It emphasizes the importance of listening and caring. But more important, it speaks to the value of developing social courage as a habit, a muscle you can strengthen. It is not something innate that you are born with, but something you can consciously develop. The way to build social courage is by practicing social courage.

My Return to NBC and the Advantages of White Space

From the moment I trusted my instincts to return to NBC from CBS, I loved my new job as vice president of News Media Relations. I'd made the leap, even though I couldn't articulate why, having spent a couple of good years after leaving Turner at CBS, the number one rated network. There, I had been a director of East Coast entertainment publicity, overseeing a bigger team of publicists and the media campaigns we pitched for mostly Hollywood-based celebrities, like young George Clooney in the one-season wonder *The Hat Squad* or emerging ingénue Halle Barry in a *Roots* sequel. I distinguished myself by injecting creativity into our campaigns in small ways (a box of cereal being stabbed by a fake knife distributed to reporters to interest them in an upcoming "serial killer" series, for example) and in bigger ones (like star-studded movie screenings). Mostly I deepened my skills in communications, especially in messaging and in selling ideas to reporters to write stories about us. But I wasn't intellectually charged by the entertainment topics. To me, to work in network news at that time was to believe you were at the center of the universe. It was almost an addiction. Your life followed the rhythm of the news cycle. That's what excited me. That was at the heart of my return.

Even with NBC in disaster mode, I realized the job was about diving into the fog and seeing opportunity where others see only confusion. Some people hate the idea of not having a clear path forward, of not knowing where to go. I am someone who loves wallowing in possibility, where I cannot see all the answers. I often use the term "fog flyer" to describe the excitement and fear I feel navigating ambiguity. And that's what I felt at NBC.

For me, post-crash NBC News turned out to be a start-up on a huge scale. It offered the kind of opportunity I call *white space*: a positive void on which you can project nothing but possibility. When I arrived, the mood at NBC News was hopeful, but just barely. So many people had been fired or had left because of the turmoil.

The department I took over was basically empty, providing me the opportunity to create a new team and be part of the reinvented newsroom that newly hired News president Andrew Lack was building.

It was the ultimate opportunity.

Andy Lack was a natty dresser, except that his thinning, dark hair was always wildly askew. He was a daredevil of a journalist, someone who earlier in his career had the temerity to take on the venerable *60 Minutes* by launching *48 Hours*, an act that won him general acclaim but also scorn among the traditionalists for being a petulant disrupter (the reason behind many of the calls trying to persuade me not to work with him). Andy's booming voice gave us all the sense that something good could happen—from questioning the accepted approach to encouraging diverse ideas, pushing people out of their comfort zones, and creating a sense of urgency around producing something new and better.

It was here that I and the team I convened literally from nothing—Alex Constantinople, John Bianchi, and Heidi Pokorny—bonded together in a mission for what could be, for turning that white space into something meaningful. We were constantly plotting and planning new ways to rid ourselves of our underdog status.

Steve Friedman, a bombastic and colorful *Today Show* producer who walked around the *Today Show* offices swinging a big baseball bat as a sign of intimidation, conceived and led the rebirth of the show's brilliant glass-walled "Window on the World" studio, originally built in the 1950s.

When Window on the World was ready, our PR team put all our energy into selling its premiere. We focused on every detail, from handcrafted invitations for our "coming out party" to major news articles. Window on the World became a statement of openness and transparency, of community—the kinds of things we take for granted now.

Late-night talk show hosts did stand-up jokes about the Window. Katie Couric and Bryant Gumbel appeared with the Window in editorial cartoons. People even planned their vacations, proposals, and retirements for Window exposure. We weren't just back—we were culturally relevant. I showed the early shades of the marketer I would become as I pushed NBC News to target new audience segments for viewership. I didn't have time to ask if an idea was okay. We were making it up as we went along.

Then there was the launch of MSNBC, which made the *Today* Window on the World launch look like an off-Broadway production. The creation of a new breed of cable network that partnered GE and Microsoft was a big deal. We generated an onslaught of content, stories, and amplification that starts slow and then gets so loud you can't ignore it. It helped that two of America's biggest companies were coming together to create the first potential competitor to CNN. But we went beyond even those expectations, and our team was recognized inside NBC and beyond for our good work.

What I remember most was the camaraderie that came with having nothing to lose but wanting nothing more than to win. Our PR team members were constantly pushing one another to get better, to do more. We spent weeks on a project we called "Witness to History" to retarget news to students. We didn't have a budget and never got one, but it didn't matter. Not all of our ideas got green-lit; the fun was in the coming together and the improvisation. It happened in tense moments, too. During any crisis or major news story (from the Oklahoma City bombing to the O. J. Simpson case) our team sat together in a makeshift media "war room," usually a conference room with four TVs, each tuned into a different news network. There we chronicled every minute of coverage in a race to declare NBC's firsts and exclusives versus the other news networks. We took the wins seriously and fought with media reporters to get duly recognized. Alternately joking, cursing, and laughing, we were "all in" at those moments—certainly I was, the frenetic race to win bringing out my competitive spirit.

And I loved working with Andy. He was a mercurial character; like in the nursery rhyme, when he was good, he was very good, and when he was bad, he was horrid. He wore his energetic spirit on his finely tailored sleeves. There was a "hail-fellow-well-met" quality to Andy. He also loved new ideas and encouraged me to try things. He never treated our team like we were "just" the PR department. In our regular editorial and staff meetings he'd ask, "What does PR think? What new ideas do you have for us?" He'd roll up his sleeves and help us write copy—he had started his career as an adman—or brainstorm campaign ideas with us. It sent a strong message that we were a valued part of the team.

Andy backed us when the journalists didn't want to be pushed to do PR (which I thought ironic for people whose livelihood was

Job Crafting

I often tell people looking for career advice, "Take the job that no one else wants." Or the job where you see potential beyond what others see. This has been a key to my career—crafting additional projects and responsibilities that help the company while giving me room to grow and find joy. With lower expectations about the role from others, you have more room to experiment. When I worked briefly for a cable television trade association as a project coordinator, I launched a newsletter to keep members informed. It expanded the role, and me. With the public access television job, I started my own local community news show, taping it in the evenings after work. It fulfilled my interests in reporting and gave the channel more content.

Researchers Amy Wrzesniewski and Jane Dutton call such efforts "job crafting." Job crafting offers people a way to actively shape their jobs to fit their needs, values, and preferences. With job crafting, they found, you shape your job to give your work additional meaning. What I like about this is that it reinforces the notion that you can use your skills—especially your imagination—to make work something special. And uniquely yours.

I know this to be true: in nearly *every* job there is room for trying new things, for adding projects, for customizing the job your way.

Here are some things to consider as you craft new parts of your job:

- Can you make the case that what you are doing will impact the business?

- Does it cost more? If so, start small to prove its impact. Establish where best to get the resources (i.e., interns, after-work volunteers).
- Are you prepared to spend time off the clock to seed the new work?
- Is someone else already doing it? Instead of grabbing someone else's work, focus on the unclaimed areas of opportunity. Every business has them.
- Convene a few colleagues over lunch and ask for input and help.

FOR MANAGERS: What are you doing to encourage self-directed work on your team? I believe in giving your team some degree of freedom to craft jobs that make them happier and more engaged, within the realm of what you have to do. Here is what I say to the teams I work with: "I don't know how long we will be working together—I hope for a long time. But my commitment to you is that you should be able to do the best work of your career here. You need to find time and capacity to do the things you love within the goals of our team."

Seed this idea. See what happens.

interviewing others). Once, believing that NBC News needed to be more relevant with younger viewers, we developed a significant outreach campign, coming up with creative ideas to pitch to consumer media that normally didn't cover television news. When we landed a big *Interview* magazine Q&A between Tom Brokaw and Shaquille O'Neal, Brokaw called me and said, "What are you all doing? My publicist is acting like a dog in heat—she won't leave me alone. Why do I have to do this?" Keep going, Andy said. (And eventually, Tom did, too.)

To this day, it was one of the best jobs I ever had. And it was one of the freest places I have ever worked. We created our own energy. We had a mission and a charismatic leader, and we created our story and made it happen.

That assignment was my entrepreneurial awakening—proof that I could be a change-maker in an organization. And it was one of my first lessons in grabbing the job that no one else wants and making it my own.

No Is Not Yet

Successful agitators for change are like prize-fighters who keep on getting hit but won't go down. The hits never stop, because new ideas never become less threatening. So you have to learn how to take a punch and keep coming back for more.

Two years into my return to NBC, the SVP of corporate communications for all of NBC, Judy Smith—who would later become the inspiration for the Kerry Washington character in *Scandal*—left the company. Most of us weren't surprised; she had come in from politics and seemed eager to work in Hollywood.

I saw myself as next in line. A big promotion, I was convinced, was my due. And then . . . nothing happened. For months the position stayed open, with no one even mentioning it to me. But I didn't step up either. I hesitated to promote myself for her job because of my lack of confidence. I had left NBC earlier because I felt my voice hadn't been heard; what would happen if I were ignored again? So I stewed silently.

I don't embrace a confrontational mentality, but a drumbeat of indignation was growing inside me at that time. Anger can be a useful provocation for action, but you can't live there. Tenacity is a better long-term game plan. At opportune moments, you must relentlessly push yourself forward, demanding that your achievements be acknowledged.

And so, six months after Judy left, I made my way determinedly into the office of our head of HR, Ed Scanlon.

Tall and lean, Ed had been at NBC since my first tenure. He had an apt nickname in the DC bureau. Whenever he came to town, people would run through the halls saying, "The Grim Reaper is coming!" He had the power to hire and fire, and people tried to avoid him.

As he swiveled to face me, I screwed up my courage and told him in as professional a voice as I could muster that I'd like to be considered for the job. Inside, I felt small. But Ed didn't miss a beat. "Well," he said. "Bob Wright and I thought of you, but you are a young mother. This job requires a lot of travel. We thought it wouldn't work for you."

I could have killed him. I was furious at the two of them for thinking they knew what was best for me and angry at myself for not stepping up earlier to make my interests known. But I learned something that day that I have never forgotten. Managers aren't mind readers. They won't know what you aspire to do unless you tell them. It doesn't mean you will necessarily get the opportunity, but at least you will both know where you stand.

Luckily, I didn't kill Ed. And I got the job.

My point isn't that in a world of self-promoters it's important to showcase your skills—though that's true. My real point is that, as an agent of change, it is not just your job but your *duty* to push change forward—whether to better utilize your skills or to promote a new idea. *Put yourself out there, with passion. And persevere.* No skill in the world can overcome a lack of perseverance.

.   .   .

In my new job working directly for Bob Wright as the head of communications across all of NBC—from news to sports and entertainment—my role was much broader than at NBC News. I was now a peer of News president Andy Lack and other major players, like legendary producer Dick Ebersol. I had a seat at the "big kids' table."

Working for Bob brought its own lessons. Bob was an idea machine—some of them absolutely horrible, some of them brilliant insights into the future—and he was always putting them out there. His ideas led NBC to acquire CNBC and then Universal.

In my new position, I oversaw the NBC Page program, made famous by the Kenneth Ellen Parcell character on *30 Rock*, and I was thrust into a series of communications situations that expanded my leadership skills—and put me on the front line of a number of crises.

Frankly, I didn't excel at the persuasion arts back then. I'm not a natural-born salesperson, at least in the "give me the order now" way. But I did excel at listening and self-control. When I heard rejection in the other person's voice, I reacted to it as muted encouragement. Through persistence I became persistent. Habits of behavior precede habits of the mind.

My efforts to persist evolved into a concept I call "No = Not Yet," something that crystallized for me while I was working under Bob. In 1998, I pitched Bob a new start-up business at NBC that I thought might take off. It wasn't going to transform the world, but I thought it could connect us more deeply with our viewers. And I was passionate about it. The idea was to create an NBC Experience Store on the ground floor of NBC's 30 Rock Manhattan headquarters, with huge display windows inspired by the Window on the World studio.

The projected return on investment was decent, but not strong enough to make it a surefire bet. And so my idea was turned down; the CFO called it economically ill-advised. I started to think it might be a dumb idea. But my "quiet courage" voice urged me on.

It told me to reach higher, leap wider, move faster. It told me to try again. So I sought the advice of others who could help me make the proposal better. I reached out to advisors who had helped the NBA launch its Fifth Avenue store. However, my second attempt was shot down as well. By this time I could "see" the store, its features, the colorful merchandise. It had to become real. I wasn't ready to give up.

It was my third attempt to sell the idea to Bob that was the charm (or the curse): I got the green light! Bob approved the budget and agreed to our request of a launch team, including set designers, technicians, and a big news director to make the experience truly unique. To quote Bob, "You make it so darn hard to say 'No'—and I really tried."

The NBC Experience Store didn't dramatically impact NBC's bottom line, but it did delight tourists for eighteen years. And it helped me overcome my natural disinclination to put myself out there and to persevere.

As I would see over and over again in my career, learning how to withstand disappointment is critical for anyone who hopes to effect change in an organization. Disappointment, delays, obstacles, recalcitrance, and resistance—they are inevitable in fomenting change. It is in how you handle yourself during the constant tussle between the thrill of a new idea and its adoption that the real work lies.

No matter how worthy an idea, you are not entitled to blind trust. There will be weaknesses in your arguments. And others will rightfully use them as a rationale for their obstinacy. The good news is they will push you to be better. I've learned that everything is feedback. It's all data to plug into the process. Try, fail, iterate, try again.

Each rejection suggests a new approach. Think too large, or become too emotional, and you become paralyzed. You have to focus on the process, on the one thing you can do today to keep momentum. It helps to break down the larger vision into smaller, more manageable bites that can be acted upon. It allows you to exert control. With the NBC Experience Store, each time we presented it to Bob, we had more detail baked into the plan—assumptions became grounded in real costs, partners, and technologies. At each meeting we presented something tangible—for example, a sample product or the diorama of an immersive theater in which to experience NBC's history.

While I was in the top PR job, Ed Scanlon and I became friends. He took me under his long, skinny wings in the aftermath of the launch of MSNBC, during which period I spent time with GE CEO Jack Welch and Microsoft boss Bill Gates. (And this time I made sure they remembered my name.) But unbeknownst to me, Ed served as my agent, talking me up behind my back.

And then the phone rang.

CHAPTER 2

THE OUTSIDER INSIDE

The Starmaker

H i Beth," the voice on the line said. It was Rosanne Badowski, Jack Welch's secretary. "Jack would like you to come upstairs please."

It was July of 1998, and the mood inside NBC was exultant. NBC was killing it. The network had made a startling transformation since my arrival in 1994. My role as vice president of NBC News had helped launch me, and I had helped launch the network back to relevancy. After becoming a senior vice president of corporate communications at NBC in 1996, I'd settled into my new leadership role as an executive and strategist. I'd built a tight, cohesive team; we were energetic, creative, and hungry to push boundaries and do more.

I knew Jack Welch a bit, but not well. I was on his radar from regular business updates and especially the annual performance reviews Bob Wright conducted as part of GE's process to evaluate senior managers. Since I had played a big role in the noisy launch of MSNBC, I interacted directly with Jack. One media event I created, a Jack and Bill "unplugged" session, brought them together with a dozen handpicked editors and no agenda other than to discuss the state of the world. Anxious and sweating everything, I even fretted over whether the smudges on Bill Gates's eyeglasses might show up in the group photo.

I grabbed my notebook and headed for the elevator. Practically from the moment GE bought NBC in 1986, there were rumors it would be sold. So I assumed Jack was calling me in to discuss details of a sale, which would be my job to position to the media.

Rosanne pushed a small, unobtrusive white button to make his impressive wood door slide open; through a window, the Empire State Building came into view, and I walked into Jack's office.

After a bit of media gossip, Jack cut to the chase. But it wasn't the chase I'd expected.

"I want you to come work for me at GE," he said.

No one had given me a heads-up, or even a hint.

The job he proceeded to define was entirely about change. Jack was just about to transition from his twenty-year tenure as CEO. But first he was looking to cement his legacy. And what he had in mind was a "horse race": a very public, multiyear contest in which three men would vie for the leadership of one of America's biggest companies. My job would be vice president of corporate communications and advertising—a position that would become, basically, the stage manager for one of the most public sea changes in American business.

Moving to GE was never something I had contemplated. GE managers frequently moved internally from business unit to business unit, and they loved being assigned to NBC. But rarely—if ever—did someone venture from NBC to GE. Media people wanted to be media people, not industrialists. I felt completely in my element pushing the boundaries inside NBC. GE would be something else entirely.

I muttered something to Jack about our successes at NBC, but he cut me off. "No, the question you have to ask yourself now is: Are you ready to leave media?" he said. "And I hope you are, because this will be fun."

Ed Scanlon—the Grim Reaper turned mentor—was waiting for me when I left Jack's suite. As I walked into his office, he stated the obvious (with a smile): "You know you can't say no, right?"

But I already knew my answer. This was a path I had to follow, even if I had no idea where it was leading me.

When I accepted Jack's offer, it meant I'd have to live near GE's offices in Fairfield, Connecticut. I immediately called our Realtor and had our New Jersey house on the market within forty-eight hours. By this time, my family had grown. I had married Chris. He had left journalism to become a "new media" executive, exploring early forms of data for television. We'd had a daughter, Meredith, when Katie was six. We all loved our life, living now in the vibrant community of Montclair, New Jersey. We'd recently finished renovating a run-down old Victorian; it had been hectic and hands-on, with Chris and me undertaking aspects like painting and wallpapering on weekends. Moving to quasi-rural Fairfield County inspired all kinds of doubts, but it had to be done.

Life was chaotic enough as we juggled parenting and careers, and we certainly weren't looking to take on more. I often think back to this time and wonder how we managed it all. I don't know how; we just did. I had too much going on to be tired. Chris and I tried to stick to our goal of having one of us home each night, and we rarely both traveled at the same time. Most travel was manageable, but there were the occasional rows over schedule conflicts, with an undertone of questioning whose job was more important. We had a series of babysitters, many of whom lived with us in a spare room. Some were great, others less so. But I believed my kids were well looked after and loved. I enjoyed our weekends, which were filled with crafts and renovation projects. I sewed a bit back then, a hangover from high school home economics classes. I could stitch together Halloween costumes: Meredith as characters from her beloved *Wizard of Oz*, Katie as the New Jersey Turnpike (a classic!). And there was "our" fifth-grade science project. Honestly, the idea was brilliant: "Hairostotle," the world's smartest hairbrush. "So smart it cleans itself." It was so good, it went all the way to the regional fair. I got really carried away with Katie's great idea, micromanaging it, almost to the point of filing patents. I had the thrill of seeing my kids' imaginations (and mine) fulfilled. There were inevitably the badly timed calls from work and endless chores that somehow got taken care of. The point is, we weren't perfect, but we did all right and we made room for curiosity and imagination.

Chris supported the move to Connecticut, although it meant a much longer commute for him at his job on Long Island. But my daughter Katie was another story. She was at sleepaway camp at the time, and there was no texting, mobile phone, or e-mail back then. But the truth is, I had the tunnel vision that comes with being in "get it done" mode and didn't even try to contact her.

I hadn't thought she would learn about my change of job until I told her. But the day Katie returned, driven home by the mother of a friend, our new Realtor had installed FOR SALE signs adorned with distinctive, fluffy sheep on the front lawn. You couldn't miss the fact that our house was for sale.

When Katie entered the house she burst into tears. Why were we moving? Where were we going? What about her friends? As she wept, Katie looked much smaller than her twelve years. To this day, I feel terrible about the unintended consequence of my career change. I'm reminded of the importance of communicating early and often as change is happening.

The Table of Lost Dreams

I jumped on the GE horse with unbridled determination, if perhaps too much haste. But the tape loop in my head kept reminding me, This is GE! My successes at NBC had validated my belief that effecting change is about focusing on what might be, always looking for new and better ways of doing things. And my new job was an opportunity to take those practices to the business world's largest stage. Although in truth, I wasn't really a student of business at that time: one of my first conversations with my new team had them talking about the upcoming 10K, and I thought they were talking about running a marathon, not filing financials.

When I got to Fairfield, my new office was bare, as if no one was expecting me. A lone phone sat on the carpeted floor, tethered to the wall by a long, tan cord. "Welcome to GE," I thought.

I came to find out that office space in our Fairfield headquarters had been designed in the 1970s with the hierarchy utmost in mind. One could determine an employee's rank by counting the number of ceiling tiles overhead: six across for managers, eight for a vice president.

I was out of my comfort zone. Fairfield was new, the people were new, even the day-to-day language, filled with acronyms and sports metaphors, was new. And I didn't fit in.

The company was a very male-dominated place back then—at GE's annual Boca Raton retreat, female executives had to made do with a makeshift restroom off the hotel kitchen because event organizers turned conference-hall ladies' rooms into men's rooms. And nowhere was this male culture more evident than at GE headquarters. A number of the executives—all men—had a reserved table in the Fairfield cafeteria where they ate every day and cut people down to what they thought was the right size. They called it "The Table of Lost Dreams." It was a black hole of negativity. No imagination. No excitement for the future. And P.S., they couldn't stand me.

The treatment I got from an Ivy League-educated functional leader was indicative. He was competitive with me and dismissed my ideas out of hand. He just couldn't believe that this woman, with zero pedigree—and from PR no less!—was increasingly involved in the kind of strategic decisions he considered his domain. In retaliation, he didn't invite me to important meetings. So I began what would become a career-long habit of inviting myself, sometimes warning people beforehand, sometimes just showing up. (Once this backfired when I showed up for a technical meeting, mistaking it for a sales meeting—you have to be especially prepared when you invite yourself.)

These guys weren't change-makers, they were gatekeepers, cheerleaders for the status quo. And they resented the fact that this new It girl from NBC, the fluffy land of media, had Jack's ear and was being given power over their fiefdoms. I didn't know the corporate world, *and* I was a woman.

Early on, I misjudged the GE culture and my role in it. I approached every day, every project—even small ones—as a wide-eyed explorer, unsure of the final destination at times but certain that there was something amazing just around the bend. And that sense of exploration and adventure always begins with asking "What if?" or "Why not?"

But the GE mothership and Jack weren't ready for that from me. Not yet, at least.

Jack loved getting press clips every day, just the way they appeared in the paper. We had a team that would come in at 5:00 a.m., cut them out, and get them ready with a glue stick so that when he arrived, he could see not only his story but where he was on page 3, or whatever.

The Introvert's Advantage

Let's face it: business is an extrovert's arena. I've had to get comfortable adopting the extrovert's way to succeed. I've worked hard to "overcome" my introversion. But I also appreciate the advantages it brings. Introverts tend to process information internally; we prefer to express our ideas after they are well formed. We may not always speak up at meetings, but we're not hogging the conversation either. You can bet we're processing the discussion thoughtfully, taking it all in. I believe my introversion has helped me be a keen observer and listener—what I've come to call the introvert's advantage.

Introversion is just one aspect of my character, not a label to define me. I think it's important to understand who we are and how it may help us. If we don't appreciate who we are, how can we ever fully focus on what we have to contribute, or what we're capable of?

- I challenge myself to ask one question or make one comment during a meeting, thinking about it in advance so that it doesn't distract me from the conversation. Bosses and colleagues who know this about me will also help by asking me for an opinion in a meeting when I've not spoken up.
- I follow up meetings with a note to my manager or the project leader summarizing what I heard and offering additional ideas and comments on how to be successful. I've become good at synthesizing discussions into core themes, and this, too, gives me a role in discussions as "the synthesizer." And it shows that I'm engaged.

- I've learned to focus intently on the idea, not making it about the person with the idea or a potential attack against me. To me this is part of the introvert's advantage—having the perspective and distance to give an idea attention and enthusiasm, and not make it personal (it's hard sometimes not to be sidelined by personal dynamics!).

- I've learned how to conserve and replenish my energy. I'll take a walk or go somewhere to be alone after an intense meeting or discussion. I will often pass on a night out to go home, or call in room service on a trip, to "recharge my batteries." Be careful that you don't use this as an alibi because you are actually nervous about socializing.

FOR THOSE WHO MANAGE INTROVERTS: It is important to realize that the introverts under you have a lot to say, even if they aren't speaking up. Tell them up front that you are going to call on them, or ask them after the meeting for their thoughts. When trolling for new ideas, be sure to plan both group brainstorming and individual and small-group time, to get the best out of the introverts who work for you.

I decided we could do that more efficiently in an electronic format. And, hey, there was nothing Jack liked more than efficiency. So one day, as we took GE's helicopter to New York City—because that's the only time we had to meet—I said to Jack, "Okay, here's a little thing we're doing with your clips. We can do this in half the time." And I gave him printouts from the web—the Internet was just beginning to explode. It seemed like an easy innovation to me.

Jack made a grumpy sound, like a garbage disposal grinding to a halt. "What do you got? *What do you got?*" he said, almost barking, and threw the papers at my face.

I was stunned, shocked that something so simple seemed to matter so much to him. But I was naïve. I didn't know Jack's mind yet. This wasn't a change he was interested in.

"That's for the next guy," he said dismissively. "I'm not going to do that."

Becoming the Outsider Inside

Despite his tough demeanor, I enjoyed working with Jack. He was an enormous contradiction, a man of immense generosity and confidence and clarity and intensity (I can still see his blue-eyed laser-like focus on me or whoever was in his line of sight). And yet, despite the change mandate that had made him famous—after being made CEO he was initially known as "Neutron Jack" to the media for shutting down factories so fast that only the buildings remained— he was pretty set in his ways. I remember asking him a few months after I arrived if there were any "sacred cows" on my team. I wanted to know where I could make changes and what was off-limits. His reply was telling: "Just one, Bill Lane," he said, referring to his long-time speechwriter. "And we've done pretty well to this point without you. Meaning, I like things the way they are."

No one I've encountered can make everything personal the way Jack could. He made it personal for every GE employee, and that's tough. It's a brilliant managerial feat to create a culture in which, beyond not wanting to let your colleagues down, 300,000 people didn't want to let Jack down. There were lots of handwritten notes, and there were stock grants and bonuses when you least expected it. Jack used to say that the GE process was all about chemistry, blood, sweat, family, and feelings. No detail was too small: At GE's big annual meetings, Jack would personally work out the golf foursomes and his dinner-table seating. He kept records so that he didn't repeat the pairings. GE was 300,000 individuals to Jack, not dozens of business units. That takes time and effort.

With Jack, there was no distinction between "I am this company" and "I lead this company." He became the face, voice, and embodiment of everything GE stood for. He *was* GE, and he felt it to his bones.

I've worked with celebrities my whole career, but I have always been struck by Jack's charisma. He oozed it. He's small in stature, he stutters, but he genuinely loves people and loves connecting. You could see it at our annual shareholder meetings. Shareholder meetings were like financial rock festivals. Old ladies came and they would be shaking in Jack's presence, as if their teen idol had shown up. Jack loved the little old ladies. He'd ask them what they did with the money, loved that they bought a second house or sent their kids to college because of GE's rising stock price.

You always knew where you stood with Jack. To this day, I try to channel Jack's raw directness, making my leadership style as transparent and straightforward as possible. That meant getting over my small-town ideas about "niceness" that I learned while growing up. Because being direct is actually *being* nice: Clarity, telling people where they stand, is a form of kindness. It is fair.

You see, with Jack, GE's culture was all about performance. You always knew how you were doing. He'd come in and say, "You're a prince today." (I was never a princess!) But other days he'd tell me, "You're a pig." Quite literally. And he meant it.

I was a prince (and got a princely bonus) when I convinced him, over the objections of my old boss, Andy Lack, who had been a former CBS producer, to orchestrate a *60 Minutes* story that made Jack shine. And I was sent to the doghouse when a positive *Time* magazine profile of him came out, naming him one of the most acclaimed CEOs of the twentieth century, because he thought it didn't get enough play.

Bearing down, his voice growing loud, he said, "I expect you to do for me what you did for Tim Russert and Tom Brokaw. You're a star maker. *Where's my star?"*

That brutal intensity, his laser focus on performance, is what led Jack to Six Sigma. In the mid-1980s, Motorola developed a quality management program based on a sophisticated statistical model called Six Sigma, which involved attempting to reduce the number of defects in their business processes to less than 3.4 per million. Within a few years, managers everywhere were demanding their organizations begin implementing Six Sigma principles.

Jack was captivated by Six Sigma and launched it across GE in 1995. It was the ultimate control system and a way to produce products that are as defect free as possible. (You'll be happy to know that GE's jet engines are produced with numbers beyond Six Sigma.) It makes processes repeatable, scalable, and perfect—the height of efficiency in a large industrial machine. It was a story with results that Wall Street loved.

Every GE employee was trained in Six Sigma methodology, and certified based on their level of understanding, from assistants to division presidents. Jack even created "black belt" positions in each business unit, Six Sigma ninjas.

I had my own Six Sigma training while I was at NBC, in 1997 when Bob Wright and I and the entire NBC leadership team took the class together with others from GE. Unfortunately, it was totally lost in translation. We were sequestered in a hotel ballroom while we learned the various nuances of defect-free processes. There were classes, tests, and more tests (if anything, this was a reminder of why I thought I never wanted to work at GE). The NBC guys stood out at these training events: they were the ones sitting at the back of the ballroom, reading newspapers and passing notes.

Each one of us was asked to identify a project to apply Six Sigma to, everything from logging phone calls to queuing videotapes to travel agendas. Nothing could escape the talons of Six Sigma improvement. It was like an efficiency diet program. Six Sigma brought with it a new vocabulary and a way of communicating across the company. It was a way to get an army of 300,000 people moving in lockstep rhythm.

But while Jack's personal leadership and focus on performance made for a tremendous upside in terms of discipline and loyalty and stock price, it also created a top-down, parent-child relationship between Jack and GE employees. Having 300,000 employees working in lockstep is powerful, but it's hard to enlist risky new ideas from people who are expected to do everything perfectly. A society that glorifies numbers—and fears mistakes—leaves little room for human imperfections.

In meetings, Jack would regularly rate people's contributions by saying, "That's got to be the second dumbest idea I've ever heard." It was always funny, but it was also a put-down. (And it made me wonder, What's the dumbest idea? Should I aspire to that?)

It was a command and control culture with one guy who gave out all the grades and permission slips. Jack would say things like, "I can't be everywhere, so I just said they can't do that." Managers shunned innovation to avoid failure. (The culture became a favorite theme on *30 Rock*, the show created by Tina Fey, that lampooned NBC and its parent company for seven seasons. One of the most popular episodes depicts an annual "Retreat to Move Forward" of "the Six Sigmas," a group of men who celebrate their "pillars" of culture: Brutality, Male Enhancement, and Handshakefulness.)

And I realized that I didn't have permission yet. GE demanded predictability and exactitude, not exploration. Jack didn't really want questions raised; after all, he had the answers. GE had become a reliable performance machine, not a place for change-makers.

To succeed in creating change, to not be picked off whenever you stick out your neck, you've got to act using the other side's language and values. You've got to act from the inside, knowing their arguments better than they do. In other words, I had to learn how to speak and act GE. That meant learning to balance myself on an organizational fault line between uniqueness and belonging, between being someone who is not blinded by cultural assumptions and has the independence to question and provoke, and someone whose sight is credible because of her loyalty to (and performance in) that same culture. I would need to make myself into someone who belonged, yet was able to be independent enough to rebel without getting fired.

A few years ago, the Franciscan priest Richard Rohr wrote an essay about living in the sacred space at "the edge." Living deep on the inside is too dark—"what might be" is incapacitated by what's already worked. Living on the outside, however, you have no influence. It is on the edge between inside and outside where you can get things done.

In other words, being the *outsider inside*. Someone who can translate the outside for the inside in terms it can understand. Someone who builds "bridges, not walls." Someone who is enough of an insider not to be rejected by the corporation's natural antibodies.

It was my performance that would allow me to build the social capital that would give me the leeway to push on the way things were done, when it was necessary. When your North Star is always the work and how to make it better, it keeps you from engaging in petty politics or hand-to-hand combat over personality issues. Putting the work first gives you a measure of protection. And I needed that.

I knew by acting as a change-maker I might never be liked or accepted. But being PR Girl, cozying up to the boys at The Table of Lost Dreams, was always destined for failure. I was never going to be a charismatic glad-hander. And I certainly was never going to be one of the boys who knew the lifetime batting average of Ted Williams.

Be the outsider inside, translating new ideas for the organization in terms it can understand. Someone who is enough of an insider not to be rejected by the corporation's natural antibodies.

Years later, I felt an odd satisfaction when I heard that after I returned to NBC again, Bill William Conaty—the head of GE HR—said to a colleague, "You know, I'll say this about Beth. It's always been about making the work great. It's never been about her."

Unlikely, but Not Impossible

With my new approach in mind, I dove into one of Jack's pet crusades, and one of the most controversial of all of GE's projects: the Hudson River PCBs fight.

In the 1940s, GE began using polychlorinated biphenyls—PCBs—as an electrical insulating fluid in the housings of the capacitors and transformers it made at its plants at Hudson Falls and Fort Edward, on the bank of the Hudson River north of Albany, New York. Over the next three decades, the company dumped about one million pounds of PCB chemicals into the river—which at the time was legal. But a series of lab studies showed that PCBs caused cancer in lab animals, and possibly in humans, and could be tied to premature births and developmental problems.

The federal government banned the use of PCBs in 1976, over strenuous complaints from GE. Even before then, the state of New York demanded a cleanup. That's when Jack came into the picture, when he was sent to negotiate a settlement with the state. With his amazing toughness and charisma, he managed to get a deal that capped the company's liability at $3 million—a small amount for a giant global corporation like GE.

By the time I got to GE twenty years later, that deal was collapsing. In 1983, the EPA declared a huge swathe of the Hudson River a Superfund site—the agency's biggest. And by late 1999, the EPA announced that GE's effort to stop seepage from the old plant sites wouldn't be enough. Dredging the river would be the only way to

Invite outsiders in to help tear down the walls, pave over the moats, and connect the company castle to a diverse flow of ideas and people.

really clean it. And GE would have to pay for the job. The starting estimate for the cleanups was $500 million.

Jack would have none of it. The EPA report was based on bad science, he railed, and dredging would make things worse by recirculating PCBs in the riverbed that were being broken down by natural processes. To Jack, the whole thing was just a leftist green conspiracy. Moreover, it was antibusiness. Inside GE, one thing you did not do—ever—was disagree with Jack on the PCBs issue.

Now, I had majored in biology in college and was a nature-loving person. So Jack's intense hatred of the EPA made me queasy. But my feelings didn't really matter. I was part of the PCBs army. It made for tough moments. Some PR people live for these moments. It's all about attack, counterattack, my message, your message. If GE was to have any hope of winning, I realized, we needed someone on the outside who knew how to fight this. So I made it my job to find somebody.

That's when I discovered Gary Sheffer, who had worked for the Secretary of the Environment in New York under Governor Pataki's administration, and, previously, for Zenia Mucha, who went on to be head of communications at Disney. Mucha had a reputation as a fiery political communicator who always won in a fight, and Gary was an acolyte of hers. I felt we had our man.

Jack brought in ad agency BBDO's Phil Dusenberry, a legendary adman who had run Reagan's campaign and who, along with Jack, had developed what is still one of GE's best taglines: "We Bring Good Things to Life." Jack approved every ad Phil and BBDO came up with, including the Reaganesque "Morning in America" ad campaign with several beautiful eagles flying over the Hudson and upstate New York. Essentially, the message was, "The eagles are back, the fish are happy."

. . .

Jack kept saying that the fight was about the science—that the PCBs that GE dumped were legal at the time. Moreover, they weren't safely removable. But as he micromanaged the PCB campaign, I began to see that Jack couldn't stand the idea of folding after he'd fought so long. He had to win.

And frankly, I got swept up in the war. As the essayist John Gardner once wrote, "All too often, on the long road up, young leaders become servants of what is rather than shapers of what might be." That's what happened to me. I was shrill, and determined to fight to the end. I didn't even nudge for change. I let my lack of experience with PCB science, and GE, quiet my inner voice.

Here Be Dragons

When we are excavating the emotional reasons behind why we do things, we tend to avoid negative emotions, such as worry, fear, and anger. But these emotions are like blazes on a forest trail. They point to problems just beneath the surface, trends, or opportunities that are emerging that nobody has spotted yet. Our fears, if acknowledged and catalogued like exotic species in an unexplored rain forest, can be valuable sources of knowledge for ourselves and our organizations.

Jack's role—and mine—in that fight over PCBs taught me a vital lesson: that one of the greatest enemies of change is what I call *incapacitated learning*, a phrase I borrowed from the futurist Edie Weiner. She describes it as a condition of "knowing so much about what we already know that we are the last to see the future for it differently." It's like carrying a career's worth of mental baggage around.

Entrenched professionals—and there was no one more entrenched than Jack—carry around a lot of hard-won mental baggage. And then, one day, all of a sudden these strange young people go rushing past them into the future carrying Patagonia backpacks. With their lighter load, they leave the old guard in the dust to rationalize their heavy expensive bags.

The unfortunate truth is, most of us fear losing what we have more than we desire winning something we don't have. The better we get at doing one thing, the less we want to work on something else. What's more, we tend to surround ourselves with people who think like we do and reinforce our biases.

It takes a lot of work to change your mind-set and continue to keep learning. Business people love to talk about disrupting markets and industries, but we rarely put forth the effort to disrupt ourselves. It's just too hard.

It may seem like I'm attacking Jack on the PCB fight, but that's not my intent. He believed in the rightness of his fight. And his winning spirit is part of what made him an admired CEO at a unique time in business history. Jack was a CEO superstar—*the* superstar of his era. And yet that era was ending. I found Jack to be an incredible teacher; I'm a better leader because of him.

Let me give you an example. Moving fast and being organized were my strong suits. If I could field phone calls with both hands and both feet, I would. The more there was to do, the more alive I felt. I loved to be productive, efficient, every to-do-list item checked. Urgency was my favorite soundtrack. I loved the energy and the thrill, and was good at keeping up with it.

So imagine my surprise when, one afternoon, I was talking on the phone with Jack when the line went dead.

I called his assistant, Rosanne, to say we had been disconnected. She said, "No, you weren't. Jack hung up on you."

What?

"He says he wants you to know what it's like to be in a meeting with you," Rosanne told me. "You're too abrupt."

Chastised, I walked up to Jack's office.

"You have to wallow in it," Jack said with his cheeky smile. "Take time to get to know people. Understand where they are coming from, what is important to them. Make sure they are with you."

I heard Jack loud and clear. My zeal to do everything on my to-do list—along with my shy nature—made me come across as abrupt and distant. I started every meeting by jumping right in. Later, with everything under control, I would jump right back out. At best, my colleagues didn't know what to make of me—and I didn't give them time to find out.

I cringe sometimes when I think of how I must have come across, and how long it took me to change my ways. Even now there are times when I forget Jack's advice. But I've learned to not only wallow in it, but to enjoy it. Having time to connect with people is as important as getting everything done. Sometimes you have to go slow to go fast.

End of an Era

My time with Jack ended with my big assignment: running the public side of GE's CEO succession.

Because company executives move from division to division so often, GE is obsessed with succession at every level. But CEO succession kicks that into overdrive. With his emphasis on performance and competition, Jack wanted a very public competition between several candidates, knowing full well that the losers would undoubtedly leave the company. He wanted to push the competitors harder than they'd imagined possible; he wanted to see their character. They would have to be professional with one another, even while fighting to the death.

In the end, the succession came down to three candidates: Jeff Immelt, a 6-foot-4-inch Harvard MBA and former college football player; Bob Nardelli, who ran GE Power Systems and was nicknamed "Little Jack" for his similarity to Jack; and Jim McNerney, who'd done great work at GE Aircraft Engines and seemed most likely to run for political office. I had to manage the public spectacle for several years, as business reporters called nonstop to get odds on the race. Jack kept his cards close to his vest, and the tension was truly unbearable.

And then, just as Jack was about to announce his successor, he saw a possible acquisition that would cement his legacy: Honeywell. Jack had studied and analyzed Honeywell for a long time; when he learned that United Technologies was talking about a merger with it, he faxed in a handwritten offer to the Honeywell leadership team.

Jack managed to push aside United Technologies and get a tentative okay from Honeywell for a $45 billion deal. When he told me about the deal, he said, "Get ready to announce that we've made an offer. And, oh, I've offered to the GE board to stay around to help make sure this happens." It would have been GE's largest acquisition to date and was a lot to swallow, especially for a new CEO.

Determined to keep military secrecy, Jack decided he would finalize the process over Thanksgiving weekend while America was cooking, eating, and getting together with family. The day before Thanksgiving, Jack called GE's board management council to tell them he was planning a phone meeting with the full board on Friday.

Then, on Sunday, he got on the GE jet in Boca Raton and told the surprised pilot to fly to rainy Cincinnati. Jack had kept the destination a secret from even the pilot until the last moment. There, Jack broke the bad news to Jim McNerney: he wouldn't be getting the job.

Then he told the pilot—still in the dark—to fly to even rainier Albany, where he told Bob Nardelli that he, too, was out.

Now, after two of the most difficult meetings of his life—telling two colleagues and, really, friends, that their GE careers were over—he flew to New York to deliver some happy news, to Jeff Immelt.

Jeff had been chosen as the next CEO of General Electric. He had grown the health care business through new products and his customer focus seemed to be just what GE needed.

The "Jack and Jeff" press conference announcing Immelt's selection took place in NBC's Studio 8H, the *Saturday Night Live* studio. In true GE fashion, we had managed the PR and media efforts with the gusto I imagine goes into a papal transition.

Jack's one-year extension came as his playbook was getting dangerously close to its expire-by date.

When Jack became chairman and CEO, at the start of 1981, GE had a $13 billion market cap; when he retired in 2001, it was worth some $400 billion. The principal source of GE's financial success was that Jack bought lots of companies—especially in financial services—to make GE's earnings continue on their upward slope. He pushed the company headfirst into finance. GE had long had a financial services division—GE Capital—that helped consumers and industrial customers finance their GE purchases. Jack pushed it to expand into other sectors, like mortgages and car and boat loans, to the point that it had $371 billion in assets in 2001 and, at its peak, accounted for over half of GE's profits. Jack then used the balance sheet of GE Capital to make financial acquisitions that could easily be sold to help fill earnings gaps on the industrial side. With this tool, Jack was able to deliver the numbers he promised, quarter after quarter and year after year. And Wall Street rewarded GE with an ever-increasing market capitalization.

But while constant acquisitions and financial services boosted GE's bottom line and stock price, they required deep cost cutting in parts of the company. In order to meet Jack's constant tightening, GE managers cut back on R&D and stayed out of risky new sectors. The company that was famous for bringing the lightbulb, X-ray machine, and unbreakable plastic to market had come up with fewer earth-shattering products in recent years.

More troubling, from Wall Street's point of view, was that GE

Capital's growth was basically turning GE into a bank—*Barron's* called it "a hedge fund in drag" in 1998. And banks didn't get the forty times earnings multiples that GE was getting.

The announcement of the Honeywell acquisition seemed to pierce Wall Street's seemingly ironclad confidence in Jack. The street was wary of such a big acquisition and growing tired of the finance hamster wheel. GE's stock began to sag. But the true coup de grâce came from Europe. It turns out that Europeans hadn't signed up for what Jack had in mind. In one short, quiet meeting, they made it clear to Jack that GE's merger with Honeywell wasn't going to be approved. As GE's stock sank and his last day in the corner office approached, the air started to come out of the GE story like a punctured balloon.

During the midst of all this change I found myself asking, Who are we? What did GE really stand for? We had a rich history that existed long before Jack appeared on the scene, seeds that had been planted a century ago. What were the things that had to change? I was still not quite 100 percent GE baked. I didn't speak GE as my mother tongue. Because of that, I could look at things a bit more objectively, and even critically.

Finally, on September 7, 2001, Jeff Immelt took over as the ninth chairman and CEO in General Electric's history.

The transition was one of the most widely covered events in business around the globe. There was a saying at GE Capital that "trees grow to the sky." And it seemed true. As the company with the highest market capitalization on the planet, we were soaring and were sure we'd continue to do so. We were ready for anything, or so we thought.

Four days later, the world as we knew it ended.

Challenges

MOTHER MAY I?

I taught class every month for early-career managers at GE's Crotonville learning center. I challenged the managers when they said they couldn't do things because "the company" wouldn't let them or their boss wouldn't let them. "Is it that they won't let you or that you are too afraid to try?" I asked.

Then I gave them a permission slip, asking them to follow through. "Give yourself permission to try just one thing that may be holding you back." And I encouraged them to share it with someone on their team. If they were a manager, I encouraged them to give blank slips to their team.

One manager told me afterward: "I did this! We had a request for a proposal that was due last month, the first for our new product, so this would end up being the template for all future requests. The initial draft was bad. I wanted to reach out to others to make it better, but our team is siloed—we don't ask others for help. I pulled a team together, including Legal, Regulatory, and Engineering, who never get included early. I didn't wait for permission! We put together a great response. And . . . we won the deal!"

Sometimes just having a permission slip at your desk or on your phone is a good reminder to take action. I keep a stack of slips in a conference room and make a big deal of symbolically handing them over to colleagues when they are stuck.

THE PERMISSION CHALLENGE

Write out a series of things you are scared of or are putting off doing. These things could range from "talking to a complete stranger" to "screaming in public." Write yourself a permission slip. (You may

```
┌─────────────────────────────────────────────────────┐
│              ┌ ─ ─ ─ ─ ─ ─ ─ ─ ─ ─ ─ ─ ┐             │
│                  PERMISSION SLIP                      │
│              └ ─ ─ ─ ─ ─ ─ ─ ─ ─ ─ ─ ─ ┘             │
│                                                       │
│   I, _____     │
│                                                       │
│   GIVE MYSELF THE PERMISSION TO:                      │
│   _____      │
│   _____      │
│   _____      │
│                                                       │
│                     PASS IT ON                        │
└─────────────────────────────────────────────────────┘
```

remember this from forging your mother's signature in high school; I was too afraid then to do it.) Decide what things you are giving yourself permission to do. Choose a permission slip at random each day, and carry out the task. Hold yourself accountable by making the act public. Have someone photograph you midscream, or tell a colleague or friend about your conversation with a complete stranger. Make the challenges as simple or as grand as you want. You have permission.

CREATE A MONTHLY BUCKET LIST

Hold yourself accountable for getting out of your comfort zone by creating a monthly "I Can Do This" list. It can be as long or short as you want, but the goal is to accomplish the tasks before the end of the month. Fill it with things like: invite a colleague for coffee, pitch a new idea, take a class to improve on or learn a new skill. Rather than waiting to do grand things "someday," a monthly list will give you a number of doable things. Start small. Start now. What can you do this month?

THE DRAGON SLAYER CHALLENGE

Whenever you feel a negative emotion related to work bubble up, take note. Get a notebook and start keeping a log. Include entries for moments of fear and negativity voiced by your colleagues and friends about their industries and jobs. Your entries don't need to be long or detailed. A sentence or a phrase will do. At the end of the week, take a look at what you've written down. Do the observations and comments add up to a larger problem or trend? What are you going to do about it?

YOUR DIY JOB CRAFTING CHALLENGE

Monday morning you are going to add one new project (that you are excited about!) to your set of responsibilities. Spend the weekend developing your thesis and how you will approach the project. Think about developing skills in a new area, for example: social media, design thinking, emerging technology, coding, finance. What will be the ways you can begin to develop the project? A newsletter, trend report, brown-bag "lunch and learn" are good ways to get started.

GET A COACH

If you worked for me and were struggling in an area of your professional life, I would likely tell you to get a coach. It's not about what's wrong with you; it's about how to become a better you. Some coaches help you make better presentations. Others help you develop more confidence. Others still focus on leadership skills. Many companies provide budgets for coaching opportunities, from classes to development advisors. But I've also paid for coaching myself in instances when I felt it was important. In hiring a coach, decide what you are hoping to accomplish. Set goals and a realistic time frame for the coaching assignment. If the coach is being paid for by your company, plan to follow up with your boss to discuss the outcome. It may be helpful to have a boss and other colleagues speak to a coach to provide input before the coaching begins. If you don't have funds to hire someone, enlist a trusted colleague for regular coaching sessions. Ask them to help you get better and hold you accountable for changing.

We all have areas to improve, whether we're line managers or CEOs. Get a handle on the areas you need to improve before a problem or weakness derails you in the future. Remember, seeking professional help is not an indictment—it is about taking a positive step forward to be a better version of you.

SECTION II

Discovery

CHAPTER 3

EDISON'S MARINES

Chaos Rewards the Bold

On September 7, 2001, Jeff Immelt took over as the ninth chairman and CEO in General Electric's history.

A few days later, on the almost cloudless morning of Tuesday, September 11, 2001, I and the rest of the communications department were all positioned in front of our office TVs waiting for Jack's live appearance on the *Today Show*, where he was launching his soon-to-be-bestselling memoir, *Straight from the Gut*. Jeff Immelt was in Seattle at the time, trudging on a hotel StairMaster.

Just after 8:00 a.m., the first plane hit the World Trade Center. Within a minute, it became clear that it was an intentional attack, and all our plans and assumptions and hopes for the future evaporated.

Immediately we shifted into crisis mode, as most companies did:

making sure employees were okay,* connecting with customers. For GE, the attacks had a major impact on our aviation and financing divisions, which manufacture jet engines and finance airplanes for airlines. Aircraft across the country were grounded for several days, and questions arose around airline security, insurance liabilities, and credit ratings.

It was only four days into Jeff's tenure, and already we were in uncharted territory. In times of chaos, it's natural to feel you should hunker down. Almost everything may seem out of your control—but your imagination and ability to take action are not among them. You have to resist the urge to think it's up to others; you have to take initiative.

While we were trying to offer solace in the face of 9/11—we moved necessary mobile units to the triage hospitals in New York, gave transformers to Consolidated Edison, and Jeff called New York City mayor Rudy Giuliani to pledge $10 million of GE money to the first responders—I decided that GE had to let the world know that while we would never forget, we were also ready to fight back and rebuild. People were lost and disengaged, and we had to show them a guiding light.

This was an incredibly awkward moment to be doing any sort of advertising or marketing. Companies were avoiding doing anything that seemed like an attempt to turn tragedy into profit. But I was sure people would find comfort in an expression of undaunted strength, so I went to Jeff and told him that we needed to put ourselves out there. With no lead time for radio and TV, that left us with print ads. That was still a big risk, but one well worth it, I believed. "We need a print ad that rallies our employees and customers and says 'We are strong,'" I told Jeff. "People are afraid. They need to hear it's going to be all right."

Jeff Immelt was a forty-five-year-old unknown to most people,

---

* Sadly we lost two people.

a mix of Ohio-bred football player, Harvard MBA, and son of a
lifetime GE engineer, who had just taken over from the CEO of
the century. Jeff wasn't as polished then—he'd walk around with a
button too far undone on his shirt, and everybody (except me for
some reason) had to have a nickname—Jim was Jimmy, Bill was
Billy, as if GE were a locker room. But he has always been the most
comfortable-in-his-skin guy you'll ever meet.

Investors and half of Wall Street were asking whether he was up
to the task. But I—and everybody else who worked closely with
him—knew that he had both that calculating Six Sigma mental
toughness (Jack Welch would have never let him close to the corner
office without it) as well as an appreciation for the "softer skills"—
including empathy, storytelling, and connecting with people, especially customers—that he seemed to have picked up while he was in
marketing and sales earlier in his career. And he believed strongly in
the power of communications, in story, as a transformative leadership tool.

When I told him I wanted to do an ad—"something iconic"—he
asked me if I was willing to accept the consequences of what happened with it. And when I said, "Yes," he told me, "Go for it," like
a football coach okaying a Hail Mary pass.

Our ad agency, BBDO, was a bigger obstacle than Jeff. They
had been GE's agency for over eighty years, and they felt their past
performance entitled them to decide what GE needed. They didn't
like—okay, they flat-out resented—that this insufficiently rever-
ent woman (me) was now, in effect, their boss. When I called Phil
Dusenberry's team to tell them that we needed to put together a
print ad that showed strength and solidarity, they wielded their apa-
thy like a cudgel. "Don't worry, we'll get you some mock-ups tomorrow," the account rep told me, before failing to do so. When
BBDO finally gave me some ideas, it was obvious that they were
phoning it in.

Now, I'm not a screamer—I get quiet, cold, and stern when I'm angry—but when they turned in garbage, the register of my voice went up. "People are scared. They want a reason to feel hopeful. What you are giving me is too corporate, too clichéd."

I finally told Phil, "Just send me everything you've done." This is a standard practice of mine: ask people what they didn't show you, the questions they didn't ask. The files they sent me were more of the same: pretty images and soft slogans. But as I pawed through the work with increasing despair, I came across a simply etched pencil sketch that made me look twice. My mouth creased into the first smile in what seemed like a year. This is hope, I thought. This is strength.

I grabbed the drawing and practically ran to Jeff's office. I smacked the image down on his desk. "This is it," I said. "*This* is the way to say what everyone is feeling."

It was a sketch of Lady Liberty, square-jawed, iron-willed, rolling up her sleeves, stepping off her pedestal, striding toward the viewer, about to open a can of American bravery on anyone who would stand in the way of her manifest destiny. A simple message ran beneath the image: "We will roll up our sleeves. We will move forward together. We will overcome. We will never forget." The only reference to us as a company was a single sentence at the bottom of the page: "A message from" and the GE logo.

Almost everyone at the company hated the idea, from our internal ad team to the account executives at BBDO. One of GE's business heads said to me it made us look like angry punks: "What is this, Lady John Wayne?" Our account rep at BBDO said we risked trivializing America's pain with a "cartoon." Even my closest friend on the internal ad team said it made her nervous because it just "isn't us."

We listened to everyone. But in the end, we overruled them. Jeff showed faith in me, and he took some heat for it, including a cascade of calls from the leaders of the business units telling him in no uncertain terms that they thought it sent the wrong message.

Just ten days after the attack, the full-page ad appeared in nearly every major newspaper in the country: the *New York Times*, the *Wall Street Journal*, the *New York Post*. The night before, I was up half the night, sweating it out, turning over every possible outcome in my head—public rejection, me fired.

I am a worrier. In part my runaway imagination is a way to prepare for every possible outcome. And partly it's just my anxiety going unchecked. I've since learned to channel this anxiety into scenario-planning; it is one way I've been able to feel so comfortable dreaming up the most outlandish, crazy scenarios for the future.

I habitually get to the office before my colleagues to get a head start on my day. It's one of my favorite times, when I plan for the day, think expansively, and tackle the biggest concerns on my mind from the night before. The day the ad was published, I arrived even earlier, just as the first light was breaking over the horizon. As I waited in my office, I could barely concentrate. What did people think of the ad? Of GE?

It wasn't long before the e-mails began to pour in from proud GE employees across the country. And our ad was a lead story on nearly every morning news show.

I only discovered the true extent to which the ad had succeeded several days later, when Jeff and I went to visit Ground Zero and the New York Stock Exchange. The smoke and dust from the twin towers choked our throats as we stared at the utter destruction of the World Trade Center site.

When we walked onto the floor of the NYSE, there was the ad, Scotch-taped to the wall of almost every trader's kiosk. People high-fived Jeff and me for giving them this image. They actually cheered.

Within days we saw our ad everywhere around New York: in Brooklyn barbershops, in Upper East Side bars, in New Jersey sandwich joints. People just *got* it. We weren't selling lightbulbs or jet engines; we were selling leadership, optimism, America.

I was so proud of the leadership GE exhibited. For GE, or any

We will roll up our sleeves.

We will move forward together.

We will overcome.

We will never forget.

A message from

company existing in this epoch of endless disruption, occasions require bold action—leaning into, and not away from, the unknown for the right reasons.

Stop Worrying, Start Planning

I believe in heeding the wisdom of Bill Gates: "We always overestimate the change that will occur in the next two years and underestimate the change that will occur in the next ten. Don't let yourself be lulled into inaction." My "Imagine it Forward" version of this is "Change seems impossible—until it happens. At which point it seems to have always been inevitable."

To combat our tendency to be lulled into inaction, I find it's useful in planning ahead to develop at least three or four scenarios about the future, including one that is wildly optimistic, one that is disruptive, and one that is incredibly conservative. I've found it's also helpful to invite in outsiders to offer differing perspectives and then marry those with, or challenge, the perspectives of inside-company experts. Red team–blue team exercises—where teams take opposing points of view—have proven valuable as a way for teams to go deep in different directions. Part discovery, part debate, these exercises allow everyone to consider the issues together.

The Call for Discovery

By the end of Jeff's first week in the corner office, GE shares had plunged 20 percent, cutting the company's value by almost $80 billion. There was a palpable sense that the ground was shifting under our feet, and it extended well beyond the change in leadership at GE or the 9/11 attacks. There were forces at work that were beyond our control, beginning with the bursting of the dot-com bubble. The collapse affected new technology businesses (good-bye Pets.com) and established ones alike (Cisco's stock declined by as much as 87 percent). And then there was the giant energy conglomerate, Enron, which declared bankruptcy at the end of 2001 in a maelstrom of scandal, followed by the dissolution of one of the world's leading accounting firms, Arthur Andersen.

All these failures combined to create a general sense that big corporations were secretive institutions that couldn't be trusted. It was around this time that the word "transparency" started cropping up in conversations about corporate America, and not in a good way.

At the time Jeff Immelt took over, GE was a disparate and complex conglomerate that included a giant television and movie company; America's seventh largest bank; a large insurance business (for humans and pets); portfolios in transportation, health care, and energy; and traditional industrial components like appliances and plastics. Growth at GE had slowed; doubts were being raised about the long-term viability of the insurance business and the dominance of GE Capital. Some economists questioned how GE had so consistently generated double-digit profit growth for nearly a decade.

Jeff believed GE had relied too much on buying other companies to support top- and bottom-line growth. His mandate was to grow from our base of technical strength. Jeff sought what investors call *organic growth*, meaning you don't buy your revenues, you *grow* them. He wanted to put the company on a course to invest record amounts in technology but also to be more connected to the world's global markets, especially those in developing countries where suddenly much of the world's entrepreneurial energy (and growth) was being generated.

That would require a new kind of leadership, one that expects judgment calls to be made in the face of incomplete data, that encourages original thinking, that values speed over perfection, that

Discovery is about engaging the world as a classroom, to extract the ideas that will create the future.

embraces change. That this would take over a decade to seed wasn't clear at the time. We knew we had to expand on the "all-in" zero-defects managerial doctrine of Six Sigma. There is a lot of good in Six Sigma, because it focuses people on quality and reduced distraction. But Six Sigma created a culture that venerated process, and along the way, our people lost some of their capacity to take smart risks and use personal judgment when making decisions.

The new GE would have to be as much about opportunity as efficiency.

The task was monumental: maintain all the expertise that made us who we are and at the same time learn how to think and act differently to ensure we are able to grow into something new. But how do you teach a company imagination that looks to create a future few can see?

I describe it as "optimize today and build tomorrow." Companies have to learn how to do *both* if they expect to be around for future generations. Good leaders know it is their job to manage the tension from this hard balancing act.

To become an ambidextrous organization, we needed to become better explorers. We needed to engage the world as a classroom from which we could learn and extract the ideas that would create our future. It was something that I would eventually codify in our workflow and come to call *discovery*.

It's hard to convey just how absurd, and even threatening, these ideas sounded to so many of GE's leaders at the time. The story we told of ourselves and celebrated then was almost exclusively a story of optimizers—our language centered on efficiency, defect removal, and process rigor, while our Six Sigma "black belts" were GE's ninja forces, guiding teams forward through continuous process improvement. How many times had I heard, "That's not who GE is." I knew the primary source of resistance to the changes we were seeking would be our own identity.

GE's Caped Crusader

As I began to assess who we were as a company and where we needed to go, it occurred to me to hire a consulting company like McKinsey to offer recommendations. But something about taking such a comfortable and predictable route during a moment of intense chaos seemed like a cop-out. I had another idea.

In May 2001, I had attended a conference with a speaker brought by Procter & Gamble named Clotaire Rapaille. Dr. Rapaille is the kind of guy who sticks in your memory, an unorthodox Frenchman prone to wearing black velvet capes and offering meandering discourses about the vitality of cheese.

A one-time child psychiatrist who founded the research and branding firm Archetype Discoveries Worldwide, Rapaille helps companies articulate their identities—and plan how to modify them for the future. And that's what GE desperately needed after 9/11. What do we value? What is sacred and what needs to change? Why?

Realizing what our brand or business is really about is critically important—especially in the face of turbulence. If a company thinks of itself only as a bank, it behaves one way. But if it begins to think of itself as a financial advisor, or as a service provider, then it starts to behave differently.

Rapaille's philosophy is driven by a belief that every culture imprints on its members a unique and distinct logic of emotion—an affective identity. According to Rapaille, the first time we understand what a word represents—*coffee, mother, love*—we imprint its meaning, and in so doing create a mental connection that lasts the rest of our lives. "Every word has a mental highway," Rapaille likes to say. Dr. Rapaille calls this the "Culture Code."

That's where the cheese comes in. "In America," Rapaille tells people, "the Code for cheese is: 'Dead.'" That's because in America,

Bring in a *spark*, an outsider who challenges the team to think differently. Be the spark!

all cheese is pasteurized, which means it is scientifically dead. In France, cheese is filled with microbes that give it a taste and a smell. In France, you never put cheese in the refrigerator because it's *alive*. The priority is different; the logic of emotion is different. The French like taste before safety; the Americans want safety before taste. "Here, the cheese is safe, and to make that really clear I wrap it up in plastic. That plastic is like a body bag and the fridge is like the morgue."

At the heart of Rapaille's work is a theory based on a three-part concept (or "triune," as he calls it) of how the brain works. The Cortex is the seat of logic and reason, abstract thought and language; the Limbic is the brain's emotional center; and the Reptilian is the area controlled by our basic human needs: eating, breathing, reproducing, surviving. All three sides of the brain exert powerful influences. But in Rapaille's world, "the reptilian always wins."

I had some reservations about hiring Rapaille—he was weird and his "science" dubious, and I could imagine Jeff's less-than-positive reaction to the velvet cape. But I felt on a gut level the need to try something new at GE, and his theories gelled with my love of neuroscience. Plus, his contract with P&G seemed to be enough of an imprimatur of respectability to justify a meeting with Jeff.

When the meeting took place in our executive conference room in Fairfield, though, it went downhill fast. It was Rapaille, me, Jeff, Bob Wright (by now also a GE vice chair), and Rapaille's assistant, who took notes and said little. Bob occasionally spoke up, but this was definitely a dance between Rapaille and Jeff. Unfortunately, the two men had no shared language. It was like Six Sigma meets the New Age, Captain America meets Inspector Clouseau. Seemingly incognizant of (or indifferent to) their lack of connection, Rapaille told the stinky cheese anecdote in its gratuitous entirety. It was excruciating.

Eventually Jeff, his frustration in full plumage, went to the whiteboard and began outlining his business strategy.

"We will invest in technology," he said, writing the words in a bright red marker. "We'll get closer to the customer. And we'll grow the company from within."

Despite being irritated, Immelt was articulate, clear, affable. He started writing numbers on the board to represent rates of organic growth within the company and revenue growth for shareholders. He drew a circle around his growth target. "This is where it has to be," he said, putting down the marker.

And then Rapaille jumped up and, with a green marker, wrote in large letters: CORTEX. LIMBIC. REPTILIAN.

Here we go, I thought, trying to contain myself. He outlined his triune theory and the principle of the culture code. "It's all about our unconscious minds," he said. "I don't understand what you're trying to say with all those numbers."

"Well, that's my business plan," Jeff replied matter-of-factly.

"And I'm telling you, it's not *in* the numbers," Rapaille replied. "The *reptilian* always wins."

I felt sick. I could see the thought bubble over Jeff's head: *I just told you what I'm going to do, what the hell does that have to do with reptiles?*

I am so fired, I thought.

But Rapaille then said something that changed the entire tenor of the meeting. "Well, all those numbers you wrote on the board: What do people have to *believe* in for all those things to happen? People don't get out of bed to work for 'the numbers' . . . for ten percent." That was a question that resonated deeply with Jeff after the upheaval we had just been through. Rapaille was searching for the soul, the raison d'être, of GE.

Jeff began talking about the corporation as if it were a living thing. "We are this giant entity," he explained, "comprised of many different businesses—great businesses with terrific customers. But we cannot just keep going out and buying new businesses. That has to change. We have an important mission now. We have many great businesses to *grow from*," he said. "We have everything you could want: global reach, technology, diversity, fantastic people, and we have all this history. *We perform.*"

Rapaille's eyes grew wide, and his mischievous smile returned to his lips. "That performance, that longevity," he said. "That's where we will find the essential truth, the Code, that drives this company."

Now he had Jeff's attention. Soon they were writing on the whiteboard together. Jeff would explain things he was trying to do with his strategy, and Rapaille would press him for the emotional needs that would make them possible. I knew it was a good meeting because it went on for at least ninety minutes. Jeff was a stickler for keeping to a schedule—he doesn't let things run over. And we definitely did this time.

Afterward, as Rapaille's elevator descended, I asked Jeff what he thought.

"Well," he said with a wry smile. "Those first few minutes were horrible, Beth. You were almost fired." It was clear that he was only half-joking. "But yes, I think it's worth it. We should try things like this, whatever it is." It was a very common utterance for Jeff: "Give it a try, Beth."

Having survived the bringing together of oil and water, I threw myself into organizing Rapaille's visits. It was not going to be easy. Rapaille's process is not a one-off focus group, but a six-month marathon. Making it harder was pushback from the people whose involvement we most needed: the discovery team I put together to investigate and lead the project.

The goal of the Rapaille process was not just to uncover GE's identity, but to find a way to present it to clients and our own employees in a way that aligned with Jeff's new growth strategy. That meant that everything was up for evaluation—we might have to go as far as changing our slogan, "We Bring Good Things to Life."

Rapaille's methodology is unique, to put it mildly. He organizes teams of employees and customers, and puts them through a three-step process of "imprinting" or "sensing" sessions. Each lasts one hour and draws on a different part of the brain, moving from the outside (logical) to the inside (reptilian). In all, the process would involve about four hundred GE employees and customers in Connecticut, New York, Atlanta, and Cleveland.

Rapaille's great value was as a catalyst, a spark, via his selection of questions. A spark is a person, usually an outsider, whose unique perspective—the more different, the better—challenges the team to think differently. Asking us to describe our tribe to an alien forced us to be our own cultural anthropologists. Posing good and discomforting questions creates distance and makes you observe yourself. This process—*discovery*—is in dialogue with the environment. And the more vital and "weird" the environment is, the more likely you are to grow.

Bring in a Spark

Early on, I was nervous about bringing in sparks, because I thought I was supposed to have the answers. Or that their difference or the fact that they made my colleagues uncomfortable would reflect poorly on me. But what I came to realize is that while their difference can cause discomfort, it is often necessary. Because they don't work in the company, sparks aren't afraid of challenging the boss or office politics. And surprisingly, people pay attention to sparks, especially when they make them think or say the unexpected.

At our first session in Atlanta, my discovery team members (there were six of them, and they represented marketing, communications, human resources, a business unit, and BBDO) bordered on hostile. The most agitated was Richard, a Brit who'd run the ad department under Jack and overseen the "Good Things" campaign for over a decade.

To Richard, I was a lightweight, and he challenged most everything I said. Now I was bringing in a crazy man to GE. Richard's body language—withdrawn, arms folded across his chest—told me all I needed to know about what he thought of this search for our code.

When Rapaille asked what the letters GE meant to our tribe, Richard mumbled, "Hmm, let's see, maybe General Electric? Or could it be Giant Eggplant?" But it was when Rapaille launched into his cheese story, which we had heard several times already, that Richard blew up. "Yes, we know the bloody cheese is *alive* in France!" he said.

The second-step "sensing" sessions were designed to take us back from our logical to our "limbic" brains. Rapaille pushed us for our emotional impressions of GE. Some staffers depicted GE as a place that was "brutal" and "kill or be killed." The notion of *Sacrifice*—reflected in comments like "I don't know my neighbors," "I live on the edge," "Stress, stress, stress," "Constant state of conflict"—was listed next to *Reward*: "It's the thrill of the kill."

After getting the people in the Atlanta group to give their brief impressions of GE, Rapaille asked them to turn those impressions into a description of the company. He had us write these on our own, to avoid groupthink. Of all the stories that came out of this first session, the one that stuck in my mind was about our toughness:

> . . . the best of the best. Tend to be successful at what they do, they
> are committed, extreme groups, they know how to survive, nimble
> enough to get it done, tough to get into.

As raw as those stories were, it was the third, "reptilian," part of the process that proved the most intense. Here, people were instructed to lie on mats on the floor and allow their minds to float back to the first imprint of GE. It was a bizarre sight: grown men and women in business suits lying on their backs in a conference room, doing "relaxation" to access their innermost feelings about the corporation. After the emotional storytelling, people were like new skin under picked scabs, so much so that I was not really surprised that, at the Atlanta event and several others, I heard sniffles in the dark.

Afterward, one young GE accountant told the group of how his fear of flying was tempered by the GE logo he spotted on the plane that was carrying him to Kansas City to see his girlfriend ("wondrous and remarkable"). Later, a consumer said, "GE protects me from certain death" every time she screwed in a lightbulb.

As we got further into the discovery sessions, something began to change in us and in our relationship to GE. We became more emotional and more reflective. We spoke of Edison and GE's rich heritage with great pride. Even Richard appeared genuinely touched by the personal stories of our fellow employees. He eventually engaged in the process and added a great deal to our final conclusions. Maybe I shouldn't have been surprised that later, after he left GE, Richard started his own consultancy, modeled on doing triune discovery and helping brands find their code.

At the end of the process, Dr. Rapaille came to Fairfield to deliver The Code we had been working so hard to decipher. Rapaille swept into the room where the discovery team was gathered. We were desperate for the big reveal; after months of work, the oracle would speak.

Without notes, he summarized the word associations, the stories, the motivating and demoralizing factors. "You are the lions, standing on a rock, looking over the plains, you can eat anything. A Great White Shark. You never stand still. GE means Get Everything. Winning is everything. You lose, you get shot. Fear is part of the drive to excel. You all have the same values: make your numbers. People have to find their own way. Do you know that no one would even give me directions to find this conference room today," he added. "Commitment. Excellence. Challenging. Thrilling. Committed. Take the hill at any cost. Work with the best. Best of the best. Perform. Win. "

We were on the edge of our seats when he finally said, "So what does all of this add up to? What is THE Code for GE?"

The room fell totally silent, as if we were about to receive the eleventh commandment from Moses himself. Dr. Rapaille smiled, clearly reveling in the attention.

"It is," he said, "the *Marines*," drawing the word out in his Frenchiest accent.

The room grew very quiet.

The Marines? That's it?

Personally, I felt deflated; I had expected something actionable, something I would instinctively connect with, something, well, *deeper*. Part of me felt he had taken the easy way out, that we had been snookered. It was what we already knew: Big. Process-driven. American. What did that add up to? The military, of course.

"The Marines?" I asked him, not in an overwhelmingly friendly tone. "Anything else to add? Something we might be able to use."

"Well, that . . ." he said. "That is your Code. Right there."

It was the first time I'd seen Dr. Rapaille lose confidence. I think his clients tended to humor the flamboyant Frenchman. But I—and all of the discovery team—had been expecting something mind-bending, something that would create an immediate before and after.

My job at this point was to present the results to Jeff. What were we to do with it? *We are the Marines; we take the hill.* After Rapaille left the final presentation, the discovery team agreed not to speak about it publicly until we presented it to Jeff in two weeks' time. We worried that people—not least of all Jeff—would misunderstand. And because, well, it sounded kind of silly.

But despite the disappointment I felt, it turned out that the discovery process had an important and lasting impact. We had become anthropologists, observing ourselves from a wholly new perspective.

Rapaille's gift was not The Code per se, but teaching us the process of discovery, the process of getting there.

GE's Most Important Product: Progress

As it turned out, the real value of this effort was less about discovering something new than about us recovering something old: Thomas Edison, who founded GE. We were America's greatest inventors. We were Edison's Marines.

Discovery had helped to focus our attention back to our roots. We remembered that Edison was not just selling lightbulbs but life-bettering imagination and a thrilling future with wow-worthy inventions.

I latched on to Edison and this insight with gusto. Our people—customers, employees, investors—needed to be inspired again. Welch had become GE's brand—and I helped make that possible. But it wasn't helpful to GE in the long run. People needed to re-believe in GE, especially now that Welch had left the building.

Fortuitously, I had an impressive tool at my disposal as we were developing these insights from our discovery: the 2002 Winter Olympics. GE was an advertising sponsor, and we had to have something to say in our ad campaign. By the time January 2002 rolled around, we were already late to begin production for ads to air during the Salt Lake City coverage.

One day, with time running tight and my frustration high at the work I was seeing from BBDO, I called John Miller, the head of the NBC Agency, NBC's in-house advertising team. I explained that I wasn't happy with what we were getting from BBDO. "You guys make great Olympics ads for NBC Sports. Can you produce ads for GE?"

"You bet. We'd love to," he said before I even finished. John was competitive and the opportunity to replace one of the big creative agencies was a major carrot.

I asked to work with Skip, who had been our go-to person at the NBC Agency. In a matter of two weeks—incredibly fast by media standards—Skip produced our ad.

It was a simple concept—short video clips of GE ads and videos from over the years, including a famous tagline from the 1960s: "Progress Is Our Most Important Product." Interjected between these historic shots were "glam" shots of our not-so-glamorous products—a jet engine, an MRI, a power generator. Over a catchy dance tune by the German Eurodance group ATC, the silky-voiced female narrator said, in part, "Our 300,000 employees around the globe create and design the technologies that promise a future without limits. Because at GE, we know there are two things that make a company great: ideas and the people who have them." As the kicker, we strategically placed a few shots of Edison moving toward the camera with a lightbulb in his hand.

"This is it," I said. I loved it. Employees loved the ad as well; it made them feel proud. Even the *New York Times* ad columnist Stuart Elliot praised its portrayal of GE as the "anti-Enron," and rated it "Gold."

Armed with a successful advertising test, along with the insights from our discovery process, I felt emboldened to ask BBDO to assign a new creative team to work with us. I felt we needed something more emotional, something grand in the messages we were developing.

We needed a mission, a rallying cry.

Every company, organization, person has a story that conveys their purpose in the world. And in business, telling that story is one of the most important things we do. To put it another way, if you can't tell it, you can't sell it. Whether it's an idea, a product, or a project, you must be clear on why it is important, what the anticipated outcome is, and why it is relevant. It's not *what* we sell, it's *why* we sell.

We decided that the simplest and best way to communicate GE's evolution both inside and outside the organization was through a new slogan, a statement of our aspiration that needed to galvanize GE inside and be shared outside. We had used "We Bring Good Things to Life" for years. It was a great tagline for its time—one of the best. But it had grown stale.

Our research told us that people heard "We Bring Good Things to Life" as bringing good things to *light*. They identified it more with GE's consumer products and couldn't find a way to connect making appliances and lightbulbs with the sophistication of making jet engines or MRIs. They identified our slogan with GE's past. To be successful, we needed our customers and our colleagues to identify with our present. We needed to state our purpose *now*.

Led by our new creative director at BBDO, Michael Patti, we shaped our discovery-based insights into a narrative that aligned with our desired outcome. There was no single *aha* moment, nobody shouting "Eureka!" in the shower. But eventually Michael and our team created a statement of purpose meant to appeal both in substance and form to the engineers who defined GE.

The beauty of the statement was that it was told as an equation, displayed on a chalkboard, in the simple language of our engineers. It became known as the GE Equation, a compelling and smart articulation of our strategy. It ended with the line "What you imagine, we can make happen."

I loved it. And the team did, too.

The equation is not strictly mathematical. We used "wow" instead of saying something about safety or speed, to appeal to the emotions of our people, to our engineers. Spend time around engineers or scientists and you'll discover that what really moves a typical engineer is the thought of solving the unsolvable, building the unbuildable, and having colleagues express wide-eyed surprise and admiration. To say, "*Wow*, I didn't think that was possible."

Once we had the GE equation set, we took it on the road, going to our key business units and training centers for feedback. It wasn't always smooth going. One engineer in Schenectady pointed out that it was "mathematically impossible to divide imagination by risk." A salesman in Cleveland said, "You really think discussing 'sweat squared' at client lunches is going to help sales?" One exec from Crotonville stood up in a meeting and threatened to quit.

And yet, there were green shoots emerging that showed that we'd chosen the right path. I was particularly heartened by the feedback of Dave Calhoun, the CEO of GE's Aviation unit, who was extremely reluctant to embrace any soft and fuzzy change. A matter-of-fact kind of guy, Dave at the time was the quintessential GE leader.

"This really speaks to me." (He liked it!) Dave embraced the need for limbic appeals, and he made it his own way of moving forward. Today, a new generation of aviation leaders define their purpose in a limbic masterpiece: "Lift people up and bring them home safely."

Bolstered by the feedback, we went back to the whiteboards to turn this into a tagline. We shrunk our purpose down to three spare words: "Imagination at Work."

Those three words served many purposes. First, they signified a break from the financialized, tough-guy GE of the recent past to one run by relentless innovators, connecting our archetype inventor-founder to our future breakthrough potential.

Second, they built a bridge from the past to the present to the future. To evolve into something new, we couldn't just cut our ties to the past. Instead, we needed to revisit and see them anew, not as constraints but as forces to harness all the new possibilities.

Finally, it paid homage to what was sacred at GE—our drive and hard work, what Edison had called 99 percent perspiration and what we now called sweat-squared. And we declared our aspiration to imagine and invent what's next.

Our new equation and tagline spoke to our desire to create a more entrepreneurial, more imagination-driven culture. But how could we ensure that these abstract ideas got translated into concrete behavioral changes? I reached out to HR, in what would become a long-standing partnership, to ask what we could do to make this statement of purpose more actionable. How could we better train and evaluate our leaders? We focused on five core traits. We called these GE's Growth Values: having an *external market driven focus*, measuring performance through the customers' eyes; being a *clear thinker*, able to sift through complex information and focus on the critical priorities and strategy action steps; having *imagination and courage*, creating environments in which others can take risks and experiment; acting through *inclusiveness*, building diverse teams and partnerships, as well as collaborating across and outside the company; and deep *expertise* as a resource to drive change.

The top five thousand people in the company would be rated on each of these traits as part of their annual performance review. To make it clear this was indeed about growth and development, and not an iteration of the previous rank-and-yank performance reviews (after which the bottom 10 percent of GE's performers were ousted—in theory—every year), we stipulated that everyone would have at least one value that was rated red (as in a red stoplight: "Stop, this needs work")—and one that was rated green (as in "Keep going; this is good"). The message: growing a company, as well as growing leadership, was a work in progress, and each one of us needed to evolve.

Taglines are not enough, of course. Too often people use them as clever statements but never go further. We needed to develop ways to live them, not just say them. For us, "Imagination at Work" became our inspiration, and the Edison touchstone worked to help reframe how we made sense of our company and what we were capable of in the future. People needed that connection to give them hope and confidence that they could actually evolve. What were reasonable actions we were expecting people to take? What was a reasonable amount of evolution to expect? How quickly?

These were questions that I was about to put to the test, personally. I had recently received feedback on my performance, too. GE, like many large corporations, has a complex and formal process for evaluating executives. For my 360-degree review, an HR leader from GE interviewed something like thirty people I worked with. The feedback was good, but also stinging: "Beth has a very independent, go-it-alone style that has made it more difficult, at times, for her to integrate with team members and peers. . . . The speed in her decision-making processes can result in people feeling left behind or unappreciated. They feel Beth's sharp, quick responses and her body language can relay a dismissive attitude."

Yikes! I started ruthlessly interrogating myself. *Where did this come from? When do I do this? How can I fix it?* Teams were engaging with me, weren't they? But I wasn't being as effective as I needed to be. Since I was making a practice of pushing myself into uncomfortable situations, this would be a new discovery—about myself and what I needed to do to keep moving forward successfully and as a valued teammate.

CHAPTER 4

A BREAKTHROUGH OF IMAGINATION: A NEW WAY OF MARKETING

Adopting a Market Mentality

The very ambitious growth targets Jeff had set would require GE to generate more than $9 billion in new revenues annually from internal operations alone. As the business media at the time put it, that's like adding the combined businesses of eBay, JetBlue, MGM, and Starbucks. No one in the world was better at producing traditional professional managers. But there was no way to optimize or cost-cut your way to those kinds of numbers.

"Listen, Beth," Jeff said. "We've got good technology, although it needs to get better, and we have a big sales force, but we don't have teams to point them in a direction and to drive new revenue from new sources. We don't have marketing."

He paused.

"I want to resurrect marketing in this company," he said. "And I want you to do it as our new chief marketing officer."

It came out of thin air, and it was a major promotion. I gave Jeff a broad smile that I hoped didn't seem as frightened and excited as I felt inside and said, "I think that's exactly what we need, Jeff. And I'm honored you want me out there in front."

No one had occupied the CMO role for twenty years when Jeff tapped me for my new assignment in early 2003. My mandate wasn't just to bring marketing back to GE; it was to help jump-start new revenue growth. As it turned out, I would also have to figure out how to make marketing into an innovation engine that inspired cultural transformation. We desperately needed growth, fueled by the power of ideas, and to get that we needed to become a GE that ventured into new and unfamiliar areas and used our intuition and imagination to turn whatever we discovered into billion-dollar businesses.

Advertising Age made the snarky observation that I was the "rare breed" of marketing chief who had never done any marketing. But I couldn't blame people for looking askance at the notion that a neophyte marketer was the key to resuscitating the ethos of Edison. At the time, marketing at GE had become what it still is at many companies, especially with businesses that do not sell directly to consumers: a way to launch a new product after it had already been developed. It consisted—if it existed at all—of advertising, trade shows, sales collateral, and publicity events. At worst, marketing was the place where washed-up salespeople went. But Jeff saw the potential—and the need—to use marketing in more proactive ways, probably because he had worked in marketing himself before going into sales.

I wasn't the most obvious choice for the role. While I had experience in communications and advertising—and I had come up through NBC, which was all about marketing—I had zero training in the fundamentals. I didn't have an MBA, hadn't grown up in GE's culture, and had never even taken a business class. Before I could think about how I was going to reinvent a marketing department for GE, and how that department would help spur massive behavioral changes in 300,000 people, I had to learn what marketing *was.* What do marketers *do?* I gave myself ninety days to get up to speed on a career's worth of teachings. I didn't know what I didn't know. But I discovered that being an outsider would be my greatest advantage.

I did what has become my signature move: I engaged in discovery, the process I expected to become the basis for the new marketing we would build at GE.

I read university marketing textbooks, especially those from Northwestern University's Philip Kotler, the "father" of modern marketing, and I became proficient in the traditional four-P constellation of marketing: product, promotion, place, and price. Before you can challenge assumptions and dislodge the status quo, you need to understand the fundamentals. A baseline.

I also reached out to headhunters to ask them which marketers were good and why, and I joined councils like M50 that convened CMOs. I'd research the examples that CMOs shared. I'd call them up and ask for more details, taking advantage of the access to ask them: "How do you measure marketing success?" I'd come to find that this was the hardest question; everyone had different metrics and different definitions of marketing.

Jim Stengel, P&G's CMO, was particularly generous with his time and advice, walking me through organizational charts and the curriculum from P&G's famed marketing institute. You can cut the time to fluency in any discipline if you can get a world-class practitioner to guide your journey. Open yourself up to be an apprentice, finding a "master craftsperson" to study under. Seek out the best in the field; take a key element of wisdom from each one, and then find a way to make it your own.

Several times, I dragged GE business CMOs with me to meet with P&G's marketing teams. On one occasion, we studied the success of the Mexican feminine products group that boosted revenues by infusing chamomile scent into the products. My male colleagues were embarrassed to even look at the product, let alone smell its "garden fresh" scent. We were a long way from jet engines.

While these consumer examples weren't exactly relevant to the work at GE, they gave us shared experiences and reasons to laugh. And they opened up our thinking. It is one of the most important gifts of a discovery-based approach.

About six months after I took over the CMO role, Jeff Immelt called me into his conference room. I assumed it was about a pending project. It wasn't. He said, "I need you to be more confident." That wasn't what I was expecting! He said he expected me to put not just my voice out there but my opinion, and to do so with conviction. I'd hesitated one time too many.

"I know how good you are, but I don't hear enough from you."

Clearly, that had to change!

As CMO, expectations were higher, as was my discomfort at not knowing all the answers. Changes in mind-set can take years—if not a lifetime—to master. So I created a set of personal challenges—small, deliberate steps—to push myself forward toward confidence. Each step, each minor victory became a small deposit in my confidence bank.

- I made sure I came to Jeff's meetings with strongly articulated arguments, and I didn't leave a meeting without adding a point of view and perspective.

- Instead of my normal "On one hand . . . on the other hand" approach, I would clearly state, "Here's what I think."
- I stopped saying, "This may be stupid, but . . ." or "I'm not an expert, but . . ." I became very aware how often my lack of confidence led me to put myself down or qualify my comments.
- I'd tell myself, You can do this. And I would congratulate myself after every small victory, telling myself, See, you *can* do this!

While I was coming up to speed, so was GE. We mandated CMO positions at every business unit. This was not popular, because few business leaders thought they needed marketing people, let alone one with executive authority. Their retort: "That is for consumer products. We're a B2B [business to business] company."

Next, because we lacked skills and people, we created a training program to hire over one hundred marketing MBA graduates every year and place them in strategic marketing and sales roles in businesses and regions around the world. Their MBA tool kit was a good way to introduce what marketing could do. But as I look back, I think we should have pushed much more on the resiliency and "figure it out-ness" of future marketers than on their fancy tool kits.

From the minute I started as CMO, this was my rallying cry: to make marketing part of the business process, at the very beginning, not just the thing you do at the end to launch something. While Jeff was preparing to invest record amounts in R&D and new technology—jet engines, MRIs, locomotives—we were coming to understand that technology untethered to a need doesn't sell well. It becomes too expensive because we overengineer it with too many features that *we* think are necessary, without knowing if the customers actually value those features. Really, when was the last time you used all the features on your smartphone or microwave?

We were unfortunately all too familiar with what happened when

Look at what isn't happening and imagine what *could*.

we didn't take customers' needs into account. The engineers at GE Healthcare refused to design an MRI or CT scanner with a wider bore—the donut hole around which the amazing magnet with the force of up to 1.5 Tesla power spins. The marketplace trends were clear: people were getting bigger, with, um, wider girths. Some people found the experience of getting an MR image extremely uncomfortable. Or worse, they couldn't fit at all. GE engineers refused to accept this; they believed that making the donut hole bigger would degrade the power of the magnets and thus create a less-than-perfect image. *Why change if it doesn't result in better image quality?* they thought. So they refused to accept the market insights and focused instead on perfecting a scanning machine that was perfect only for engineers, and perhaps a few academic radiologists. And as a result, they lost market share as competitors came out with wider-bore MRIs, solving a big need for radiologists, imaging centers, and today's patients.

The job for our new marketing teams was to look through the eyes of the user to find gaps in the market, to look at what isn't happening and imagine what *could*. To create something that didn't exist before. To satisfy unmet—and sometimes unexpressed—needs.

Marketing, as I was starting to see, was about taking the name seriously—living in the markets and then bringing the outside in. And that meant making the company way more open. You have to get out of the office, out of the spreadsheet, and into the marketplace. It all starts with a mentality that I'd come to call a *market mind*, fueled by discovery.

The secret to successfully adopting a market mind was looking and doing and feeling things from other people's points of view. An easy way to induce a roaming mentality is through a practice I call *mental grazing*. This is the seeking stage of discovery, where we playfully attempt to stray outside our comfort zones to encounter

To get an edge on the future, you have to be willing to go weird.

new experiences, new tools, and new people outside our networks. We ask people to be more creative, more innovative, generate new ideas . . . but we often forget that new outputs require new inputs. It's like demanding milk from a cow without allowing it to graze first.

I began to barrage my team with every concept that interested me, much to their frustration at times (one of my colleagues later described me as the incessantly distractible dog from the animated movie *Up*, which barks and barks at one shiny object until the next quickly grabs his attention). This can be annoying, to be sure, but you never know which interactions will catalyze innovation. To get an edge on the future and graze on something new, you have to be willing to "go weird." A fear-laden word in most workplaces, *weird* has taken me from a South Korean underground dance contest in search of consumer trends, to scouting an F-15 fighter with members of the Israeli military to learn about how they impact the country's start-up culture, to being one of only a few non-thirty-year-olds on a cruise ship with one thousand start-up founders under the age of thirty. I meet often with artists, poets, fringe scientists, designers, theologians, musicians, and a range of others who seemingly have nothing to do with my business but do offer a new perspective on how we and others view ourselves.

Over time, I came to realize that my role—and that of marketing—was foremost that of an instigator of change. To move marketing from theory into practice.

Imagination Breakthroughs

"Leadership needs to understand new ideas that lead to new revenues is now part of their job. Here's an idea how to do it," Jeff said one morning, handing me a business magazine article chronicling an industrial company's attempt to create a corporate incubator to grow ideas into new businesses. "See if you can do anything with this. It should be led by marketing," he said, as if he were putting in an order for tomato seedlings at the Southern States supply store.

This would become the riff that we developed over the years: Jeff giving me his "seed of an idea, maybe a bad one," shooing me out of the office with a quick "See what you can do with it," and me heading off with a million questions buzzing through my head, yet oddly eager to begin the process of discovery.

I enlisted a few of the newly hired marketing MBA grads, and we did research on incubation models (the company in the article—Danaher Corporation—was our blueprint) and then drafted a rough plan to grow new revenue by reimagining existing offerings or developing new ones. I got input from the business CMOs, who were both excited and nervous: "How will we do this? Where is the budget?"

We dubbed the incubation initiative *Imagination Breakthroughs*, and went back to Jeff with a rough outline of a system to generate more usable product or service ideas. As I explained the project to Jeff, he reached over across three chairs, impatiently grabbing the papers from my hand. (This would become our regular routine.) Jeff would scribble over everything. Nothing is ever fully finished when he's involved; I call him The Serial Iterator. This could be frustrating for those with a "checklist efficiency" at GE. They wanted to be told what to do and head out, assuming that if they did it, it was done—not something that will be refined several more times. When you are seeding something new, it's all about iteration and refinement. This is maddening at times, but necessary. With the teams I work with, I've learned to say, "We're going to iterate this several times. Get ready, and don't wait for perfection." Too often we take so much time waiting for all the inputs and data, preparing the most beautiful presentation, when all we really needed to do was punch the idea around and fiddle with it. As I would learn later, taking something to a client that is less than perfect is actually a much more effective way to work.

Out the other end of this process came our mandate: Each GE business had to come up with two or three ideas of new lines of business or product applications, geographic areas, or customer bases. They had to generate at least $100 million in new revenue within five years. And each team had six weeks to come back with their ideas. Ready, set, go.

A few weeks later, at GE's quarterly convening of the business leaders, I explained the concept, and Jeff told them he was serious about Imagination Breakthroughs, or IBs as they became known. "I expect Marketing to lead it. Got it?" he added. The room was silent. Afterward, I was the recipient of their grumbling—"Marketing? . . . Not sure we have time or resources for this . . . Frivolous."

When the first IBs came back (on time—GE's ability to execute was never in doubt), it was clear the ideas were neither imaginative nor breakthroughs. People had dusted off old plans that had been sitting around for months, if not years—the old-products-with-added-features kind of idea. But it was a start. So we picked out a few that were promising, and Jeff sent a note to the division CEOs and their CMOs saying, "Here's the list of the IBs I like. Take another stab and come back to Beth with an updated list. By the way, I expect you to pay for these breakthroughs, so tell me how you're going to do it."

"We have to pay for these?" was the universal outcry. Now Marketing had their attention. Clearly, many had picked ideas that seemed interesting, but perhaps not essential, because they thought "Uncle Jeff" would be paying. I learned an essential lesson about business innovation in this exercise: people have to be invested. They have to have "skin in the game." When they do, mysteriously, better ideas are selected.

We started with about thirty-five ideas—a small number for a company of our size—from a dual card for consumer finance that would let consumers use their store credit card in other locations to a hybrid locomotive for GE Transportation. One of the simplest and quickest came from GE Energy: a plan to yield $200 million in two years by segmenting existing markets in the Middle East, finding new customers who needed power generation equipment, and targeting existing customers with more offerings. I used this one as the clarion call to show what good marketing could do, even if it wasn't particularly "breakthrough." It was a way to get quick financial returns, show marketing's impact, and hopefully get "permission" to go for longer-range ideas. It was a way to get an early win.

Some of the early ideas were inevitably duds, of course. Our appliance group suggested an unnecessarily complicated "double range" that you couldn't install in contemporary kitchens without ripping out a wall, and the CEO of our Universal Studios unit practically spat when he saw a Plastics division idea for a "self-crumbling" DVD that reduced itself to dust a few days after being exposed to air. It petrified customers—it seemed unhealthy—and Netflix made the product obsolete before we could introduce it anyhow.

But perfection wasn't the point. The Imagination Breakthrough process was meant to shake loose revenue-generating business ideas, but it was also a vehicle to propagate my outside-in, be-the-customer idea of marketing throughout the company. It was indirectly teaching the company discovery—by forcing executive teams to scour their businesses and their markets on idea scavenger hunts.

A year into the program, eighty IBs had been identified and qualified. Led by marketing, businesses were jumping into new markets, generating more ideas for new revenue and finding new needs to solve, like "unbanked" consumers who couldn't get access to traditional banking. Jeff devoted hours every month to reviewing these projects with me and the teams, holding business CEOs accountable for investing and CMOs for pushing leaders to develop a new mentality that looks to the market for what's needed.

On average, he and I would review eight Imagination Breakthrough ideas every month, with the eight program managers sitting around the big conference table. Behind each one there would be a photograph or mock-up of what that person was working on—a new locomotive engine, perhaps, or a desalination plant. Power-Points were outlawed. That didn't last long. I'm still trying to kill PowerPoint—the ultimate business security blanket. People feel safe with their well-honed presentations complete with business plans that contain a "hockey stick of growth"–exponential growth that is always three to five years away. But it was rarely, if ever, that easy in reality. Jeff would pluck the one-page profile from each manager in the pile in front of him and go around the room asking, "What is the biggest technical barrier? What is the biggest external barrier? Are you on time? How many resources do you have on this project?" He wanted more discussion, but he, too, went back to the death-by-PowerPoint ritual.

The fact that Jeff would devote a day a month to digging into an organic revenue-growth and marketing process delivered a clear message to the organization about the new importance of discovery, idea generation, and marketing. Still, there was tremendous resistance at first, because inevitably, some of the ideas would fail, and too often, managers do not want their names associated with failed projects.

That is why it was so vital that we find a way to protect new ideas and their authors. With Jeff's full buy-in, IBs became what I had dubbed a "protected class of ideas," fully funded business bets that could not have their budgets cut because of a tight quarter, giving them space to take risks and grow into something valuable. We had to convince people that it was okay to have a failed idea, that this would not be held against them financially in a promotion review. I told them this in no uncertain terms, but people had to believe it in their hearts. And their bosses and division CFOs often said otherwise. The tension could be thick.

I told Jeff, his business leaders, and really anyone who would listen that they needed to tell people they supported them in their efforts to try. And if and when they failed, offer absolution. Without that, people wouldn't feel secure enough to give themselves permission to dream. We had to protect people from an ingrained corporate culture that is intolerant of losers.

We pushed for GE's best people to drive the effort and committed $5 billion over the next three years to fully fund IBs. I presented our progress to GE investors, who seemed underwhelmed by the smallness of the early ideas and the length of time it would take to see a return. They were used to big, instantly gratifying acquisitions. And they just couldn't get their heads around why this effort would be led by marketing. Traditionalists, they saw marketing as the advertising department, rather than the key driver behind growth and change.

In time, IBs were expected to deliver $25 billion of additional revenue growth, and by 2005, twenty-five IBs were generating revenue. There was a new Life Sciences platform built from umbilical cord blood that grew into a thriving Cell Therapy business a decade later, an air-taxi concept that gave rise to the small engine-powered Honda jet a dozen years later, and a new line of appliances—Café—targeted to millennials living in their parents' basements.

One of my favorites was a simplified way to deliver anesthesia in a chaotic operating theater. The health marketing teams identified a grave problem: alarm fatigue, when a truly life-threatening event is lost in a cacophony of beeping monitors and cluttered medical equipment that are all calling out to capture doctors' and nurses' attention. It's a systems failure that results from technology driving processes, rather than processes driving technology.

As we dug deep to address the issue, the team learned that our customers—the anesthesiologists—couldn't tell you what exactly they did in the heat of the moment. As they considered this, they asked, "Who else finds themselves in such life and death situations, navigating all kinds of inputs and monitoring equipment?" And they had a startlingly useful realization: an airplane's cockpit is remarkably similar to an operating room. So they invited pilots to observe surgeries and help GE identify the problems. That turned out to be fairly easy, as their industry had faced an almost identical problem decades before. In the 1980s, the airline industry had been about where the surgical room was in the early 2000s, with complex systems and conflicting requirements that needed to be harmonized. And just as designers of cockpits eventually consolidated and prioritized the gauges and alarms into the three screens aircraft have today, the pilots helped our medical group come up with the very successful 2007 GE Aisys Anesthesia Machine, which has three separate screens: physiologic monitoring, anesthesia machine management, and anesthesia information.

We had learned a crucial lesson. We had to "get outside the jar," as one designer described it to me. In other words, we needed an "outside-in" approach to generating insights to improve a product or process. You can't see a jar's label from inside the jar. You need a different perspective.

What was amazing about Jeff's sponsorship of the IB idea was how it forced GE's entrenched leaders to take it seriously. "Nobody is allowed not to play. Nobody can say, 'I'm going to sit this one out,'" Jeff said.

As we moved forward with Imagination Breakthroughs, I convinced Jeff to tie a percentage of executive performance and compensation to the ability to grow top line and market share, especially generating new income from new sources. We added customer feedback metrics like Net Promoter Score and experimented with others. Now, business leaders had to up their game with skills that were harder to measure: discovery, strategy, and customer psychology.

My job in all of this was as chief instigator and shaper of "the new." Our team kept track of the IBs to find patterns in the losses and wins of our teams. It was a grand apprenticeship in marketing and innovation, one in which we were making small bets and, more often than not, failing and starting over again.

The next step was to create a formal process and code around

The STAR System

Ideas need time to develop before you can show someone the money. I've come to believe that putting out ideas and defending them until they are ready is part of my obligation as a change-maker. Here's a mnemonic framework that I call STAR that I've found helpful in keeping ideas alive and twinkling with possibility.

Shelter it: An idea starts as a seedling, sometimes something that you can't even articulate. Maybe it comes to you on a walk or on the train, or it builds on top of something someone else said at work. Noodle it, let it breathe. Ignore it and see if it still comes back to nudge you again.

Tell it: We have a tendency to keep new ideas secret for fear of someone else stealing them or of looking silly. The irony is that the more you talk about your idea, the clearer it becomes. Ask people for help in making the idea clearer.

Ask yourself: How much do I believe in this idea? There comes a time to test your passion and commitment. Do I feel strongly enough about it that I'm willing to devote the time to refine it and test its viability? Can I handle the criticism I may receive from others when I put it out there? Do I feel so strongly about it that I want it to happen with or without me?

Repeat: Be resilient. *Don't give up.* Find more people with whom to share the idea, more ways to bring it to life. Sometimes the timing may be wrong. The company may be wrong. The boss may be wrong. Keep at it.

this. In 2006, HR hired Vijay Govindarajan, a professor of strategy and innovation at the Tuck School of Business at Dartmouth College (Jeff's alma mater), to be GE's first Professor in Residence, based out of our Crotonville education center. Known as VG, he would become a marketing lifeline to me, giving a new voice of authority to the programs I was leading. VG introduced us to a simple tool that was classic "business school." It turned out to be so crucial that I advise all aspiring innovators to use it. VG taught us to look at our growth investments as a portfolio of three boxes: Core, Adjacent, and New. The Three Box Approach—or what I've come to call *3D budgeting*—was all about strategic planning, a way to continue to protect the established business lines while at the same time innovating at the edges, in unknown and uncomfortable places.

BOX 1	BOX 2	BOX 3
Core	Adjacent	New
Now	Next	Future
Winning the present or near term (18 mos)	Near future (3–5+ years)	Long term (5–7–10+ years)
Incremental innovation still matters!	Existing tech/product to new market or new product to existing customers	Create the future: market making, disruptive offers
Up to 70% of resources allocated here	15–20% of resources allocated here	10+% of resources allocated here
Profit metrics	Market Share metrics	Viability metrics

3D Budgeting

Budgeting for innovation allows organizations to become more nimble and position themselves for entrepreneurial growth. The Three Box Approach has withstood the test of time for me. I still return to it and have found it a useful framework for how I think about budgeting with my teams—always ensuring we have up to 10 percent of budget, and time, for exploring the new.

When I say resources, I don't mean just project investment dollars or capital expenses but also people. It would take me a while to learn that you require different skills and capabilities for innovating at the core versus the new, and that measurements or benchmarks need to be aligned accordingly—it's hard to measure profit on an idea that doesn't even have a viable customer yet! But sadly, well-meaning companies do this.

Time is an overlooked resource as well. I make sure I carve out at least 10 percent of my own time in any given workweek for exploring what's new. For example, I carve out Friday afternoons for discovery, whether it's meeting with an expert in a new field or reading about a new topic. I created "Field Trip Fridays" once a month to take my marketing team to visit an emerging company or even an exhibit or art installation.

In my personal life, the percentage of time I spend in discovery is much, much higher. I search out new products, venues, exhibits, and experiences as a way of life. An adaptation that I've challenged myself with is to create three segments, along the lines of Things I Love to Do, Things I Have to Do, and Things I Hate to Do. It turns 3D budgeting on its head, with me attempting to have more things I love (Box 1)—like reading and exploring—while finding creative ways to outsource things I hate (Box 3)—like doing laundry!

But even as we were gaining traction, the sharks—both inside and outside the company—began to circle. For one thing, people had huge doubts that a big and slow corporation like GE could make itself agile, swift, and innovative. We needed a clear, unmitigated success, validated by the one traditional metric that will always matter most at GE: huge profits in billion-dollar markets.

CHAPTER 5

ECOMAGINATION

Y ou're going to make us look like idiots!" John shouted from the
back row.

I was standing at the front of the Lyceum meeting room in GE's
Crotonville executive education campus during our quarterly corporate executive council meeting (CEC), which brings together
forty-five top business and functional leaders from around GE. I
remember thinking that, even for a company that prides itself on a
kind of raw clarity in its feedback, those were pretty powerful words
for a division head to be directing at the CMO.

I was presenting a radical new company-wide initiative through
a just-finished commercial that featured a dancing elephant named
Ellie. But it wasn't just the gyrating elephant that got our execs concerned about their image (though the elephant was an issue). Rather,
it was the essence of the initiative: to reinvent ourselves from an
environmental Godzilla—to our critics, a lumbering capitalist beast
leaving total destruction in its wake—into a tree-hugging corporate
Jane Goodall. That's not how I presented it on that day, but seeing
their fuming bewilderment as my talk unfolded, that's certainly how

they heard it. Innovation is not just about generating, analyzing, selecting, and publicizing ideas. It's about getting an entire community of "customers"—in this case, the company's executives and employees—to adopt new behaviors and practices. It's a slow process. And, as was becoming painfully clear, the Imagination Breakthrough program was only the start. Real company-wide adoption would take years. But the bigger and bolder the effort, the faster we could move forward.

Nine months earlier, Jeff came to me with one of his "quarter of an idea" observations. He told me that in client meetings, business reviews, at the coat rack after sales dinners, and in industry conference elevators, customers—especially those in the energy and rail sectors—were cornering him with various versions of one muffled fear: They wanted to do right for the environment, first because it was the right thing to do, and also because of pressure from enhanced regulatory standards in the EU and United States. But they feared they could risk financial ruin in the process of converting to expensive technology.

They wanted help.

"Is there something we should be doing about our technology and the environment?" Jeff asked. "Go check it out."

Of course, not every energy and rail executive told Jeff the same thing. Far from it. It was that their words, taken together, created a pattern that was identifiable to someone with the orientation to see it. In the executives' anxiety and fear, Jeff recognized a pattern of environmental tension that couldn't be found on any spreadsheet— weak signals or repeated anomalies that register as "Hmm, that's interesting" among the noise of the day-to-day business landscape.

My friend Joi Ito, director of MIT's Media Lab, uses mushroom-hunting as a metaphor to explain how pattern recognition—what he also calls *peripheral vision*—works. It requires immersion without

Try brailling the culture. Use all your senses to recognize patterns that you don't yet see.

absorption—a broad awareness of the environment, while resisting the pull to fixate on any one thing. When you go mushroom-hunting, if you focus too deliberately, you won't find any mushrooms. With your task-oriented mind switched on, you'll filter out the weak signals, the visual hints of delectable fungi that are nearly, but not quite, hidden in the nooks and crannies of the forest underbrush; however, when you stop looking so intently, suddenly your pattern recognition kicks in and you'll see mushrooms everywhere.

Futurist (and spark) Faith Popcorn calls her version of the method "Brailling the Culture," which I love because it makes you think about using your senses in different ways to recognize patterns that you don't yet see. After Jeff asked me to look into the signals he picked up, my job was that of a sense-making machine—examining early signals picked up in discovery, going deeper and collecting more information, and seeing if patterns emerged of something bigger. And if they did, what could GE do with that knowledge?

To build our case for (or against) an environmental initiative, I convened a small working group to survey the effects of environmental regulation on business and make suggestions on what, if anything, we could do. My first questions were, "Is this bigger than these few industries? Are there more dots to connect? When you connect them, what image and opportunities do they create?"

At that moment, we already had a trend of three. British Petroleum had left its maiden name behind and rechristened itself BP (or "Beyond Petroleum"), Toyota also was messaging about a cleaner environment, and now there was the expression of unease among our own customers.

We spent all of 2004 figuring out how we could connect technology to environmental and economic outcomes, from retail to railroads, and do it credibly. David Slump, the CMO of GE Power, and I formed a sort of ying-and-yang team. "You dive off the board and go deep, and we'll survey the pool from the lifeguard's tower," I told him. David's Power team delved into details—they knew the

technical realities of our products, what our customers were buying and not, what our energy-generating competitors were doing—
and put together a granular report on issues like how Europeans
were using renewable energy, such as wind turbines, differently. My
marketing team went wide, looking at trends on the horizon, com-
paring issues not related to the power-generation space, like how
Toyota's success with the Prius could be applied to products in the
power-generation space.

Our marketing team also set about to research macro trends on
the environment: What did consumers say versus what they did?
Were other industries leading in green technology? What efforts,
if any, were taking place in GE's industries? What was the science
about carbon emissions and the environment? Is global warming
real? What did our scientists believe about it? What could we really
do about it?

One of my GE Water business-unit colleagues told me, "Yes,
but you don't have enough subject expertise to understand my industry or what my customers need." Exactly! Looking at the world
horizontally means considering ideas outside of our direct expertise.
And because of that, we could see opportunities that deep domain
experts cannot. Never underestimate the value of viewing things
through a different, wider lens. You need to have both: ideas born
in deep expertise and then a challenge by someone asking, Where
else can this apply?

When we finished our first wave of research, it was clear we
had discovered a theme emerging across our different businesses—
energy, rail, water, aircraft engines—that was bigger than any of
these businesses alone. The opportunity was real, but vague, broadly
focused on emissions reduction, energy efficiency, water usage, and
what I would call generally the economics of scarcity. What wasn't
clear was what GE could do.

I worried that a pure messaging campaign wouldn't be different
enough from what BP was doing with its rebranding. Moreover, I

feared that if we engaged in that, people would accuse us of green-washing. After all, we had a difficult environmental legacy. Our position on PCBs in the Hudson had sparked the wrath and fueled successful fundraising efforts of NGOs like Greenpeace and Bobby Kennedy's Riverkeeper. I also knew there was a lot at stake in pivoting our position on the environment—a move that had the potential to baffle and enrage our internal constituency and maybe make us an even bigger target for environmentalists.

"Why are you messing with this?" one sales lead asked David. "You are going to piss off our customers!"

To veer away from an intramural debate, I created something we called Discovery 2015, a future "Dreaming Session" with our thirty biggest utility customers. Some of the top players in the industry—CEOs like Jim Rogers of Duke Energy and scientists like David Rutledge of Caltech—came to Crotonville and listened to Jeff Sachs from Columbia University talk about global warming. In addition to the thirty customers, we had our top GE management, sales, and R&D leaders in attendance. We debated and dreamed aloud about technologies, especially the timing for renewable energy such as wind. Most of the utilities are subject to local regulatory bodies that must approve price increases, so cost issues were critically important. Jeff also floated the idea of doing something on public policy on greenhouse gases. Debates were robust. But we also made room for dreaming.

This environmental Dreaming Session was a critical hinge event for GE, because it helped to show that we could go beyond improving management practice and indulge in business innovation. It was one way to show the organization that it was okay to stick your neck out and even to make customers a little bit uncomfortable from time to time.

On a very basic level, change is a conversation. The more vibrant, the more diverse, the more animated and sometimes agitated the

To be innovative, you have to learn to be comfortable with some level of "maybe."

conversations an organization is having, the more likely you'll find an adaptive organization that's gotten good at learning, creation, innovation, and change.

In that sense, our Dreaming Sessions showed us that management can discourage innovation by an overdependence on the scientific method, by demanding innovators "prove it" before "it" is really understood. To be innovative, you have to learn to be comfortable with some level of "maybe."

To this end, we asked our energy customers at our environmental Dreaming Session to peer into the future to the year 2015. We picked a time frame—and we were very deliberate in choosing ten years out—that was near enough to be actionable, but still far away enough that CEOs could "dream" and not feel competitively threatened by sharing insights with one another. "What technologies would you like GE to invest in?" we asked. "If you had a billion of GE's dollars to invest, where would you place it?" We laid out options for new technologies, such as cleaner coal, wind, solar, and geothermal energy.

We facilitated the discussion, posting notes around the room. Jeff in his usual fashion jumped in whenever the debate heated up and needed moving along. There were a few utility CEOs who just didn't believe GE would be able to deliver benefits like emissions reductions; others feared what it would cost. "What happens if we get ahead of regulations that never end up existing? Who pays for that?" said one CEO. It was the kind of feedback we needed to intelligently invest more money and resources into solutions such as solar energy or "clean coal."

While GE executives listened carefully to the input, ultimately we would make our own investment choices. "I love customers. I get great insight from them, but I would never let them set our strategy for us," Jeff said. But by talking to more customers, we saw patterns emerge, where they were alike, and where we could develop offerings that scale.

Deep investigation into customers' lives and needs was vital when GE's Achilles' heel was that it often engineered the product first and then had to figure out how to convince customers to pay for it. The new plan was to ask, "Let's first figure out what they want to pay for."

As we developed our ecological business initiative, my team and I worked on a parallel track talking to NGOs, government leaders, academics—the very people we had been fighting for years. We asked them what they thought GE could do to make a difference. It was the first time some of them had heard us asking questions instead of going in and telling them how right we were with our point of view.

Their first reaction was suspicion. Eileen Claussen, the head of the Pew Foundation on Global Climate Change, said, "Let's just say that I've been waiting a long time to have this conversation with you guys. And I never expected the day to arrive."

"How will this be perceived?" I asked her. "How do we make it credible? What do you expect GE to do, Eileen?" But it was slow going to make even a tiny crack in her suspicion. I found her lack of trust understandable, but ultimately irritating. Finally, at a meeting in her office in Washington, I blurted out, "How can we make it so you and your colleagues can accept that we're telling the truth?"

Eileen had been around—at the EPA, the Department of Defense, Booz Allen Hamilton—and she was known for her frankness. "Let's think of this another way, from another industry: Arms control treaties are based on trust, right? They have to be, but every one, I promise you, is verified by an arms control observer group. Trust, but verify." (Eileen would become the longest-standing member of our Ecomagination advisory board.)

I nodded. "Verify," I said.

"Yep."

It was at this point that it became clear that to convince skeptical customers and third-party observers, whatever we did would need to be measured by a trusted outsider, a referee whose judgments would not be doubted. That would be absolutely crucial to our success. We needed an outside force to say, "GE has cut greenhouse gases by Y and saved its customer $X in the last twelve months," and have people believe it. We needed a scorecard.

I talked to green activists, government leaders, and other forward-thinking industrial firms, and one name came up repeatedly: Green-Order. We commissioned the New York strategy firm to evaluate the environmental performance of our innovations and grade them on detailed economic and environmental scorecards. To qualify as part of this new program, a product had to show considerable and *demonstrable* benefits both for the planet and for GE's bottom line.

Because GreenOrder was well respected and connected, they also helped us sort through the many NGOs and green activists who had concerns about us. Accompanied by GreenOrder, we spent months talking to over two dozen groups to hear their concerns and test our ideas. We developed an advisory board composed of NGOs, customers, and venture capitalists, whose role was to verify our actions and advise us on R&D investments.

We started to believe this new initiative could change GE. So we took the scorecard that GreenOrder's Andrew Shapiro helped us build and began auditing our products. We were pleasantly surprised to discover that we already had $5 billion in product sales in the pipeline that met our standards—for products like a hybrid diesel-electric locomotive that beat EPA standards and energy-saving water desalination programs. We were already on our way to becoming a green economy leader without knowing it.

But Jeff was blazingly clear: this could not be just a feel-good project; for this to work, we had to have a positive economic outcome. Jeff kept saying, "Not just ecological; it has to be economical."

We debated our actions around Jeff's big conference table. I was on what seemed to be the greenwashing, lunatic fringe, with GE chief legal counsel Ben Heineman on the other extreme. In between sat Jeff, GE's chief communications officer Gary Sheffer, and Steve Ramsey, former chief of the environmental enforcement section at the Department of Justice.

"You don't understand the legal precedent here, Beth," said Ben. "Steve and I have been steeped in this for years. There were sound reasons we fought bad science. You just can't throw that aside. GE will look ridiculous." Steve opted for the "hold on" approach, choosing to school me, the marketing chief who was clearly overwhelmed by all the science. And Gary would repeat various versions of "But what will the media and NGOs think of our sudden change of mind?"

"The world is moving in this direction, and we have a chance to be industry leaders," I replied.

"Why do we have to make a statement about being green?" Steve said. "We manufacture a lot of technologies that aren't green. Unfortunately, most of manufacturing isn't green!"

"But it turns out so much of what we do and so many of the technologies we created already *are* green," I countered. "We have something concrete, something real to build upon! Why would we not use that to grow sales and mindshare?"

"We can't put our customers at risk, making them a bigger target than they already are, inviting in NGOs like Greenpeace and more regulation," Ben said.

"Our customers are in the crosshairs *now*," I said. "They know if they don't do anything, it's only going to get worse. They're clearly asking for our help."

Jeff had listened long enough. "Strict standards like those from the EU can be good for GE. We've proven we have the technology to meet and beat emissions standards. We can do this. Our customers need us to do this. But neither they nor we can go broke doing it. What the marketing team proposes here positions us on the right side for them and us. We're doing this."

In other words, green had to be about doing what's right for the environment *and* our customers. That was our commitment. It had to be ecological and economical.

Then Ben blurted out, "Green is 'green.'"

It was the perfect expression of our mentality. Our goal was to harness the collective power across all of GE's business units to deliver new products to solve big ecological challenges—fewer emissions, better fuel efficiency—while at the same time improving our customers' P&Ls. Customers from rail to air to power generation had said they wanted to do the right thing in terms of using technology that was better for the environment and that met tougher standards—but that also wouldn't break their budgets.

The team was on board; maybe not all in, but we were moving forward. All we needed now was a name, and a story, and a launch plan. This part of the process—the packaging—fell to me. We couldn't roll this out with some dull dressing, like GE Ecological Portfolio. BBDO was pushing GE Plus, with a green plus sign. But I wanted something with more spark.

The name we finally settled on was Ecomagination. It wasn't perfect. I had pushed for the neologism because I thought it allowed us to be unexpected and attention-grabbing, and to reinforce that our imaginations were at work. But as imperfect as it was, the name, both cute and deeply serious, *worked* because it encapsulated all we meant to say. It stated our mission to deliver on two versions of eco— ecological products that offer economic benefits—while using our imagination, our most limitless resource, to find newer and better solutions to our limited energy resources. Our core positioning to customers was simple, too: "Invest in the future of the planet, meet and exceed industry clean-energy standards, but don't go broke doing it."

I remember Jeff saying, "You need to present this to the CEC," our corporate executive council. Which brings me back to the shouting match that opened the chapter.

.   .   .

Standing up in front of that room in Crotonville was intimidating. The place is designed with auditorium-style seating, but intimate, like a gladiators pit. On the back wall someone had hung a cheesy motivational wolf poster that read "Only the strong survive." Jeff teed me up, saying, "I think we're on to something. I like what Beth and the team have done here, I've asked her to present it." Then he added, "This is somewhat controversial. We're taking a stand on something."

The meeting started ugly and got worse. I kicked off with a presentation on what Ecomagination was and the myths and realities of green business—things like "It's Too Expensive" versus "It Makes Money"—and then ran into our big promotional blitz, most notably with the ad of Ellie the elephant dancing to "Singin' in the Rain," and these beautiful images of our wind turbines mixed with sunflowers.

Some of our people *hated* it. Some GE executives believed we'd embarrass ourselves with such a position, given our long-standing Hudson River issues. Others believed we didn't have the technologies to make the performance commitments. And many didn't want us to get ahead of our customers; they feared these declarations would incentivize more federal regulation, or worse, make our customers *not* want to buy from us. And they especially hated the name. "Oh, my god, that's ridiculous," one said, which quickly became a chorus.

I have to confess that the reaction to my Crotonville Ecomagination presentation was deflating. But I had put so much on the line for this. I knew in my heart and my gut that this was an important effort. It was tapping into the mission that people so desperately wanted from us. We'd found a way to make purpose tangible, and profitable. I'd been a passionate driving force behind the design of Ecomagination. It must have been tempting at this point for Jeff to backtrack, to tamp down my enthusiasm with a lot of qualifiers, and allow me to shoulder the blame for going too far, too fast, down a road that our customers weren't ready to take. He could have apologized for taking bad advice, and allowed me to take the fall. But he didn't. He saw the potential, too.

Instead, he became a champion of Ecomagination. A few times every year, he would look at the leadership team and say, "Hey, I've got a really good idea right now. I've listened to all of you, but here's where we're going. Get in line. We're doing it my way." Ecomagination was one of those times.

It takes commitment and courage to go forward when you know that you risk being criticized, by customers and investors. The best leaders exhibit humility in their strength, and vice versa. They embrace where they must lead and the changes in themselves that it requires. Not long after we launched Ecomagination, Jeff backed off from GE's most complicating environmental legacy—the strident fight against the EPA—and agreed that GE would pay to dredge the Hudson to the tune of an initial $460 million.

Jeff also stood up to customers pressing him to back away from environmental issues. As we unveiled Ecomagination, the boss of the energy company TXU, John Wilder, called Jeff personally to tell him that he was so disturbed by our program—he feared it would draw unnecessary government regulation—that he was going to withdraw his business from GE to the tune of $100 million.

And you know what? Jeff bravely asked us to push Ecomagination forward, because he believed it was both good for the environment and good for business. Jeff never told me about the loss of TXU. I only learned that years later. That's what good leaders do; they absorb the shock waves and anxiety in moments of radical change.

Luckily for all of us—especially for me—sales were lifted. We launched Ecomagination in 2005 with the first seventeen products, and we pinpointed $10 billion of revenue from products tapping renewable energy sources, such as the sun and wind, during the first year after launch. By mid-2006, thirty-two products across our businesses had been Ecomagination certified, including things like the GEnx jet engine, which saves 22 percent on fuel compared with conventional engines, saving airlines over $350,000 annually on each plane; our 210-ton, 4,400-horsepower hybrid diesel/electric Evolution locomotive, which burns 15 percent less fuel and pumps out 40 percent less pollution than conventional trains; and our Harmony washing machines, which use 75 percent less energy than old-school models.

We created ecoTreasure Hunts with customers as a way to help them better reduce energy and water usage and emissions. The idea of the "treasure hunt" was to find untapped savings within a company that would reduce emissions or energy and water usage and save money. At GE, we had given ourselves stringent targets for reducing CO_2 emissions in our factories, and for reducing energy and water consumptions, and in the process our employees took the challenge and helped us exceed the goals. It made it easy to share the blueprint with customers—a franchise of Wendy's fast-food outlets—and in turn helped them get greener and strengthened the GE relationship. The lesson here is that there are many ways to engage employees and customers together to deliver a solution that has meaning and economics; our "gamification" of it added a twist, and with enough examples, made way for a simple application that sales teams could use with prospective customers.

Ecomagination offered a big lift both operationally and in terms of our brand and reputation. According to a study by the independent branding group Interbrand, GE's brand value increased by 35 percent at one point, in large part because GE began to mean Green Energy. In 2005, GE saw $10 billion in Ecomagination sales. By 2017, our annual Ecomagination revenues paced at over $35 billion annually.

Of course, Ecomagination's success required an enormous amount of commitment and passion. Plunging into customers' fears and turning them into a product—turning ecological worries into Ecomagination—is not done easily. Telling our biggest industrial customers to get ahead of regulation was in a sense telling them to accept that by having dirty emissions they were behind on preparing for the future.

There is also the ongoing tension of funding newer, cleaner technologies that require time and investment to develop and scale versus incumbent technologies that generate cash and operating profit. Over the duration of Ecomagination, its mission would be tested as GE grew its Oil & Gas and Energy businesses through a series of acquisitions—most notably, in 2016 when GE acquired Alstom, the French power generation company, for $15 billion. While Alstom had a good base of renewable energy (mostly wind, hydropower, and smart grid), it also came with coal-burning technology. Given the pace of economic growth in Asia, it meant that there was still much need for established power generation, providing near-term profits that GE (and investors) needed. Accordingly, Ecomagination expanded its industrial strength, being applied in tougher-use cases like flare-gas capture, and renewable hybrid power and water reuse at gas drilling sites. Some customers, like Norway's Statoil, became early development partners, proving that there are almost always forward-focused customers, despite fears to the contrary. But for carbon-based technologies, the pace of change would come faster than even the early adopters imagined.

Jeff championed Ecomagination proudly as he hedged his options. He bulked up on legacy tech and he invested in the new. He made room for Eco, for debate with our teams and external advisors (especially on solar energy, about which I became a fanatic, a pain in the neck, even. But it was hard to break through because solar seemed far off, even as new models were launched by challengers. "How will GE make money?" was always the question and the answer). Annually we convened a meeting of the country's top ten utility CEOs, and every year we noted declines in energy usage due to efficiency; that energy technology was becoming more decarbonized, distributed, digitized, and democratized; and that renewables were scaling faster. A few utilities had been able to spin off new units that harnessed these changes; others weren't able to shake their regulators or investors, or they got lost in their gaps of imagination.

With Ecomagination we instigated a cleaner, more relevant future. Of that I am certain and proud. We succeeded in many ways. Yet, frustratingly, we could only impact so much despite that the potential to make the future was profound. This is the change-maker's dilemma. In GE's case, despite all the momentum, Ecomagination could only reach so far through the layers and layers of complexity and denials of change—across GE, across our customers, across the ecosystem, across financial markets. There were business managers and investors who dismissed Ecomagination as "just marketing." Time would prove them right: Yes, this *is* marketing. Ecomagination stands as an example of what new marketing does well—live in the market, create a new business strategy, meet change early, build a coalition of those willing to work for a new future, deliver new growth.

Because tomorrow always comes, change-makers can't be afraid to share their vision and declare their aspirations for it loudly, even before they've built it, done it, won it. This is how you grab mindshare. And you need mindshare before you can capture market share. You need to sell a vision, devise a plan, and invite others to help build it. This is how change gets harnessed.

It's not without frustration or peril. As Jeff told a newspaper reporter several years later, "There were only two of us who thought this thing was a good idea." For my sake, I'm fortunate that Jeff was the other one.

To be a change-maker, think mindshare before marketshare.

Challenges

SEEING THREES

When you're trying to recognize a pattern, it can be difficult to determine which signals you should pay attention to. One handy rule of thumb is what I call "Go On Three." The idea comes from newspaper "trend" stories (i.e., "Everyone's Wearing Bowties!"), in which the rule is that one event is an occurrence, two similar events form a coincidence, and three are a trend. Many futurists use a similar method. Alvin Toffler, whose *Future Shock* got attention in the 1970s with its bold (and accurate) predictions, is said to have employed a method whereby he kept stacks of newspaper clippings on topics around a room; the stacks that got bigger became his heat map for new trends. At a basic level, patterns start with a hunch or a hypothesis, and each data point serves to strengthen the insight.

I often advise people to practice this in simple ways: For example, alternate your routes to work in the mornings to see what new things stand out when you do. Read about other industries, and see what kind of similarities you can spot. At the airport newsstand, observe the range of magazines. Buy a few that you've never read before (*Backpacker* magazine will surprise you!). What observations do you make? What questions start to form?

SEEING THE FUTURE

Here are a few of the Imagine It Forward scenario planning tactics I use to better "see" or anticipate the future. Try them out with your own team or company:

- Opposition: Assume the opposite of convention. Good is bad. Bad is good. For example, what if fats were good for you, sugar were bad for you. All electricity we generate were powered by the sun.

- Worst-case scenario: What is the worst that could happen? Work back from there, and see what kind of ideas emerge to prevent or address that.

- Parallelism: Put yourself in another's position. You are the competition. You are the client. You are a colleague. What ideas might you generate from this perspective?

- Time shift: What if it took no time to create a solution? What if it took five years? Ten years? What would change in terms of the solutions you seek out?

- Control shift: Imagine a shift in governance or technology or nature brings about a shift in power. Technology did that for Uber in competing against local taxi authorities.

- Roadblock-busting: How would you approach the problem if the roadblock didn't exist? Or if you could remove it easily?

- Phantom problem: What if it's not really a problem at all? What if money isn't a challenge? Or if the boss isn't standing in your way? Or if the competition doesn't have a better product? What would you do differently?

- "Ungranted": What happens if something goes away that you've taken for granted?

- Strange bedfellows: What interesting or unlikely things can be combined to create something new?

- Wrong problem: What if the problem isn't what you think? For example, the issue isn't that we don't have enough skilled jobs, we just have a mismatch in skills.

Sky's the limit. Are you thinking big enough? Yahoo! developed a search to narrow parameters. Google had a grand vision to search the entire Internet.

THE POWER OF CONSTRAINTS

Constraints fuel creativity. Sometimes having a smaller budget and a tighter deadline—especially in the early days—forces you to hone your idea. Look at your constraints as a source of *creativity* rather than as a temporary hardship to overcome.

The next time you are tempted to say, "We don't have enough money to do X," or "My manager will never green-light the budget for this," or "We'll never get this done with such a short time frame," STOP. Such thinking will only quiet your imagination. Let it sing. Instead, ask:

How much faster can I come up with a good idea here?

How much budget do we really need to get to the next phase?

Who else has done work in this area that I can learn from or build on?

If you manage a team, turn budget and project requests into a challenge. Reward people who generate the best ideas with the most constraints. Can you establish a measurement for innovation efficiency or innovation throughput—more ideas in, better ideas out, faster?

BRING IN OUTSIDE SPARKS

- Succinctly identify one issue or problem area where help is needed.
- How do you think an outside spark can help shine light on the issue?
- Identify your spark, ideally an outsider. I've found that good places to find sparks are at industry conferences, trade publications, and universities. But you can also find experts in other teams or departments within your own organization.

- Invite them to address your group, using a relevant case study. Most people are flattered to be asked to speak. It doesn't have to be a formal presentation. Invite them to a team lunch.
- Leave time to facilitate a discussion and seek feedback. Ask your team: Has this new perspective changed your point of view?
- Spend time with your sparks to help them with the natural "lost in translation" issues. For example, don't have them offer a series of consumer examples when addressing a B2B company.
- When introducing your spark to the group, explain to the group, "She's here to bring in a radically new perspective. You may feel uncomfortable with her comments. Stick with us." Leave time for discussion and debate.
- You may need to act as a facilitator. Help to translate the spark's unusual perspectives into your team's workflow.

Finally, if you can't bring in a speaker to serve as your spark, you can channel new perspectives by distributing books or articles to your team. Offer an overview of why you selected this material and why you think it could challenge your team or help them to think differently.

LOOK FOR THE WEIRD

- Ask yourself what trends you find bewildering and even a bit unsettling. Go from the big headline trends to the little ones, the trends that seem odd rather than threatening. Start with what seems like a novelty, something made purely for fun.
- Record any unsettling trends or observations as you see them and think. Don't pass judgment. Just keep a running list of

weird things you encounter. Return to it often. See if your observations have changed your perspective.

- Seek out unusual or weird experiences: Challenge yourself to go to one event or exhibit or read one book that seems odd or out of the ordinary. Ask people you know what's the strangest thing they've seen lately.

Agitated Inquiry

CHAPTER 6

NAYSAYERS AND THE DIGITAL ONSLAUGHT

The Valley of Death

At GE, rising executives are regularly moved to new, unfamiliar, and uncomfortable situations. In fact, if you aren't moved just as you're getting comfortable, you can be pretty sure you aren't going anywhere fast. Two years into my job as CMO, with Ecomagination showing real momentum and Jeff's faith in me validated, it was time for my call.

It came in early November 2005. NBC Universal's longtime CEO and GE vice chairman Bob Wright made one of his regular visits to the Fairfield headquarters. I'd worked for Bob in my last stint at NBC, so we were old friends of a sort.

Bob asked to see me up on the expansive, quiet executive floor. Bob's office was packed with photos of him with NBC celebrities.

There was something about Bob that was always a bit more down-to-earth midwestern (in a good way, although he grew up on Long Island) than Hollywood. Highly intelligent and emotional, Bob was never shy about expressing ideas, even if they weren't always clear.

We sat in two easy chairs in Bob's office. He blurted out what was on his mind: "Beth, how would you like to come back to NBC? We need someone with your . . . uh . . . creativity?"

I was surprised, but not completely. Wright needed new sales and marketing models, and was starting to get antsy about digital media. He had just come off the big acquisition of Universal, which gave him a way to grow earnings, but he saw that NBC wasn't dynamic enough, wasn't in touch with the changing media landscape. New niche cable competitors continued to nibble away at the ad sales revenue over which the networks once had near-monopolistic control, and a new generation of marketers, increasingly aware of the data websites were generating about their audience, was demanding a more intimate, data-rich connection to viewers. It was a chaotic moment.

Bob had brought my name to Jeff and Bill Conaty, GE's head of HR. In his vice chairman capacity, Wright had seen my success in changing GE's brand positioning and in introducing Ecomagination to a resistant workforce. The media world in general, and NBC in particular, was under siege from the piano-playing cats of YouTube and the pimply teens at Myspace.

Dismissive and condescending toward the upstarts, few people in media understood how quickly and brutally these kids would transform the media landscape. My mission would be to make NBC accept a reality it didn't want to acknowledge. It's a recipe for constant conflict, although I didn't know just how mean-spirited it would get.

I now know it can't be avoided. There is a wide chasm that separates insights about a changing market and important new ideas generated in the discovery phase (or R&D lab), and the commercialization of a new product or service. Venture capitalists call that

Most of us are adverse to conflict. But conflict is the primary engine of creativity and innovation.

chasm the "Valley of Death." To me, the Valley of Death is the unstable transition where the tensions between vision and reality, idea and action, must get reconciled. Not to mention confronting all the messy and often conflicting personalities and agendas. Ideas without a committed team to lead them turn into something interesting without results. It is why so many ideas die. There are politics to navigate, short-term thinking to overcome, capability gaps to address, budgets to allocate, coalitions to build, and many difficult conversations to work through.

What's needed are the skills of a social architect, someone who is committed to collaborating in a psychologically safe zone that allows for what I call *agitated inquiry*. Agitated inquiry is the practice of evolving an idea into action steps through heated exchanges and debate.

If discovery is about capturing the exotic conversations with the world outside your company's walls, agitated inquiry is about the abrasive, but essential, conversations between the people within. Most of us are averse to conflict. But there really is no getting around it when attempting to drive change. On the one hand, conflict is dangerous; it can damage relationships. On the other hand, says Ronald Heifetz, founding director of the Center for Public Leadership at Harvard's John F. Kennedy School of Government, "conflict is the primary engine of creativity and innovation."

At heart, innovation is a twelve-tone symphony of conflict and resolution. Lose control of the notes and the music will descend into chaos. Learn to conduct it and you can create something transcendent.

NBC wasn't the only big media player to realize that the digital onslaught was going to involve more than a few cute kitten videos on YouTube. In July 2005, News Corporation announced that it was paying $580 million for Myspace, which set off a frantic scramble among the rest of the media world to ensure that we weren't left without a big digital property.

Be Like Abe (or How to Deal with Conflict)

If everyone agrees on the same approach to an idea, perhaps you're not pushing the boundaries hard enough. Perhaps you haven't sought enough divergent views. Good leaders recognize that tension is inevitable, and they learn not just to navigate it but to use it to fuel creativity.

1. Learn to accept that conflict can make your idea or product better. Perhaps your problem is that there *isn't enough* conflict in your process.
2. Recognize the underlying conflict; identify it. I'll ask to meet with people privately and address the issue in a group setting only where necessary.
3. State the issues as you see them. Then ask the other person to do the same.
4. Give the conflict a name, something funny or memorable to cut the tension.
5. Ask the person or team to address the conflict while avoiding the personal issues that too often arise. Keep talking until the issue is resolved.

Or be like Abe. As Doris Kearns Goodwin tells us in *Team of Rivals,* Abraham Lincoln invited his biggest rivals from the presidential campaign to be top-level members of his administration. At the outset, this produced a great deal of confusion and a titanic clash of egos. But as each member of his cabinet saw that their voice was being heard, they felt comfortable expressing their opinions. For Lincoln, having difficult conversations and managing conflict was a way of governing.

The Myspace buy felt seismic. Major recording artists like R.E.M. and Nine Inch Nails had introduced releases by streaming them on the site, and advertisers like P&G and Sony Pictures advertised there. The media responses were a predictable mix of urgency and fear; half of us stuck our heads in the sand while the rest ran around like headless chickens looking to acquire web companies to join the game. Our entry into the digital sweepstakes was iVillage, as I'll describe in the next chapter. And it would prove to be a knotty mess.

One of the hard lessons I learned during this period is that a good idea itself is not enough. Making NBC digital was the right thing to do. But for an idea to become a successful innovation, to generate revenue and renewal, the harder part is the people: How do you mobilize people to open up to change and then adopt it? There's no smiley-face version of how this goes down. You have to agitate the water.

The traditional top-down style of leadership—here's the answer, now do it—won't work. Often, the person leading the change doesn't *know* the answer, only the need for a new direction. How do you get people to work toward unseen opportunities?

I knew from the start that NBC was going to be a very tough assignment. That I had worked at NBC before only exacerbated the situation, because my colleagues pictured me as I had been. They had little appreciation for what I had accomplished at GE.

I knew Jeff Zucker from my previous stint at NBC, when I was rising through the ranks of PR and Zucker was the dynamic, hyper-competitive young wunderkind of the *Today Show*. A 5-foot-6-inch Harvard grad from Miami, he had won his high school class presidency based on the slogan "The little man with big ideas."

Zucker jumped straight from running *The Harvard Crimson* to a job as the researcher for the NBC Olympics in Seoul, in 1988. From there he leapt to producing *Today*, where he rose at warp speed, revamping it at age twenty-six and starting its sixteen-year run atop the morning ratings. He won because he was willing to take the

most chances. People called him Machiavellian. Yet, no one under-
estimated him for long. He'd won two bouts with colon cancer. He
was a gritty survivor.

Jeff was prone to hissy fits that turned his face beet red, the kind
of tantrums you eventually learned to let pass. Jeff and I had our
disagreements, like the time I called him out for trying to negotiate
his contract in the media. After the negotiation was done, Jeff made
sure to call to tell me that he'd badmouthed me to Andy Lack. "You
know I talked to Andy and he said you were out of bounds," Zucker
told me, his voice shrill and breathless. "You don't really matter
here. You need to know that's what Andy said about you." Nonethe-
less, we were genuinely friendly in a work sense. We'd sit together
and pass notes at Lack's staff meetings.

At my return to NBC, Zucker's position was infinitely more
complicated. After a decade of prime-time dominance, NBC had
sunk to the ratings cellar—in fourth place, behind Fox. *Queer Eye
for the Straight Guy* was fading at Bravo, Katie Couric was unhappy
at *Today* (she'd leave for CBS News in May), and, after a miserable
2005, ratings in 2006 weren't looking any better. Worse, when GE
reported its earnings in January 2006, NBC Universal was the only
division whose profits shrunk.

As someone who'd been thrown into difficult situations, I sympa-
thized with Zucker. Before becoming head of the TV group, Zucker
had led the NBC Network and the Entertainment division, and had
overseen the network's plunge. A lot of people were asking in back-
office whispers and media leaks why he'd been promoted instead of
fired. Jeff Immelt supported him fully and understood that television
was cyclical. But this was GE, and Zucker had to meet his numbers.

It was a chaotic situation.

When for a second quarter in a row NBC was the only GE division for which profits fell, Zucker and I began to have turf battles
over our scarce resources. At one meeting, we talked about how
we could combine some of our sales efforts to offer the iVillage and

nbc.com digital platforms to TV advertisers. The TV sales leaders thought digital was a distraction, however, the money too small for the amount of work. "You expect me to trade in analog dollars for digital pennies!" Zucker burst out.

The room fell into an uncomfortable silence. I could tell he'd been waiting to deliver that line for weeks, to cut the digital folks down to size.

Soon "analog dollars/digital pennies" became his go-to mantra wherever he went, from the media to industry conferences and GE business reviews. My digital team was frustrated. When a top exec belittles you in front of the whole division, spouting, "Come back when you guarantee me $500 million," it undermines our efforts to try new things. And it was incredibly shortsighted. You have to believe that those pennies will become dollars. And they did, a decade later. Today, online video streaming services have market caps of $100 billion or more.

Being an outsider, building a network, telling our story had been a strength of mine at GE. But when I returned to NBC, I also signed up for a lot of publicity. The job became as much about my personality as it was about NBC. I did a lot of interviews, and I was the subject of a lot of articles, complete with glam shots of my hair blowing in the wind.

My goal was to make sure people knew we were serious about NBC Digital. And in much the same way I had done at GE, I tried to be the living embodiment of that, an evangelist on a mission. But I let it go too far. NBC was a place of dueling egos. I could have saved myself a lot of tension by lying low at times. Instead of proselytizing in the media about why digital was great, I should have been spending more time fighting it out inside NBC. Retail politics is what begets real change inside an organization. You have to build "local majorities." Businesses in many ways aren't run from the top, especially now.

I was certain that NBC needed to embrace a digital future. But I was failing to sell my vision to the swing voters.

My relationship with Jeff finally fractured over my attempts to make budget cuts to one of "his" units. Zucker had been incredibly supportive of me in some things, like the launch of two creative studios, one that would create *BuzzFeed*-style digital shorts and the other creating content for advertisers. But he grew increasingly upset when I tried to make changes in the NBC Agency, which John Miller had run forever. The NBC Agency had a team of 250 that did all the NBC on-air promotion. They were the ones who came up with "Must-See TV," and Zucker loved Miller.

As good as the NBC Agency was, it was bloated. I tried numerous times to discuss the cuts with Miller, but he brushed me off. Even though I was technically his boss, he had protection from the corner office.

So I had no choice but to go to Zucker. I told him that the costs were high compared to other agencies, and with my GE–certified thriftiness, that leanness would breed more innovation. It wasn't just about the money—the group needed a shake-up. With each rationale, Zucker waved me aside. "Don't mess with Miller—he's an icon," he said. "Focus on something else." Finally, I couldn't continue the dance, and my insistence gave way to a demand. "Listen, Jeff," I said, "I really need you to support me on this."

Zucker stood up. He stomped over to the easy chair where I was sitting and physically lifted me by the collar of my shirt and walked me back to his office door. "Just get out of here! I can't take you!" he yelled, with a childish temper, and slammed the door for added effect. It was like a scene out of a bad movie. I wish I could say I had stood up for myself the way Jennifer Lawrence or Sandra Bullock would have on screen. But I was too shocked to act.

I went back to my office, closed the door, and cried tears of pure frustration. I had this stunning corner office on the fifty-second floor of 30 Rock, overlooking Manhattan and the Hudson. I was up in the clouds but feeling as if I couldn't sink any lower.

It was a moment of truth for me. I realized I needed to learn to handle conflict better with my peers. You have to use release valves in the office to let the tension out. You can't avoid it. In fact, you have to surface conflict continuously, *before* tensions mount too high. Tension is the price of admission when you are innovating. I should have confronted Jeff Zucker long before and told him that his actions were unacceptable. And I should have stated my position up front—I was in charge of the NBC Agency. I didn't need his permission to run the agency. I had backed down to preserve the peace, but as I was coming to realize, appeasement is the antithesis of innovation.

My relationship with Jeff Zucker didn't grow any more tranquil as the months passed, and the iVillage acquisition turned into the iVillage nightmare. But business failure wasn't the cause of the moment that truly broke our relationship. Instead, it was sunk by the most natural of human emotions—the fear of being pushed aside.

As Bob Wright approached the "not-official" retirement age, the media began to buzz over who was next in line. Soon, news articles began to appear saying that Zucker's ascension wasn't as sewn up as it seemed. I was an unlikely "dark horse," they said, who had the support of Jeff Immelt. "She's the one set up as a competitor to him," one nameless source told the *New York Post*. "That's the way GE works, as they typically pit two people against each other."

Imagine how Zucker must have seen things at that moment: profits and ratings down at NBC, GE breathing down his neck, and a mole from Fairfield planted in case he failed. To him, I was a threat. How many of us have lashed out privately, if not in public, at someone who is yapping at our heels?

On September 15, 2006, an item in the *New York Post* Page Six gossip column froze me where I sat.

As the Dalai Lama once told me, your enemy is your best teacher.

Comstock—who once headed p.r. at the network, and marketing at GE—is said to be building an empire through the Internet, using her talent and charm. "She's lethal," said one insider. "She could take out your kidney and you wouldn't know it was gone."

It was the ultimate drive-by attack. Someone was out to cut me and my ambitions down to size. I was out in Palo Alto. On the phone with people at NBC, I tried to joke it off, saying I was honored to be thought of as a corporate samurai. But inside I was devastated.

I called a friend who was then the head of the Weber Shandwick PR agency and asked him to check with his sources at the *Post* to see where the quote had originated. He called back quickly. "I got some bad news. I can't find out who, but it's coming from within."

I had become the enemy. Was it Bob Wright's PR chief? Somebody on Team Zucker? Zucker himself?

In February 2007, Jeff Zucker took over for Wright, as everyone knew he would. He said the right things about change coming faster than ever, about digital media being the future, but my antenna was up. Soon enough, I received proof that the turf war was still on. In April, a story in the *Post* said I was "losing credibility" according to half a dozen sources "close to NBC." One said, "People are beginning to question why she has been given so much responsibility relative to her performance."

I felt so alone. When the article came out, I was at a GE leadership meeting—a golf outing on Kiawah Island—along with Zucker. Since I don't play golf, I walked the beach for hours, turning everything over in my head. I felt publicly humiliated and betrayed. And I felt like I was falling off the radar.

Leadership is not for those with weak kidneys. You can't stay above the fray and still be an effective leader.

I had taken to talking to Zucker only when absolutely necessary and only about our disagreements over digital and cost-cutting. The real solution, I realized later, was to seek out more genuine, more open, more emotional engagement with him to better offer feedback so it's not seen as criticism. But I didn't understand yet how powerful that kind of conversation could be, or how necessary it was to have the tools to do it well. I had a lot to learn.

I once worked with a man named Gavin; he *really* irritated me. He frequently talked over me, he didn't ask for input before deciding the answers to complex questions outside his realm, and he generally needed to have the last word in everything. I would get anxious heading into meetings with him, fearing that we wouldn't make much progress. Then one day, I tried a new tactic. I asked myself: What can I learn from Gavin? Instead of being indignant that he didn't work hard enough and took too much of the credit, I decided to use him as a teacher of how to work differently. I asked myself, What can I learn from him about working smarter, not just doing more work? Cultivating that new perspective helped me, and eventually I forged an imperfect but functional relationship with him. He didn't change, but I did. There are still people in my life who can irritate me. Instead of seeing them as adversaries, I have learned to change my mind-set, to think of them as potential teachers.

While attending a session in Boston between the Dalai Lama and a group of business leaders, the Dalai Lama said to us, "Your enemy is your best teacher. I lose my temper, yes, but deep anger, no. I've learned to look first at the human level. I'm just like you."

All In?

As the Page Six attacks escalated and my fights with Zucker grew bitter, I thought a lot about loyalty. I felt like I'd been tossed to the wolves—and worse, that Jeff Immelt had done the tossing.

That's when Steve Jobs called.

At the end of 2005, NBC signed an iTunes try-out deal with Apple under which we sold TV show episodes for $1.99 each, like everyone else (Apple set the price). When I started at NBC we'd already pulled in $2.5 million, a third of that from *The Office*.

As NBC's new head of digital, I'd been working with Apple to push more of our digital content to iTunes, and I got to know their team as the relationship grew. I met with Steve's right-hand man, iTunes VP Eddy Cue. Eddy later approached me about working for him, as a general manager for iTunes. I had also gotten to know Allison Johnson, their head of advertising, and Phil Schiller, their CMO, through my marketing network.

When Steve called me to seal the job offer in November, it came so out of the blue that I couldn't think of anything to say, except that anyone would be stupid to not consider such a great opportunity. I went to Cupertino as a next step, meeting with a number of people at Apple, culminating with Steve himself.

I was led into Steve's stark-white conference room next to his office. Steve seemingly materialized out of nowhere in his black mock turtleneck and jeans. He was smaller in person than I expected. Our meeting lasted an hour. We talked a lot about GE's ad campaigns, about Ecomagination, which he liked a lot, and about NBC and digital content. He didn't make any specific offers or mention a title other than iTunes management. I realized I was being felt out. It was all very Jedi.

A few days later, he left a message on my cell phone. "This is Steve Jobs. I just wanted to say how much we'd like to have you work for us at Apple. We're about to make something really big happen. You haven't seen anything yet," he said on the message. "If you have any questions, I'm happy to talk to you directly."

I felt honored and excited, but queasy. Could I just leave NBC? In 2006, Apple wasn't yet the juggernaut it would soon become with the launch of the iPhone. An inveterate planner, I focused on all the reasons I had for turning Apple down.

The environment seemed very command and control, and I had been trying to get away from that environment at GE/NBC. Allison told me that although Steve was hard to work for, she did her best work there. If you want to be tested and made better, she said, Apple was the place to do that. And that resonated with me.

Yet I was excited about what could happen by merging digital and video. I believed there would be more opportunities in content; I wanted to be a storyteller.

Although I was torn, in the end I said no.

Two months later, I was surprised when my cell phone rang with Steve calling me again. "I understand why you didn't take that role with iTunes. I get it, it wasn't big enough for you. But I have an idea for another role. When can you come to see me?" When I told him I had plans to be in San Francisco in two weeks, he suggested that we "take a walk."

At first, he talked about the concerns on his mind—energy consumption, landfill issues with computer waste, packaging and shipping. Then he asked me to tell him more about what we had done with Ecomagination. He was particularly interested in the advertising that we had done at GE. I talked a lot about our dancing elephant and the imagery. He saw our efforts as imaginative and "bold."

"I want you to work at Apple. So here's what I have in mind. You'll work directly for me. I need someone who can help us get a better handle on the environment. We're not where we need to be, and I'm committed to doing a much better job on the green front. And I think there are other things you'll do down the road."

At home, I spent the weekend obsessing over what to do, driving my husband, Chris, crazy. Chris is a great problem-solver. His easygoing, calming influence is just what's needed when I overthink things. He simplifies, cutting through my layers of complexity.

He listens. Once, when I jokingly called Chris "my therapist," a woman asked me, intrigued, *Really?* You married your therapist? He's not, he's a journalist turned business operator, someone who is really good at steadily moving things forward. We spent hours at the kitchen table walking through the Apple offer, doing the math on whether we could swing the move to California. Then I stayed up half the night, making worksheets, methodically listing the pros and cons about my role at NBC versus Apple.

By now, I made a long daily commute to New York City from our home in Connecticut, which had been convenient for my GE job. Truthfully, we didn't love Connecticut. While it was beautiful, there was a coldness, some of my own making as I basically focused on work and family, making little time for more. I had few acquaintances beyond mothers of my daughters' friends. "I can't believe none of your neighbors brought you a pie to welcome you to the neighborhood," my mother once remarked. I felt certain if I did get a pie, it would be frozen. (Knowing my mother's friendly ways, she would have gotten to know everyone in town in the first six months.) I felt guilty seeing how Katie had struggled to adapt as a young teenager to a new school in a new town where relationships are hard to navigate at any age. I worried about uprooting Meredith, who was just starting high school. Meredith told us she would turn "goth" if we moved. I still laugh at that. As if wearing black clothes and thick eyeliner was the worst thing that could happen.

While my relationship with Zucker and the iVillage team was two months deeper in the toilet, I was also nervous about taking an assignment that was so vague. I had been burned by the NBC role, where I had a title and responsibility without accountability. And I wanted to be part of content creation more than technology development—perhaps run a cable network or a consumer digital company.

I called Steve back on Monday. "Steve, you've given me a lot to think about. It is exciting," I said. "But I can't take the job. I just can't move my younger daughter right now. It was hard for my older daughter, uprooting her to Connecticut. I vowed not to repeat that."

I think Steve was surprised, but his tone was very empathetic. "You have to take care of your family first. I understand," he said. "I'm sorry. But I understand."

Not long after I turned Steve down, Zucker started to ask if Apple wasn't getting a better deal with iTunes than they should. "We really should get more for *The Office*, considering how hot it is," he said. "We're making iTunes, not the other way around." And so, about six months before the contract came up for renewal at the end of 2007, we made it known we wanted a new deal. It quickly escalated into a war, with Jeff Zucker and Eddy Cue sending caustic e-mails to each other, and Jobs stepping in to calm the waters.

Apple refused to budge from its one-size-fits-all pricing. And soon enough, Zucker got so angry that he sent NBC PR to the *New York Times* to tell them we weren't renewing the contract. Jobs went ballistic, and for almost a year there was open warfare between NBC and Apple. It was not until September 2008 that NBC and Apple announced that NBC content would be back in the iTunes store.

Later, I felt turning Steve down may have been one of my biggest missed opportunities. Not the money, although it hit me a few times how much I could have made in stock options. The thing that nagged me most was the missed chance to be tested, to grow and be made better. And yet, in my gut, I worried that I might not have thrived in that environment. There may have been too many constraints on my ability to grow and innovate.

There would be a few other times I talked to companies about open roles. I've never considered it disloyal to discover new potential paths and understand your worth outside your current company. Usually I'd return with a renewed commitment to the mission, and especially to the team.

CHAPTER 7

FAILING FORWARD: IT TAKES A VILLAGE

L ess than a month after I started at NBC, Mark, my head of business development, told me an investment banker had called to say that the women's community site iVillage was on the block. Although it had been on our radar, I didn't really have an opinion on the site at first. But the more I looked at it, the more I felt that its community and content could be a strategic value for us if we worked it in with our own women-angled properties, such as Bravo and especially *Today*.

It wasn't perfect, of course. Mark called it a "premium-priced fixer-upper." While it had good sales, it was still a Web 1.0 company, a glorified online magazine. The big upside was what Mark called "the power of NBCU programming meets the passion of community"—that is, we could make our content interactive for a passionate audience that would access it on platforms from laptops to the smartphones that were just starting to appear on the market.

iVillage was led by CEO Doug McCormick, a seasoned salesman who had packaged the site well by emphasizing the community piece that most interested us. It wasn't a sexy, YouTube kind of property, but it had this incredible community of women. We had intense debates over whether or not we should buy iVillage. I remember sitting in my car in Westport, Connecticut, having a conference call with Bob Wright, Darren Feher, the CTO of NBC, and other members of our team. We were in the final stages of the deal, trying to get a bid in as rumors flew that other media companies were going after it. Darren had just reviewed iVillage's tech and he wasn't impressed. "The technology back-end is bad," he said. Bob asked what I thought. I said the audience is what we wanted and the ad sales would jump-start our digital team. Then I bounced it to Darren, to ask if it could be fixed. "Challenging, but of course, we can fix anything," he said confidently.

After a pause, Bob's voice came on the line: "Let's keep going."

Jeff Immelt called me after we had pitched the deal, and the heat was on for us to make a formal bid. The price was now $600 million, much higher than our starting point, but by now everyone was in—even Darren. We had reworked the financial plan several times to find a way to get the payback terms that GE needed to fund it. It was a near frenzy of irrational exuberance.

"So you like this deal?" Jeff asked me, "Bob is really hot for it."

"I like the strategy. It moves us toward the future with community, even if it's only one step." I was six weeks into the job, and honestly, I didn't have enough expertise to make that call yet. But I had trained myself to project an image of preternatural calm at such moments. It was only years later that I learned to trust my doubts, and express them candidly to others.

Learn to listen and
trust your doubts.
And don't be afraid to
express them to others.

In the end we did the deal. The competition was rumored to be closing in, and the price kept going up. Bob was the lion in for the kill, News Corporation's Myspace acquisition taunting him. We were all following close behind, cheering him on.

I dubbed the acquisition the cornerstone to our digital strategy. But the first crack appeared immediately: the iVillage management team left within days of the purchase. I remember feeling particularly peeved at McCormick, who had led such a fierce bidding contest and then couldn't wait to exit. He left pocketing about $25 million. Why was he in such a hurry?

After watching much of iVillage's leadership jump ship, our most pressing responsibility was to create an integration team. We quickly chose the head of the Bravo network, Lauren Zalaznick—who worked for NBC programming head Jeff Gaspin—as integration leader and general manager. Lauren had had a spectacular run heading Bravo after NBC acquired it, building on programs like *Queer Eye for the Straight Guy*. I thought that, depending on how things went, she could become iVillage CEO.

Lauren's brilliance at Bravo had been to hone the network as a kind of entertainment boutique, serving a small but hip and affluent audience, exactly the one advertisers wanted. Quirky and creative, Lauren is prone to mocking the very bureaucracy she expertly navigates.

I pushed hard for Gaspin and Zalaznick's involvement. And in the early days of integration they were excited. Lauren loved her new job, because she got first dibs on our new property. Much of NBC was psyched to help, too. The interactive director of *Access Hollywood* asked to be included, and Jeff Gralnick of NBC News suggested streamable video by health and science correspondent Robert Bazell, which could then be promoted on *Today*.

For the first sixty days, the team focused. But as Lauren and Gaspin and other division heads dug into the iVillage integration, staff started to ask why money and attention was being showered on

an outside women's platform when they'd rather create their own—
via Bravo, *Today*, and NBC TV stations. They had their own digital
teams. Why weren't they being given the love?

At meetings, when I'd throw out an idea such as linking the
Bravo and iVillage communities, or creating an iVillage women's
health series for *Today*, Lauren and Gaspin began to imply that the
other pieces of NBC refused to cooperate. "My team is already
building one," Lauren was told, or, "*Today* is on that already."

People stopped concentrating on the fact that iVillage had a robust community of engaged women and strong sales that we could
all leverage. Instead they focused on all the things that were wrong
with it. Lauren complained about the amount of astrology on iVillage. The iVillage audience was America's heartland, not the hip
demographic she was aspiring to reach. And the technology *was*
bad—much worse than we had thought.

In the face of rapid change, people tend to retreat into their silos
and guard their own turf. The question was, How was I going to
overcome those walls and fiefdoms? How do you get a company to
embrace the new?

I could have asked Bob Wright to get more personally involved,
but it didn't seem right. I'd grown a lot since leaving GE—I shouldn't
have to say, "Because the boss said so." I had been hired to handle
this. So I fell back on old habits and tried to go it alone. That's
tempting but also foolish, I would come to find.

Innovation is a social activity. One person's ideas build on another's. Someone else reframes it through the eyes of the customer. It's
never clean or linear. To create an innovative team environment, the
person leading the effort needs what entrepreneur Margaret Heffernan calls *social capital*. Social capital is the mortar that connects
team members, the feeling of safety and trust that allows people to
ask crazy questions and provide slightly less crazy answers without
embarrassment, to iterate to greatness. But social capital has to be
built, banked, and stored. That means engaging in practices that are

Invite the Critic In

Most of us don't like conflict—I know I don't. At times, I've seethed in silence (or rolled my eyes in exasperation), as opposed to listening to critical comments as signals in and of themselves. But learning when and how to work with your critics is an important step in managing change.

Spend time with your biggest critics—invite them in. Perhaps they have valid points that can improve your plan or make your project better. By incorporating their input, you may find new allies.

- Acknowledge that you and your critic have a difference of opinion. But see if you agree on something. For example, do you both agree that the project is worthwhile? Is it just the tactics that you disagree on?
- Give the critic a starring role. Tell him or her that you need divergent voices in the process. Provided he won't be disruptive, you need him to challenge the team.
- Create ground rules. Here's one I love: "No But." Critics have to offer a solution or build a bridge to another idea—they can't just say no. Or carve out time in regular meetings devoted to "objections," allowing everyone, including critics, to make well-articulated rebuttals to key elements.

BEWARE: Some people are just negative. They don't want to offer solutions and aren't in pursuit of better. You may decide they can't be part of the project, because they aren't attempting to contribute anything beyond negative energy.

antithetical to a world that measures people by how well they meet their numbers. In that environment, asking your employees to make time for more idle chitchat sounds ridiculous.

That was precisely the lesson Jack Welch taught me when he instructed me to "wallow" more in the informality of office life. Some companies mandate prohibiting their employees from eating at their desks. They are encouraged to share meals—and conversations—in the lunchroom. Some leaders schedule ice cream breaks for the entire team to encourage people to talk about things outside of work.

The point is that the more time team members spend together, the more social capital, trust, and honesty they build. And the more innovative, risk-taking, and productive they are.

Building an innovative team is about creating trust, not just hiring stars. No one person dominates the conversation; everyone talks equally. Team members are socially and emotionally attuned to the needs and feelings of the others. (Perhaps not surprisingly, the most successful teams include a range of diversity, including women and more diverse thinkers.)

Instead of putting Lauren in charge as the star, in the wake of her success at Bravo, I should have spent more time cultivating an iVillage *team*, putting members in situations in which they could honestly argue and exchange ideas in order to make iVillage better. Innovation is not polite; disagreement, conflict, is inevitable. But you have to feel safe to disagree.

Unfortunately, that is not the atmosphere we had at NBC when it came to iVillage. People came to meetings, raided the division like a shared fridge that nobody was stocking, and went back to their lives. It was becoming clear that the change I needed wasn't going to happen with Lauren at the helm. We never had a big confrontation, just a gradual erosion of support. Tons of fake smiles; lots of resistance to change.

I was experiencing one of NBC's least pleasant behaviors: the "grinf*ck." At GE, people took a kind of plucky pride in calling

When you are innovating, tension is the price of admission.

you an idiot to your face. Media people resisted that kind of head-on collision. People said they were going to do things that they had no intention of doing. They smiled and said they were behind the deal. But when it came time to integrate iVillage into their brands, they'd go back to protecting their fiefdoms.

To go forward, I decided, we needed an outsider to run iVillage, someone with a digital and a women's branding background. Someone tough enough and with enough of an outsider perspective to deal with NBC's resistance to change. Our headhunter recommended Debi Fine, who recently had been the president of Mark, a millennial cosmetics brand from Avon that had shaken up the industry. I called Avon CEO Andrea Jung, whom I knew as a member of the GE board. Andrea said that Mark never would have happened without Debi. Then she uttered the magic phrase: "I would hire her again."

That was enough for me.

A few weeks later, a member of our HR team went on a hike with the former head of HR of Avon, who had a different view on Debi—that she was excellent, but that it was all about Debi. This is a worrisome attribute for a team leader, especially for a troubled property that desperately needed to build a team. HR wanted me to find someone else. But I persevered: Debi was strong willed and aggressive, I said, just what was needed to combat the feudal tribes of NBC.

I soon saw that I should have considered HR's advice. As we negotiated her contract, Debi said she wanted NBC to pay for a car to bring her to and from NYC from her home in New Jersey. She had been used to the amenities of a scaled company. But iVillage was a scrappy company, not yet scaled.

And then there was the redecoration of the iVillage offices. Or, should I say, *her* office.

The division's Garment District offices were the kind of open-plan cubicle style that brought the word *sweatshop* to mind. I green-lit office improvement funds, because I thought it was important that the team felt like we were investing in them.

A few weeks later, when I showed up at iVillage, I couldn't hide my surprise at finding Debi's office beautifully appointed in a white sofa, new desk, and new carpet. Money had gone to her office and new carpet for the executive areas. There was a clear line where those areas ended and the old, stained carpet began—where everyone else worked.

What we needed was a leader, convener, and bridge builder. Was that who I hired?

To her credit, Debi was fearless in going after revenue and marketing. We upgraded the site, launched an ad campaign, invested in community. Debi bonded with sales, and they got off to a strong start courting big customers like Walmart and driving up pricing. The business plan that we handed to Debi was overly optimistic. She was quick to call us on that, and yet she didn't use it as an excuse to slow the hunt for growth. I gave her a lot of credit for speaking truth to an unrealistic plan. I was also coming to realize the conundrum that can accompany acquisitions: revenue projections and deal "synergies" are often unrealistic, leaving the team that has to execute left holding a lighter bag of goods than planned.

But when Debi needed to expand beyond her capabilities, she sparred with her COO, Ezra, who had a strong background in building digital media companies. Worse, Debi brought in her own digital "guru," who appeared from time to time as a disembodied voice on the phone, like Charlie from *Charlie's Angels*.

"Any comment on our plans for the new comment widget?" I asked him on the speakerphone during one meeting.

Heavy breathing, and then the utterance: "Beware the interface."

Instead of growing iVillage into a new child that everyone owned, iVillage was becoming the village idiot that everyone avoided. And I didn't have the political savvy yet to woo people in NBC to work across platforms to save it.

I pestered and reiterated with ideas for integrating Bravo with iVillage. One day Lauren spun around to me to say, with some irritation, "You just don't stop, do you?" My tenacity had served me well up to this point as a tool for managing up. But as an operational manager, I needed different tactics.

And then came the TV show.

By this point, we were desperate for someone, anyone, inside NBC to partner with iVillage. In November 2006, the NBC TV stations group pitched us on doing a live daily talk show, called *iVillage Live*. The show would be produced by Miami-based NBC station WTVJ at Universal Studios in Orlando, and syndicated across all of our NBC stations and offered to affiliates. It was supposed to be a first-of-its-kind lifestyle show that mixed a curated online community with a live audience. Viewers would be able to log on and send in questions or comments, or watch it streamed live on the Internet.

I was thrilled to have an opportunity to show what iVillage could do.

David Zaslav, NBC's president of cable distribution, tried to convince me to reconsider. I wrote off his warning to his not wanting us to succeed. It was hard not to be a little paranoid when it came to iVillage.

"The Stations division isn't good," he said. "Don't give them the iVillage brand. You need to protect the franchise. They are going to screw this up."

I told David that we weren't really in a position to turn down an opportunity. Plus, everybody on my end was excited. We convinced ourselves that we would create something the world had never seen.

We worked our tails off for the December 2006 premiere, and the show launched to great fanfare. I remember sitting down to watch the first episode, excited, jittery, nervous. And within minutes I realized that it was . . . *terrible*. The three novice hosts the Stations team hired to seem more like the "real people" had no chemistry. It was like a community access version of *Live! with Regis and Kelly* with a studio audience and the online community, except when they went to take questions no one called in. And a nearby roller coaster at Universal Studios kept drowning the hosts' chatter. We were a laughingstock.

Worse, it wasn't innovative.

Bravo stopped replaying the episodes three weeks after the launch, claiming (rightly) that it did nothing for the brand. We quickly reconfigured the show, moved it to Chicago, and relaunched it with slightly better-known hosts as "In the Loop with iVillage." But that only seemed to make the media critics attack it more savagely. No one was surprised it lasted only a few months after the relaunch.

Looking back, if we had successfully married iVillage with *The Today Show* (or any NBC property for that matter), we would have built a community around *Today*, with engaged viewers and insights to make viewers, producers, and salespeople happy. It's tempting to look back and think we had our shot at a Facebook. Of course, Facebook had only just emerged out of a Harvard kid's room at that point. But we did see the possibility looming on the horizon. It was within our grasp, if only we could get out of our own way. Instead, as is too common within established companies, iVillage was wounded before it could even challenge. It stumbled along alone in a sort of twilight, making it look like the failure it was.

With the TV show spinning in the breeze, an idea surfaced to move iVillage from Manhattan to offices in Englewood Cliffs, New Jersey. The state was courting digital firms with substantial tax credits. I fought hard—it was a horrible decision, one that would disrupt the franchise at a delicate moment. But Bob disagreed. "The financial reasons are clear. Your people will come to like it."

By move-in time in the fall of 2007, half of the employees had resigned. The move tore the heart out of iVillage. The new offices were (finally) stunning, but they were empty. Our footfalls echoed as we walked the halls. iVillage was still moving, but it was the aimless shuffle of the walking dead.

In the years since iVillage, I've discovered better ways than fancy work spaces and lighting to help create that high-quality environment between team members. Harvard Business School professor Amy Edmondson coined the term *psychological safety* to describe the kind of environment we needed, where people feel confident enough to go out on a limb in the pursuit of a new way of doing things. Edmondson found, counterintuitively, that top-performing teams made *more* mistakes. Or rather, that they *admitted* to making more mistakes, because they felt safe enough to do so. It was everything iVillage was not.

CHAPTER 8

GETTING IT RIGHT

In mid-December of 2005, *Saturday Night Live* cast members Andy Samberg and Chris Parnell, and two new *SNL* writers, gave birth to the modern Internet when they filmed a zero-budget rap video parody called "Lazy Sunday." Samberg and Parnell played two not-quite-gangster rappers singing the praises of Google Maps and Magnolia Bakery cupcakes, and mixing Pibb soda and Red Vines candy ("Crazy delicious!") as they head to a matinee showing of *The Chronicles of Narnia: The Lion, the Witch and the Wardrobe* ("We love The Chronic—What?—les of Narnia!").

The video was anything but what was considered professional at the time: they recorded the song on a used computer they bought on Craigslist and filmed the video with a borrowed camera. The fast-cut short just screams, "Anybody can do this." The creators doubted that it would ever see the light of day. But an hour before SNL broadcast on December 17, 2005, show creator Lorne Michaels gave the thumbs-up, and "Lazy Sunday" went on the air.

Within the week, "Lazy Sunday" broke the Internet.

During its first week on YouTube, "Lazy Sunday" was viewed over two million times. Within a few more weeks, it had gotten five million views. It wasn't the Internet's first viral video. But it was its first mainstream hit. The problem for NBC was, we weren't getting a dime.

Suddenly it was clear that if we didn't figure the digital world out, we would end up having our own Kodak Moment.

In those early days, YouTube cast a big shadow. I saw user-generated content as a real advantage to whoever was running a community. I'd ask show producers, "Why don't you put out a clip and ask users to edit it?" But people were too afraid of being consumed by piano-playing cats to do it.

Even the earliest iterations of YouTube were foretelling a remarkable shift from passive viewers gazing at a big black box waiting for the next sitcom, to users clicking actively through YouTube's visual kaleidoscope, leaving comments and sharing those that inspired their awe (or ire). People were putting their stamp on the media, making it their own. And NBC needed to be there.

NBC Universal had put some money behind a digital creative studio, bringing in young digital natives to figure out how to create this kind of experience. It had been started with a fairly big budget of several million dollars. By the time I arrived, a combination of organizational arrogance ("Look at those amateurs!") and fear ("Where's the business model? What about IP and rights?") had conspired to cut the studio's budget. But not its enthusiasm.

Seeing this ignored white space, I saw a chance to innovate. The remaining half dozen film producers and directors, twentysomethings who had come out of digital and advertising agencies, just needed a mission and someone to believe in them. So I commandeered the team.

iVillage subsumed me not long after, and the digital studio band eventually broke up. But while my crackerjack team of digital turks

Change is not a single act or initiative. It is an ever-evolving dynamic in which you prod and seed the environment with a range of friction-causing catalysts.

didn't produce any blockbuster victories—they did create a few viral hits of the day like "Microwave Gorilla" and "The Easter Bunny Hates You." To see such initiatives as failure is misguided. We fall back on doing so because we are used to big versus small, success versus failure. But we do so to our detriment.

Change is not a single act or initiative. It is an ever-evolving dynamic in which you prod and seed the environment with a range of friction-causing catalysts. This is why you need *sparks*, be they people, projects, or perspectives.

A change-agent is like an early-stage investor. You put down a lot of small bets, and a few large ones, on the belief that one or more will blow up big and lead you forward. You learn from each failure in this evolving portfolio of strategic experiments. There is a larger class of experiments that I call *challengers*: the creation of a corporate-funded competitor functioning independently outside the mothership, or (as you'll see in the next chapter) the formation of an internal digital marketing team to compete against the existing department. They are high-stakes challengers to the status quo. And of course, defenders of the old order inevitably pile on to kill them. But challengers are what lead companies to qualitative leaps forward. From my years launching Ecomagination and Imagination Breakthroughs at GE, I knew the advantages of Red Team/Blue Team exercises, when you set up two opposing teams to work on the same project, to inject more ideas and a competitive edge into the process. At GE, we used Red Team/Blue Team in Imagination Breakthroughs as a way to consider new ventures with opposing points of view—to tease out the tension, arguments, and counterarguments. With Ecomagination, we pitted a group of researchers tasked with proving climate change (the Red Team) against a team refuting it (the Blue Team). In the end, the Red Team's evidence, based on the science, was so compelling that the Blue Team capitulated.

The Red Team/Blue Team mentality came out of the military, as Bryce Hoffman describes in his book *Red Teaming*, and is now playing a bigger part in the corporate world. In one form of it, one team tries to find holes in the organization's security system; a second version involves something called "alternative analysis" in decision-making, in which one team is charged with trying to find facts that disprove existing hypotheses in order to get past our all-too-human tendency to look at information selectively as a way to support or confirm existing biases.

To free us from our "Lazy Sunday" paralysis, I felt we needed a Red Team at NBC, an outsider who could challenge The Way Things Are Done.

In July 2006, Viacom reached out to David Zaslav, NBC's head of cable distribution, to suggest we form a "Broadband Joint Venture." The plan was basically that NBC and Viacom would create a walled hub of shared content. Each of our network-based websites (nbc.com, bravo.com, MTV.com) would continue to have their own video content, but all would be aggregated in the NewCo joint venture, which would be ad supported; the owners would share the returns. Eventually the discussion expanded to include Fox. The code name of this Red Team was "Project Caterpillar."

The Red Team never got off the ground, though, as the media partners obsessed about protecting their own turf, how they would make money, and making sure no one got something on the other.

Then, in November, an unforeseen event sent the media world into a frenzy. Google bought YouTube for $1.5 billion, which totally changed the landscape (and infuriated Jeff Zucker, who felt that YouTube's value was built on the back of the *SNL* video). With Google's backing, the digital onslaught we had feared was suddenly very real.

Prompted by Google's YouTube buy, NBC and Fox returned to the drawing board and came back with a new venture—NewCo #2, for now—based on new momentum led by my deputy, NBC's chief digital officer, George Kliavkoff (known as George K) and our digital team. The Fox side would be led by Mike Lang, their

EVP of business development and strategy, and George would be interim CEO.

We hoped it would become the online source for premium video content. It would give Fox and NBC a two-way digital relationship with viewers, and it would create real community among the viewers, who'd be able to enjoy content online anywhere.

We were deeply excited. But I feared that the motherships would fight us. When we brought together the launch team—one hundred staffers plucked from NBC and Fox—at a grand kickoff meeting at a W Hotel in Manhattan, my worst nightmares were realized. The meeting disintegrated into a chaotic turf war designed to ensure that each team did not lose a single inch of its "own" property.

As Mike Lang, George K, and I watched the chaos of the meeting at the W, and the media's reaction to it, we agreed we'd need a great CEO to make this work. My experiences with iVillage had taught me some painful lessons about what start-up digital leadership required. We knew that it was imperative that we hire an outsider for our NewCo CEO, someone without preconceptions, allies, and turf. It was also important that we bring in someone who was skilled in building a sort of pioneer team that worked toward one goal, without the ossified processes and the old ways of thinking of our parent networks.

Hulu

Jim Citrin of Spencer Stuart introduced us to some very impressive executives like former Ticketmaster CEO John Pleasants; and Travelocity CEO Michelle Peluso. But we kept coming back to one name: Jason Kilar. Before leaving to take a break from the grind, Jason had spent nine years at Amazon, building up its DVD service from scratch before moving to other roles.

What attracted us to Jason was that he'd grown up under Jeff

Bezos's theory of innovation management. As an Amazon executive, Jason had attained a Zen-like mastery in managing conflict. To Jeff Bezos, workplace harmony is overrated; conflict is the spice that leads inexorably to innovation. Executives at Amazon are inculcated in Bezos's management notions, such as #13, Have Backbone; Disagree, and Commit. "Leaders are obligated to respectfully challenge decisions when they disagree, even when doing so is uncomfortable or exhausting. Leaders have conviction and are tenacious. They do not compromise for the sake of social cohesion. Once a decision is determined, they commit wholly."

If you're going to innovate to greatness, you have to be able to give your colleagues candid feedback on their ideas—and be prepared to face the same firing squad yourself. Striving to maintain harmony is dangerous; it silences honest criticism and allows people to serve up polite praise for bad ideas.

Real innovators can be disagreeable; they don't require the social approval of their peers to move ahead with disruptive ideas. On this point I believe Bezos is demonstrably right, as uncomfortable as I know this is. Research shows that creative tension promotes stronger idea generation and group problem-solving. Constructive dissent and debate encourage people to reexamine assumptions and make room for creative thinking. In the words of Pragmatist philosopher John Dewey, "Conflict is the gadfly of thought. It stirs us to observation and memory. It instigates to invention. It shocks us out of sheep-like passivity, and sets us at noting and contriving."

Bottom line: You have to get up in the morning and fight for what you believe in. And you have to create a climate in which your people have permission to do the same.

That is exactly why we all liked Jason immediately. The problem was, he wasn't as excited about the job as we were. After leaving Amazon, he had gone on a year-long trip around the world with his wife and two young children, blogging from nineteen countries as he hashed out his next move. He worried, with good reason, that having two corporate masters would kill the business we were trying to create. He doubted that he would be given the independence he needed. And he really didn't like some of the contract terms.

"Listen, Jason," I told him, "you justifiably have doubts about how adaptable and fast we'll be. But we are completely committed to making you successful. We need this to work. And we need someone like you to lead this. Not a media wonk."

Jason sighed on his end of the phone call. "I need freedom to make fast decisions on behalf of my people. I need to prototype things quickly and trash things quickly. I need to pay people in stock, because there has to be an upside to match the risk."

"I totally understand. This is about making something new, and about making it work," I said. "Have faith, Jason."

One big issue that had separated us was equity in the new venture. Like everyone who'd worked in the start-up world, Jason knew that equity grants and options aligned employees with the NewCo's interest: if they stayed and it succeeded, they won big. But that was anathema to GE. Jeff once was close to signing a deal to acquire a start-up and keep it separate, and Jack killed it at the last moment, saying, "We have one currency at GE: GE stock."

Those kinds of edicts take a long time to die, I discovered, as I pushed for the crucially necessarily tool: non-GE equity. The issue was how much ownership to give and how much freedom Jason would have to give it. My challenge was to get the NBC/GE system used to the fact that NewCo employees would have a different "currency." It was an uphill fight. When I pointed out that this was a fifty/fifty joint venture and the new team needed to have an ownership stake in that venture, Marc, our head of HR, worried that people in NewCo might get richer than people at the same level inside NBC. When I noted that they were taking a huge risk joining a start-up, he fell back to the "one currency" argument.

To my delight (and the chagrin of many others), Jason got most of what he wanted in the end: the ability to offer equity and the ability to run the new company with near total independence.

Even before his first day at the headquarters in Santa Monica, Jason traveled to Beijing with a few minders from NBC and Fox, where he introduced them to Eric Feng, a twenty-eight-year-old poker buddy from Seattle. Jason and Eric had never worked together, but Jason had tried Eric's software at Mojiti, a year-old online video start-up, and he had loved it. Jason was convinced that Eric would make the perfect CTO to build the tech he wanted. The folks at Fox and NBC thought that Eric was too green for a project this big (even Eric admitted that he wasn't sure what a CTO actually did). But Jason got his way.

Jason's phrase for building a fast-moving, dynamic, and rebellious dream team was "the Ocean's Eleven approach." He hired buddies from Amazon and classmates from Harvard Business School, anybody he knew and trusted to spend eighteen-hour days arguing and coding in an almost suicidal bid to get the NewCo site running within ninety days. You can't confuse credentials with character, competence, or chemistry. When your aim is to disrupt the status quo, you have to know the team has your back.

My experience at iVillage had encouraged me to believe that the conflict and tension inherent in change inevitably equated to an atmosphere of nasty infighting. Yet Jason's approach made people engaged and happy. He kept them focused on what mattered. He fought the battles with the mothership. The employees I saw in the offices were a tight team, and they seemed thrilled to be there. Jason had installed himself in a tiny office just off the main project room and attached whiteboards to the walls. He and his launch team had put together a mission statement that united them in a quest. It was a mission statement defined by frugality, meritocracy, and ownership (they all had equity). Jason and his cohorts wrote, in part:

We are in the business of building and innovating. . . . We invest in whiteboard wallpaper. We invest in flat, highly talented teams. We invest in Costco snack runs, particularly the M&M trail mix. We see it as all of our jobs to make it as easy as possible for builders to build and for innovators to innovate. In this, we serve each other.

One of my HR managers wrote to me to say he had been "hearing some concerns about how Jason is making some decisions too autonomously." Jason signed people up without confidentiality agreements, committed to equity plans without having them approved, and removed IP language from offer letters. Our people wanted him to act like an entrepreneur, but they didn't know what that meant. Tension ran high.

Jason was a youthful executive at the time, both in appearance and energy. During my initial visit to the NewCo headquarters in Santa Monica, he acted like a kid excited to show me his new room. Fox had rented offices that befitted a big-time media company—replete with a swanky corner office with high-end Steelcase furniture for him—which went against every fiber of Jason's start-up being. "Can you believe how big and wasteful this is? We don't need this much space. We're going to sublet it," he told me. And the fancy furniture? Gone, replaced with a few Costco desks and a shared printer. The food? He held up a big plastic tub of pretzels. Costco, of course.

"Come here," Jason said, taking me by the arm into an office furnished with only a folding table that was surrounded by a gaggle of twenty-year-olds. "Look at this, I've hired a dozen interns from USC and UCLA; they are digitizing all the clips from *Saturday Night Live*. Your lawyers are so slow to give me permission, so I'm just doing it. I'm sure we'll be able to use them by the time we're done digitizing them. If we waited for the legal folks, we'd never get anything out."

He was baffled we had hired Price Waterhouse Cooper to help with strategy. "What on earth does a start-up team need with consultants? They make more in a month than I can pay the team in a year. Gone!" he told me, giddy with movement. Jason dumped everything.

Jason was doing exactly what needed to be done: he was exceeding his authority based on his need. Amidst all Jason's seeming chaos, the vision—the direction—was always there: we are going to create the future of television.

It was eye-opening to watch Jason dance on the edge of his authority, constantly pushing the limit of what others thought he ought to be doing. The need to go beyond what you are authorized to do can be a positive trait when you are pushing to change the way things are done. The secret is to know where the boundaries lie. Some who resist your efforts will tell you you're "pushing too hard." Others, just as resistant, will encourage you to "go for it" because it makes you more likely to be fired. The key is to learn how to push the limits without being seen as unacceptably subversive.

Later, the press would describe the first months at NewCo as a chaos of crazy ideas, with whiteboards filled with wild notions of what could be.

Jason kept pushing the limits. "Consumer behavior is one of the hardest things to change," he said. "The gap between the existing and the new has to be so materially better that it shocks you into a behavior change." Jason's maniacal obsession with the user experience is a large part of why NewCo was successful in creating a service that one customer called "brain-spray awesome."

At the time, though, Jason's maniacal obsession seemed petulant and out of bounds to many. I remember getting a desperate call from Darren, the CTO at NBC, asking for help convincing Jason to use the digital video player that Darren's team had built. They'd spent $5 million (a lot, even then!) and were proud of it. And they were convinced it could help Jason move up the launch date.

Don't be afraid to go beyond what you are authorized to do when you are changing the way things are done.

But Jason's response was unequivocal: no. To him, it had so many doodads; he said it looked like Tokyo at night. He wanted a service so easy to use his mother would understand it. "My team can build something that suits our needs," Jason said. "The video player has to be a superb experience. NBC's is not." It became clear that we couldn't—in fact, shouldn't—make Jason do anything. I think that had NewCo been a wholly owned subsidiary of NBC, we would have forced him to use that clunky player. Or we would have had ten meetings about it and lost weeks deciding what to do.

Jason transgressed every "rule" at NBC in his push to disruption— from the video player he wouldn't take to the older shows he insisted be recoded into HD to the sacrilege he committed by telling NBC's bosses to not only limit the number of ads viewers saw but also give viewers the ability to choose which ones they saw. And our executives pushed back. You don't digitize old shows. You don't open digital rights. You don't ask producers for special content. And every time, Jason went around them.

A few years down the road, many of his ideas became industry best practices. It serves as a vital reminder that it is the outsiders, the rule-breakers, who possess the kind of disruptive intelligence that cultures have always relied on to catalyze reinvention and renewal. On the other hand, weirdly, I believe having gatekeepers is a positive. Constraints and obstacles are as necessary for the mischiefmaker to produce great work as it is for a poet to create a great poem. The most creative ideas are often triggered by restriction and scarcity.

Jason tried to dub the service Cream, "because it rises to the top," which elicited a groan from NewCo's advisors. Thankfully, Jason's new CTO, Eric Feng, had a better suggestion. Why not call it Hulu, he said; it meant "vessel" in Chinese.

Jason continued to drop bombshells, of course. He wanted to open with an invitation-only beta site so that he could keep iterating before the real launch. And the search engine his team had built would display results for all broadcast video across the Internet, not just from Fox and NBC. Both those ideas drew the ire of the TV people. Showing a beta site was like letting people watch a film before it had been edited. And putting the competitors' content alongside our own? Jeff Zucker and Fox COO Peter Chernin were furious at the very idea. But Jason was adamant, as always.

The friction between Jason and the higher-ups at Fox and NBC illustrated one of the inherent difficulties for challengers like Hulu: the role of top leaders in "green-lighting" the structure. We set up a Hulu board with Chernin and Zucker as cochairs. I was on the board, with George K and Mike Lang. Our job was to oversee and green-light his efforts. But those efforts—like including competitors' content—often ran up against the parent companies' turf interests. NBC and Fox had each committed $25 million to funding Hulu, which created tension at the parent companies.

Exacerbating the tension was Jason's apparent allergy to making money, at least at the start. He was obsessed with creating constant feedback loops with the user by requesting actual comments and tracking user actions. His laser focus was on the user experience, not on revenues. He didn't plan to introduce advertising until later. It was in complete contrast with my experience at NBC, where I was fighting with Zucker over the number of ads we could allow on TV. During one meeting with Zucker and our financial strategists, we looked over another dismal month of ad revenue, and Zucker asked, "How much more could we make if we dumped another ad block in *ER*?" I squirmed; *ER* was our top-rated show. My sense was that viewers were already drowning in ads. "Couldn't we find different ways to price the ads? Like better targeting? What if we charged advertisers different rates based on how well their ads hold viewers?" I said.

But Jeff waved me off. In the end, though, I believe choosing profits over the user experience is one of the things that made broadcasting so vulnerable to disruption, something Jason knew intuitively.

Challenger Brands

Hulu's mission statement—its "culture document"—reads like a manual for why and how challenger brands are so effective in creating the conditions that foster innovation: small teams, autonomy and freedom, insulation from the practices of the parent company, relentless focus on solving consumer problems, an approach that encourages experimentation (with no stigma attached to failure), and a reverence for creative disobedience.

Successful challengers aren't just agile relative to legacy companies; they share Jason Kilar's indignation and purpose. To change an industry, you must be driven by a passionate conviction for how that industry should be—that is, you must have clarity around what the business or team believes and the change it's trying to bring about. You're always fighting for and pushing against something—for the consumer, generally, and against the self-satisfied established practices of the market leader.

Hulu's mission statement included the words "the world has long since exceeded its quota in the mediocrity department. . . . We are aiming to dramatically improve and change the way that media is distributed, discovered, and consumed."

Hulu thrived because it was insulated from the parent culture while at the same time enjoying its plentiful resources. I helped to make this possible by acting as a kind of Yoda, taking on the political battles, calling in favors, and carefully navigating the existing order of the company.

Challengers need someone to play that role, because they have none of the advantages granted the incumbents. Their budgets are smaller. They have less time. They can't get away with incremental improvements. The challengers must take big risks, because they know they have to produce something—a product, a service, whatever—that is so much better and more persuasive and easier and more exciting to use that users are almost forced to change their behaviors—such as, "From now on, I watch TV on the Internet."

I believe creating a challenger brand is an effective way to introduce entrepreneurship into organizations. We weren't "managing" Jason, we were watching a brilliant and unpredictable garage entrepreneur. To me, he demonstrated the real value of creating a separate space to build something with an existing corporation. The role of the parent company or mothership is to seed innovation and make tough choices, as well as to give the entrepreneur the permission, space, and freedom to take only what's valuable from the large entity and move quickly to build what is next. Challenger brands create value only inasmuch as they are led by someone who knows how to challenge.

As I watched Jason struggle, fight, and, more often than not, win, I was beginning to formalize my ideas about challengers, especially new brands, as one of the most effective mechanisms to drive rapid change.

Hulu finally launched in beta in October 2007, and then for real several months later. I remember the first time Jason showed us the demo. The design was simple, elegant, beautiful. He walked me through the user experience, explaining the intuitive features they had put in place. He explained the back-end development and the data they were collecting about the user. Every decision was made to support a great experience for the user. It was the living example of what I had failed to convey in my time at iVillage. This was the gold standard.

It seemed that the rest of the world—and most important, users—agreed. The site was simple, elegant, and minimalistic—exactly what nobody expected from an online video service parented by two media giants. The viewing window for watching video online was a third bigger than previous services, the image resolution was true TV quality, and the interface was totally uncluttered—easy enough for Jason's mom to use. Even the tech-world intelligentsia who had mocked it as ClownCo were forced to offer their respect ("[B]oy did [Jason Kilar] make me eat crow—a well charred crow on top of that," Om Malik later wrote on GigaOm).

The investor world gave Hulu its stamp of approval as well. In October 2007, at the time of the beta launch, private equity heavyweight Providence Equity Partners invested $100 million for a 10 percent stake. This was important, because it would keep Fox and NBC honest; our coinvestor would want for Hulu to succeed as the future of TV, not as a way to protect our media butts. Outside money also served to validate the model.

A month after the site went fully live in March 2008, it ranked tenth on the Internet for streaming video. In 2009, it made $120 million; by 2012, it had three million subscribers and $695 million in revenue. Even better, for data-obsessed people like myself, was the information Hulu gave NBC and Fox. Hulu only showed a quarter of the ads that viewers were forced to sit through on TV, but we had demographic information on each viewer for each show, gathered when they registered for the service. And viewers provided feedback on ads, which allowed us to more precisely target them. No more Geritol ads for twenty-five-year-olds—precisely what advertisers wanted and were willing to pay for.

NBCU digital revenues jumped past $1 billion in 2009, more

than double the digital revenue in 2006. NBCU's combined web properties, such as NBC.com, CNBC.com, and MSNBC.com, went from being a top one hundred destination in 2006 to a top ten destination by 2009. We launched the Peacock Equity Fund and put down almost $100 million in early-stage investments in digital media companies. We even took Peacock to successful exits, with the sale of Adify to Cox and Bigpoint games to GMT.

Hulu was, for me, a validation of my approach to marketing. Jason showed how entrepreneurs have to think outside in, but always with the user as their North Star. The user and her "unmet needs" was at the center of everything Jason did. He took a discovery-based mode of inquiry that starts with questions that look beyond the current reality: What if there was a place where all the high-quality premium TV and movies could be watched? Whenever and wherever people wished? And in HD quality? And in a video player that was elegant and clutter-free?

How might we . . . ? These are the questions that change-makers must ask, and continue asking.

In the years after Hulu became a success, Jason still found himself the target of attacks from the media giants who owned Hulu. The tension came to a climax in February 2011, when Jason posted one of the most controversial memos in media history on the Hulu blog. The memo was ostensibly meant to announce that *The Daily Show* and *The Colbert Report* were returning to Hulu. But after spending a few words on that, Jason doubled down on a deeply felt and, sadly, a professionally reckless manifesto about what was wrong with TV.

Jason didn't mention the three broadcast partners that owned Hulu, but he didn't have to. His memo was a two-thousand-word indictment calling them doomed Luddites and nitwits. How did he say that? By saying that traditional TV has too many ads that angered consumers and charged advertisers for nothing, whereas Hulu's sparse ads were twice as effective? Check. That consumers want TV to be more convenient and not scheduled as it is in broadcast? Check. That consumers decide what gets renewed and what dies via responses on social media, and content creators have to listen? Check.

Eventually Netflix and Amazon would get this right, and become scaled disrupters to the television networks. Hulu could have been the broadcasters' (or cablecasters') answer to Netflix, if they could get out of their own way. Eventually, they still might do this. In Walt Disney's 2017 proposed takeover of 21st Century Fox, Hulu was seen as a factor for survivability in a digital age.

By early 2013, Jason was gone. He cashed out for a reported $40 million. He'd fought long and hard, and created a great product, against everyone's expectation.

Battling for Yes with Dr. No

Like everything involving change, you have to keep working it. Frustrating as it may be. Like Jason, I was always at war with some version of "Dr. No." You know Dr. No—they are everywhere (maybe you've even been one)—and they stand as a particularly malignant example of staff resistance. It's like they have a PhD in saying no; no is the answer to everything. "We've tried that before." "The customer won't like it." "We can't do that."

And too often, I allowed a Dr. No to be my foil. In addition to digital, I also oversaw the NBC Universal teams selling television advertising—this represented over $6 billion annually and was core revenue for NBC Universal. Brand marketers—the CMOs of our ad clients—were expressing concern about television media because marketers weren't able to get the data insights they needed from us. They wanted to know more about the viewer than they could get on their own, and they were willing to pay more for it. (Money that in later years, Facebook and Google would commandeer.)

I had all kinds of ideas for driving change in ad sales, and enthusiastically created one of media's first branded content studios and expanded our segmentation of target customers by interests—wellness, environment, women's issues, pets—beyond what we'd done for decades by selling a daypart (i.e., late night) or a traditional demographic (i.e., women 25–54); and I tried in vain to develop a data-driven viewer loyalty program. Along this path, one Dr. No drove me especially crazy.

She was a hard-charging sales department head. Influential and outspoken, she made it clear that no one messed with her. She oversaw sales for important dayparts—meaning big revenue—and had been at NBC for what counted as forever. Whenever the marketing or digital teams suggested something vaguely different, she'd say, "No, that won't work." Or she'd trot out the name of a big buying agency: "I just talked to Julie of Zenith Media, and she doesn't think this is a good idea." She was an immovable force. No matter what it was—a digital banner ad, video pre-roll in digital video, branded content—the judgment was always the same. Always brutal. Few people would challenge her.

I tried, or so I thought. I set up meetings with her, sometimes with her boss (who reported to me) to try to "educate" her on the new trends in media marketing. I brought in clients so we could hear from them together. But she wouldn't budge; and I got more frustrated. I'm not proud of it, but ultimately I just started working things on my own. I essentially gave up on Dr. No, and went rogue. I was determined to "show" her how it was done. And while I had some success—forging broader relationships with key clients like P&G and GlaxoSmithKline; landing a first-of-its-kind $30MM branded content deal with American Express and launching innovation testbeds with several media agencies—I essentially had given up on the organization by doing these things alone.

A change-making colleague described Dr. No with ruthless clarity: "You know, she is like a cancer. She just infects everything with her attitude."

Sometimes an overly resistant Dr. No must leave. But getting rid of Dr. No isn't always possible, or wise. Nor would the NBC system have let me fire her—she had deep expertise, grew good client relationships, and brought in revenue. I should have worked harder at amplifying the ideas of other change-makers already in the sales organization, not just battle the human barrier wall. When you create a surround-sound of change, those resistant usually adapt. I could have been more candid and patient with Dr. No, instead of giving up on her. Distrustful people, I find, end up isolating themselves and alienating others.

Today, the media landscape is closer to what I was pushing to build back then. Media companies now have in-house creative agencies and branded-content studios, and streaming video services have scaled. I was gone from NBC long before media started to change the way it engaged with audiences and advertisers, long before Hulu became a household name.

Some of the conflict I experienced at NBC came because people were threatened by change or my fervor in driving it, and some came from my avoidance of conflict with people. That's clear to me now. My relationship with Jeff Zucker never improved. He barely tolerated me, and I him. Until he didn't have to any longer.

In 2008, I got a call from Jeff Immelt during one of my regular "check-ins" with him. "What do you think about coming back to GE?" he said.

I'd not really thought about it, I told him. I figured I'd keep working at NBC and eventually take over one of the networks. "Things are starting to take root here," I said.

"We need you back at GE," Jeff said, after a pause. "We need a bigger push in marketing and sales."

It was not a request. I never knew if Immelt prompted my move or Zucker did. At first, I didn't know how I felt about that. I realized that when Immelt sent me to NBC, he had suspected the mix of a dysfunctional culture, outside disruption, and my lack of a power base would make my job incredibly difficult. Now, being called back when I was, I felt somewhat betrayed. I had wanted Jeff to stand up for me through the NBC attacks and conflict so that I could achieve the kind of large-scale success I so dearly wanted and fought for. But I couldn't really blame him for not diving into that shark-filled pool. That wasn't his job, nor as it turns out, was it mine.

On my last day at NBC, Marc in HR organized a midafternoon reception with the leadership team. We had the standard sickly-sweet cake and champagne. Zucker came in, raised a glass. He comments were brief. "Beth, thank you and good luck."

I looked at the small group of executives assembled and said, "Thank you. I've learned so much from all of you. Everyone should be as fortunate as you, to be as passionate about the work you do." I meant it. Their passion for their livelihood, for the industry, meant everything to them. But I knew it also held them back.

Jeff Immelt later told me that my time at NBC was the closest he had ever come to firing me. It was, he said, the only time that I had lost my skill at flying above the fray. Instead, I had dived into it. And he was right. I had jumped down from the balcony into the mosh pit, losing my perspective.

As a change-maker, you will have your share of failures. It's the nature of the job. The important thing is to learn from them. I had learned, painfully, the importance of confronting and not running away from conflict. I had discovered the importance of co-opting the resisters. I learned the importance of never giving up and constantly moving forward. Of creating a challenger brand to help drive change throughout the organization.

Challenges

HANDLING CONFLICT

When you find yourself getting irritated, here are some tactics I've learned that can transform a challenging situation into a learning experience.

Learn to recognize when you're getting irritated in the first place. In poker, everybody has tells, little quirks of gesture and voice that reveal when we're bluffing. (Me? Disgusted look on my face—gives me away every time!) The same is true of anger and frustration.

1. Learn what your tells are (your colleagues are probably better at this than you are, so consider asking a few you trust). Recognize when they're happening.
2. If you don't know why you're irritated, then ask yourself "when." When did your irritation arise? Did somebody say something? Was it an e-mail that came in? Something you saw or read? Is your irritation future-focused or about something that has already happened? Is it about a person? Is it irritation directed at yourself?

That last question is particularly useful, in my experience. Often, when we're frustrated, it's because we didn't seize an opportunity to speak up and disagree, ask a question, or propose an alternative. Sometimes anger and irritation can be jealousy in disguise. The other person is less important than your reaction to them.

TOWARD INNOVATION, OR HOW
TO UN-GRINF*CK A TEAM

Make the work about learning, not just performance. I should have framed iVillage as a way to learn how this new thing, digital media, might be successful, and told everyone that their ideas were vital. It could have become our digital learning lab, instead of "the cornerstone of our digital strategy." We needed an atmosphere of intellectual and creative interdependence, not one based on hitting the numbers. We would have been wise to confront the fairy-tale nature of our business plan up front. Unrealistic financial projections are common in new ventures, in an effort to justify a return.

Admit you're not perfect. Don't be afraid to ask for help. Express your doubts. It takes a confident leader to admit what she doesn't know. That is how you get buy-in from the rest of the team.

Ask a lot of questions. By asking team members questions, you force them to formulate and own their ideas. Never dismiss or mock an idea, no matter how ridiculous it may seem. Patients die and planes crash when team members sit on problems because they are afraid of being belittled.

Ideas trump hierarchy. Show your distain for groupthink. Embrace divergent viewpoints, especially from junior members. Look at Israel, where there's a miraculously vibrant and innovative start-up culture. Entrepreneurs there get their formative leadership training in the country's compulsory military service, in which the country's rabid antihierarchical ethos encourages even a private to question a general if he identifies a weakness or believes he has a better tactical solution. In some of the executive courses on innovation that I've helped create at GE, I insist participants visit Israel. They stare with disbelief at the raucous free-for-all that passes for a typical business meeting there, as the CEO is invariably probed and challenged on every declaration. It is an incredibly vivid example of psychological safety.

Confront, but don't make it personal. Resist the urge to become defensive or, worse, attack the person critiquing your idea. Work to build social capital through informal conversations and activities. Reinforce the fact that you work for the same team and that your success is a function of your interdependence. Creating an atmosphere of psychological safety means creating an environment that can be demanding and argumentative. People fight out of passion. That's why it is worth the fight.

COULDA SHOULDA WOULDA

The French have a great phrase: *l'esprit de l'escalier*, which translates to "staircase wit." In other words, thinking of the perfect reply when you're already on the staircase heading out the door. I suffer from it chronically.

If you're a worrier (like me), you can drive yourself crazy replaying the things you should have said, but didn't. As much as I think on my feet, I am always so much more brilliant in my mind after the fact. But life is not a Hollywood movie. We rarely get a do-over. And you don't want to be *that* person who sends awkward e-mails or asks for a follow-up to explain yourself.

Here's a simple practice that I find helpful. I jot down the conversation in my notebook, as well as what I wish I'd said. I draw two lines down the middle of a blank page. I label column one What He/She Said; column two What I Said, and column three What I Wish I'd Said. It allows me to stop obsessing over it by getting it out of my head and on paper. And it serves as a reference for the next time. It's also often a good reminder that what I said wasn't so bad after all!

HAVING DIFFICULT CONVERSATIONS

"Conversation is a meeting of minds with different memories and habits," British historian and philosopher Theodore Zeldin says. "Conversation doesn't just reshuffle the cards: it creates new cards."

That is why constantly talking with colleagues and, even more so, detractors is so vitally important. Here are a few tricks I've learned over the years to conduct those difficult conversations, and to co-opt those with whom you don't necessarily have a positive relationship, in order to turn conflict into momentum.

1. Keep the opposition close. It's vital to do things like have coffee with the person most dedicated to seeing you fail. I should have sat down for coffee with Jeff Zucker—often.
2. Ask your opponents to articulate *their* vision for success. I didn't ask Zucker several vital questions about NBC and digital: What are your goals? What does success look like to you?
3. Be candid. Turn conflict into the basis for an alliance.

BUILDING TEAM TRUST

I have a rule: No team outings that involve bathing suits. I was once scarred by an early-career outing that involved bathing suits and team races with rubber chickens between our legs. Let's just leave it at that.

Trust can't be coerced. It is earned, one action at a time. Being vulnerable (and not in a Speedo) is a good way to set the tone: Admit what you don't know. Ask for help. Tell a story of adversity. Share a good laugh at your own expense.

A friend of mine uses a great icebreaker for a dinner series we host. She asks: Tell us something about yourself we can't find out from Google. Then she kicks off the round by telling a story of her high school arrest . . . (for a silly prank). It's amazing how well you can get to know people when you open up, even just a little.

Trust yourself to trust others. Don't be a chicken.

Storycraft

CHAPTER 9

REWRITING YOUR STORY

Story Disrupts the Dark

When I came back to GE in early 2008, I was exhausted.

At the end of one phone call Jeff made to me to "check in," I told him about the job offer from Steve Jobs I had turned down. "I want you to know I'm all in." But what I really meant was, "Don't take me for granted."

I had added responsibilities—in particular, sales—and I was promoted to senior vice president. But I felt undervalued. I was back to that eerily quiet third floor of GE headquarters, where I moved into what had been Bob Wright's office. It was like some kind of reverse feng shui. There were ghostly reminders of Bob everywhere, like the now-empty glass shelves that had once been filled with celebrity-studded photos of Bob and his family.

There was a panic button hidden at knee level in Bob's old desk.

Grieving Your Workplace Failures

The downside of trying new things and taking more risks is that sometimes you are going to fail. It's okay to grieve what could have been; after all, it is the death of what you had hoped for.

I try to give myself the time and space to feel bad when things don't work out. To say the words (until I am quite convinced) "It didn't work" so that I can get past them. This is especially hard for get-it-done people, because we tend to try every possible option before declaring defeat.

At times like these, I summon the words of Samuel Beckett: "All of old. Nothing else ever. Ever tried. Ever failed. No matter. Try again. Fail again. Fail better."

Next time you fail, ask yourself, What did I learn? What will I do differently next time? Now share it with a teammate or your manager.

For those who manage teams, conduct regular postmortems or project "autopsies." I have found it a good practice to gather teams right after a project launch—in good times and bad—to review what worked and what didn't. When a project works spectacularly, challenge the team to talk about what didn't work well. Be humble. When a project fails, start the discussion with what worked and what to feel good about. Then end with lessons learned.

Remember, failure prepares you for future success. Even if it doesn't feel that way in the moment.

I wondered, what kind of panic would cause one to push it? Would anyone even arrive if I did?

On the other hand, the past has never held as much sway over me as the future. I began to imagine how the things I'd learned at NBC—new digital tools, data, creative content—could be applied to even bigger, better use at GE. I rediscovered the possibility and power of story at GE and in my life. It has the potential to reinvigorate companies, launch new products, and create new markets. It is muscular and real. For example, I see myself as a curious, courageous protagonist, a fearless explorer. It is a narrative that has always held regenerative power for me. Beth the change-maker, ready to take on the gatekeepers protecting "the way things are done."

I realized I had been telling myself the wrong story, focusing on slights and missed opportunities at NBC rather than on the promise of what lay ahead.

The power of a positive attitude has been supported by research. Martin Seligman at the University of Pennsylvania, who pioneered the field of positive psychology, conducted studies showing that those who attributed setbacks to the larger, imperfect world ("It's not all my fault"), who framed periods of adversity not as personal failures but part of a process of growth ("I learned so much"), were less prone to depression and more resilient.

Or as my husband, Chris, would say to me at the end of many long, soul-searching conversations, "The NBC experience was something you needed to go through. As painful as it was, I feel like it will one day serve you well."

Even as I rebounded personally, by 2008 GE was experiencing its own trauma—one so severe, in fact, that GE's survival would be called into question.

The New Normal!

After topping out near $60 during Jack's last year, by late 2007, GE's stock had climbed back to the low $40s. We had begun to refocus the company's efforts, pointing us to technology like green energy and our inventive roots.

The problem with this was that the story was only partially true. Half of our company was still GE Capital, and that half was driving healthy earnings, just as it had under Jack. Jeff had to feed the beast and, in fact, had built up the commercial real estate and consumer-lending portfolios. Like nearly all public-company CEOs, Jeff was beholden to his shareholders and the consistent quarterly earnings they demand. GE business leaders accept that they have to deliver the financial plans they promise. "No surprises" is the motto. But as we had seen since 9/11, the world was becoming more volatile.

Our business model at GE Capital was to borrow money at a low interest rate, lend it out at a higher rate, and bank the difference. We raised money via short-term bonds or "corporate paper," loaned it to companies and consumers, and made money on the gains that flowed back into GE Capital, which then boosted the profits, and shareowner returns, and offset the more modest returns from GE industrial technology.

In 2007, though, Jeff started noticing deals coming into GE Capital where math just didn't make sense.

A subprime mortgage crisis had been percolating under the surface of Wall Street for years. GE, as one of the largest non-bank financial institutions, had some exposure to these mortgages. The inherent risks of GE Capital gave Jeff qualms (as it did everyone who looked at it closely). Faced with these worries, Jeff asked the consulting firm McKinsey to do a $3 million study of our credit risks and how to face them. "I mean, are we *really* okay?" he asked.

McKinsey swooped in and did its Excel magic, and sixty days later, they came back to Jeff with good news: Absolutely! This is the new normal! As they explained it to him, money from nations with a trade surplus, like China, and sovereign wealth funds from places like Qatar, among other investors, would provide enough liquidity in the financial system to fuel lending and leverage for the foreseeable future.

Then, with perfect irony, Bear Stearns collapsed and launched the financial crisis, almost killing off GE in the process. McKinsey's people had built a model out of mining knowledge garnered from clients across industries, many of them our competitors. But they only dealt with what they knew, using the data they had. They didn't use their imagination to interpret clues as signposts to the future, which is what was needed to predict the arrival of this Black Swan event. But few did.

The backbreaking straw was, of course, Lehman Brothers. In September 2008, after hordes of its clients had fled and its stock had plunged, Lehman Brothers was told by the Treasury Department that it was not going to bail them out. With no other option, Lehman filed for Chapter 11 bankruptcy protection, and just like that, American's financial markets plunged into panic.

At GE, we found ourselves on the brink of collapse. We couldn't sell our bonds; we were in a liquidity crisis. The government declared us a systematically important financial institution (or SIFI). In other words: too big to fail.

Our stock dropped at one point to an ominous $6.66.

Jeff said ruefully to me after the Lehman bankruptcy, "In the words of the immortal philosopher, Mike Tyson, 'Everybody has a plan till they get punched in the mouth.'" Or my version of his sentiment: it works until it doesn't. Too many times people assume their models will work . . . forever (aka "Trees will grow to the sky!"). As happened at NBC Digital, change often happens in barely perceptible ways, before, surprisingly, it disrupts—the same way Mike, in Ernest Hemingway's *The Sun Also Rises*, went bankrupt: "Gradually and then suddenly." Emergent change seems impossible until it happens, at which point it becomes inevitable.

One of the biggest challenges that faces established-company leaders is giving credence to alternate scenarios of the future. It's one thing to imagine change, it's another thing to give up on a model that is working, especially with investors breathing down your neck. Especially if you've been trained to keep your promises. A kind of magical thinking takes place. We convinced ourselves we were doing something that made a difference—"We're on it!"—when in fact, we were just working harder at the same things.

It's as if one can just *will* reality to go one's way. That's the magical thinking at work. And sometimes Jeff subscribed to this. His optimism made him an incredible leader—a motivator, communicator, and often an advocate for the future and today at once. Jeff has a gifted way of framing tough issues within the arc of a grand strategy, prescribing which steps to take first. But GE's golden rule was chiseled into his DNA: always deliver on your commitments, always with integrity. But looking back, delivering the numbers consistently made his—and the GE teams'—job much harder.

Every day, I'd see Jeff as he hunkered down in his conference room with his core financial team, desperately searching for buyers to take our bonds and let us escape our capital crunch for another twenty-four hours. Jeff and CFO Keith Sherin and their GE Capital and treasury teams threw around piles of paper and screamed on the phone as they slogged through the list of bond buyers. We were in the crosshairs.

One day Jeff pulled me aside after a meeting and looked at me with sleepless, haunted eyes, his normal optimism hijacked by the bond traders. "You know, Beth, every night when I get home, and it's always late, Andy wakes up to talk to me," he said, mentioning his wife. "Every night when I tell her about my day, she says, 'It will be all right.' Last night when she said that, I said, 'No, honey, not this time.' I really don't know."

Jeff isn't one to let his emotions show. He never shows how concerned he is. I had never seen him flinch. His default is to just work harder, dig deeper, keep moving, and he expects others to do the same.

In the short term, the Federal Reserve and Warren Buffett saved us, giving us desperately needed cash infusions. The Fed bought over $16 billion in our short-term paper when no one else would, and in October we announced a $12 billion stock offering to raise desperately needed cash; Immelt convinced Warren Buffett to invest $3 billion in GE by paying him a 10 percent annual dividend.

But we were like a heart attack patient who had been stabilized with a jolt from a defibrillator: alive, yes, but not long for this world unless we seriously changed our plan, our story, our narrative.

Making Sense of the Senseless

In the 1980s and 1990s, organizational psychologist Karl Weick coined two terms that I believe help to describe the issues GE faced after Lehman collapsed. The first of those is *cosmology episode*—that is, the sudden loss of meaning that people and organizations experience when faced by a traumatic event (such as the death of a child in the case of a parent or, in 2008 for GE, the bankruptcy of Lehman Brothers and a looming global financial crisis, or as would happen again for GE in 2017 with another leader transition and investor activism). Cosmology episodes shatter our cosmos of beliefs and the stories we tell ourselves about our companies, our careers, and our lives, unsettling us to our very core.

The path from the impossible to the probable to the new normal used to take years. Now it seems like we have a new normal every few months. The world has become so uncertain that economists

We can't make
uncertainty go away.
But we can change
the way we react to it.
Every uncertainty is a
new potential future.

have come up with an acronym for it: VUCA, which stands for volatile, uncertain, complex, and ambiguous. (I'd add another A, for anxiety.)

And acceleration. We are communicating faster, working faster, innovating faster, and by some accounts even talking and walking faster than we did in previous decades. (It's not your imagination—studies show we're actually walking 10 percent faster in cities than we did a decade ago.)

We can't make uncertainty go away. But we can change the way we react to it. Every uncertainty is a new potential future. Seen in this light, uncertainty doesn't need to be a source of anxiety; it can be a signal that it's time to change.

That brings me to Karl Weick's second term: *sensemaking*. At a basic level, sensemaking is the process people and organizations go through to understand unexpected, traumatic, or confusing events (those cosmology episodes). In its simplest form, sensemaking involves collecting data about the unknown and the ambiguous, and synthesizing that data into new and revised stories and frameworks that make sense of the unknown. It acts as a springboard for collective action.

Too often, most of us think "story" is what you add at the end, the colorful wallpaper that gives your room (or company) that decorator touch. But telling your story in a coherent way is not spin. It allows you to describe the actions you are taking and to bring everyone else in the organization along with you. People spend so much time focused on the synergies of the merger, of a product's new revenue growth trajectory, that they lose sight of the essence of their company. I would argue that *strategy is a story well told*. And if your story doesn't hang together, perhaps your strategy isn't sound. Of course, story alone does not make a business strategy. But traditional business strategy too often does not bother to create a story or narrative about its actions for its employees and the world to gather

**Strategy is a story
well told.**

around. For the strategy to become reality, people need to see themselves in the story and then take action to make the story happen.

I realized we were faced with a desperate need in late 2008 and the early months of 2009 to create a sensemaking project to understand GE's identity in relation to the world around us—or risk sinking into irrelevance.

"Beth, you are the chief storyteller here," Jeff said to me early on in the crisis. "We need you to help us get ahead of the story. Because we're not looking like the good guys right now. How can we tell our story, our way?"

In the first months after the Lehman Brothers collapse, our VP of communications Gary Sheffer led the crisis communications effort with Jeff. With Gary focusing on day-to-day crisis communications, I turned to the strategic perspective.

With OSOW—our story our way—top of mind, I strode into my weekly communications meeting, and asked three simple questions: Who are we *now*? And what is our value? Then, How do we tell that story louder and faster, and more often?

We were just coming off the presidential election of Barack Obama. Fresh in my mind was a series of stories documenting how modern political campaigns were being reshaped by Big Data and cutting-edge social science. Political campaigns were, in essence, aggressive sensemaking operations—precisely what we needed. Political candidates lose when they allow themselves to be defined by their opponent. And when they win, it's because they are able to tell their story more effectively, loudly, and have it resonate with enough people to carry the day. Why not bring a guru from the political campaigns into GE's sensemaking efforts?

I started calling around my network of people I knew from NBC News and beyond, looking for introductions to the Obama team, and spoke with political journalist Chuck Todd of NBC News. Chuck had spent most of the previous year following the campaign, so I was sure he knew the key players in Obama's election campaign. But his answer surprised me.

"The best is Steve Schmidt," he said. "From the McCain campaign," he said to my stunned silence. *"He's a fighter."*

"The McCain campaign?" I thought to myself. But Chuck was convincing, and a fighter was what we needed. So I called up Steve, and we set up a meeting.

I still wanted someone from the Obama campaign, however. I decided we needed David Plouffe, who had run the grassroots ground game that allowed the Obama campaign to connect so intimately and authentically with voters.

When Steve strode into the offices at 30 Rock, I was hooked from the second he caught me in his icy blue stare. Tough and relentless, Steve was the kind of guy you knew would rather die than lose. In the HBO movie about the McCain campaign, he was played by Woody Harrelson, the actor who starred in *Natural Born Killers* and, later, *True Detective*.

"Steve, people here feel under siege. The media and analysts are questioning our financial model, questioning us! Our own people no longer know what GE stands for. How do we fight for our reputation and good name?" I said.

Steve leaned forward and barked, "Okay, this is the number of negative stories," he said, holding his hand a foot above the desk. "You're not going to be able to control that." Then he held his hand three feet above the desk. "What you can do is ramp up the volume with the stories that you want to convey to customers and the public. But to do that well, you have to gather feedback to answer some vital questions: What are those stories? Who do we want to tell them to? How do we want people to act when they hear them?"

With him on the team, he said, GE would attack, attack, attack, always selling its story. Campaigns, he reminded us, aren't won by the candidate or the company with the best character, or product, but by the one with the simplest and most clearly told story.

Pick a simple story, he said, and tell it again and again and again. Republican operatives called him "The Bullet." With his focused tactical ferocity—and the shape of his shaved head—I could understand why.

David Plouffe was the polar opposite of Schmidt: soft-spoken, thoughtful, almost delicate. He calmly laid out the keystones of Obama's success almost as Zen koans. David valued strategy above all, playing the grassroots ground game, using the art and science of microtargeting authentic messages to individuals or small groups. Almost quaint in a Facebook world.

We had the Zen Master's yin to match the Bullet's yang, the strategy to match the tactics, the Ground War to match the Air War. Steve and David were sparks who could act as catalysts for change in behavior and perception. But they became more than sparks; they became teachers, coaches, confidants—even therapists.

Jeff and our team were attacking the business issues around GE Capital and the parts of GE that weren't working and needed fixing. But we needed a renewed narrative, as much inside the company as out, to rally our 300,000 employees together and to clarify what GE stood for.

To create the feedback loops that collect data about the company, we surveyed eight hundred people outside the company across the country about what they thought of us in light of the financial crisis. We called our subjects "the likely voters." We segmented the people we needed to target, and then asked them questions: Is GE a company you're likely to buy from? Is GE a company you trust? How does GE's innovation compare to Google's?

With our baseline data, Steve created a sort of cockpit, full of feedback dials and instrumentation. This one tells us how Washington, DC, influencers view us in light of bank regulation. What does the general public think of us in terms of innovation? What happens if we disseminate videos of our newest MRI scanner leading to a healthy outcome for a sick child? In other words, what happens if we spread the word about some of our amazing technology in the field of medicine and its ability to diagnose and treat patients?

The dials Steve helped us create were much more sophisticated than any we had had before. (And seem a bit quaint now.) And he was brutal, creatively and combatively engaging with the data that was coming in—and fiercely challenging the messages going out. Along with Greg Strimple, who was his political data ninja, Steve parsed data and repackaged it into small insights that built to a crescendo.

One of my colleagues made the mistake of suggesting that we run commercials with Jeff Immelt talking to the camera about GE's accomplishments.

"That's absolute bullshit!" Steve bellowed. "We need to flood the world with tight messages, not that boring corporate mayonnaise."

Steve was famous for his almost tactile sense of story, his ability to simplify big issues into powerful images. Surprisingly he was also an advocate of traditional advertising, telling Jeff in meetings that we didn't spend enough money telling our story. We were constantly battling and negotiating with finance over the size of our budget. Even today, there are misguided beliefs that only retail companies should advertise. In reality, every business is fighting for a share of customers' minds in an effort to win a share of their wallets. For many of GE's products, the sale is very complicated, with multiple decision-makers influencing the purchase. HBR/Corporate Executive Board estimates that 5.4 people are involved in the average B2B buying decision.

Our days of selling ourselves as a financial services–powered conglomerate were over—although it would take several more years for this to be true. Big iron and tech, I decided, would be our new campaign. We had already found success focusing on our clean energy and health technology. Steve boiled down our message to a thing of pure beauty: GE is a builder, America's builder. Steve relentlessly tested these ideas in our feedback loops, tightening them as much

Human Sensing Machine

The creation of a feedback loop is a central element of the sensemaking process. There are many ways to break down sensemaking. The process we developed with Steve Schmidt involved four basic steps:

1. Collect responses from multiple sources—not just your customers but also your suppliers, investors, employees, and even your competitors and the public at large.

2. Invite others—sparks like Schmidt, for example— into your sensemaking program. Tell them your observations and opinions, and listen to the observations and interpretations of people who have different perspectives from yours. We'd have fierce debates with Steve and researcher Greg Strimple over their interpretations of the insight versus ours. Sometimes the process was frustrating, but we always got to a good place, and the new messages tested better and gave us even more insight.

3. Use each set of responses and observations to shape experiments that you can use to test your ideas. For example, test out headlines, dozens of them, with readers using social media. Constantly iterate your messages. New questions inevitably arise. This can drive teams crazy because everyone wants to be done, to check things off their list. But with a continuous feedback loop you are never done.

4. Don't fall back on the frameworks and worldviews you've used in the past. Be open to new

> interpretations. And try to avoid sweeping gener-
> alizations, or oversimplicity, like good versus bad
> or science versus art. I find that viewing issues on
> a spectrum is helpful, as it allows you to set the
> dial for more nuance and context.

as possible, just as he distilled Arnold Schwarzenegger's successful
California governor campaign to one word: cooperation. And with
the arrival of more digital tools and media outlets, we could better
target both our message and who received it.

We now had a structure in place so that we could craft messages
that would give us new relevancy. What we didn't have was a lot
of time to play around. We needed to get our new messaging out
now. Jeff went on CNBC one day, just before a quarterly close, to
say that the quarter was in the bag. But the quarter *wasn't* in the bag,
and several weeks later when we came out with our earnings, we
missed. Jeff had breached the golden rule at GE. We *hadn't* met our
commitment.

The day after we missed our earnings report, Gary Sheffer came
in to tell me that Jack Welch was on CNBC and would be talking
about GE's earnings. At the time, Jack was showing up regularly
to do guest hosting gigs on the channel. His bluntness made for
good soundbites. And so, the day after we reported our earnings
miss, Welch was on CNBC and someone asked him, "Jack. What
if Jeff misses again?" Jack barely skipped a beat before saying, "I'd
be shocked beyond belief, and I'd get a gun out and shoot him if
he doesn't make what he promised now," he said. "Just deliver the
earnings. Tell them you're going to grow 12 percent and deliver 12
percent."

One misstep and you're executed? Jack's statement battered the
internal story of nearly every GE employee, rattling our psyches.

Magical Thinking

I confess: I read my horoscope daily and have since I was a teenager. (I'm a Virgo.) I used to travel with a small hamsa given to me by a Middle Eastern colleague to "keep me safe." But I'm not alone. A number of us bring superstition into the way we work. Just try finding an elevator button to take you to the thirteenth floor. Or listen to how many times in a week you hear someone say "knock on wood" in a business meeting.

Many of us have quirks and rituals to bring us luck at work, to close the deal, to get the job. (Jack Welch carried "Mr. Lucky," a gnarly brown briefcase given to him by his mother.) Lucky charms and rituals do have a positive effect. Researchers at the University of Cologne found that superstitions boost confidence and, in turn, serve to help our mind push for better performance.

But beware when a person, a team, or a culture gets locked into habits out of fear—or pursues goals based on magical thinking.

During World War II, indigenous people in the Pacific Islands, after observing airplanes landing on military bases, came to believe it was the runways and the strange motions of the helmeted men that summoned the planes from afar. When the war ended and the planes departed, these native groups built their own runways and staged rituals on them, imitating air traffic controllers waving landing planes to safety.

It's all too easy for companies to develop their own rituals to sustain magical thinking. We come to believe that if we just conduct the same series of meetings and generate more of the same reports and utter the same

> reassuring phrases, we'll be okay. I believe this behavior made change harder than it needed to be at GE.
>
> The next time you find yourself scheduling a meeting that has lost its purpose, or you find yourself writing another report that will never get read, ask yourself, Have I joined an island cargo cult? Mistaking magical thinking for important actions can be fatal. Get your team to try another way, to take a step in another direction—just once. But never on Friday the 13th.

We couldn't be the legendary deliver-the-earnings company if we couldn't hit our numbers. Clearly, there was a lot of resetting to do.

GE Works: Authenticity Begins at Home

Armed with our political survey data, I called together all of the various creative media agencies working for GE—from PR to advertising and digital and brand marketing—to help us create a new master narrative. For two days straight we locked ourselves in a hotel suite in Manhattan, blank paper on the walls for notes, cans of Diet Cokes, plates of cookies on every table. If I couldn't rally them, maybe the sugar and caffeine would.

"The economy is suffering, people are losing their jobs. Some economists estimate that it may be 2017 before the economy fully recovers. As a country, as a company, we've got work to do. So here's the assignment," I told them. "How do we rediscover the important work GE does, and how does it make us more relevant in these times?"

I challenged our agencies to swim in one lane, to function as a relay team rather than individual competitors—without a lead agency. Without individual glory. It was a profoundly creative session. We were a team on a mission: To deliver the words that would define us. To unlock our strategy, through the power of story.

In previous eras, marketing was about creating a myth and selling it. Today, it's about finding a central truth and sharing it. Manufactured myths just don't stand up these days. With a few clicks of the mouse, people can discover almost anything about a company and instantly circulate it to an audience of millions. It is the organizations that are confident enough to share the truth—warts and all—that succeed.

I believe this passionately. And it was something we had seen from the early days of Imagination at Work. Authenticity begins at home. Most important, our story had to resonate within GE, or it would never resonate with our customers and the world. As Steve Schmidt and David Plouffe would say, seed your message with your base. Because it's their story, too. And they become your best ambassadors.

Our team, as well as representatives of our agencies, traveled to our factory sites. We wanted to explore anew what it meant to work for GE, starting on the factory floor. There, craftsmanship meets sweat meets high technology. We canvassed our colleagues, asking them simple questions that cut to the essence of who we are: What do you do? Why do you do it? What do you love about your work? Unlike with the Rapaille work, when we brought people in for deep thinking, this time we were field anthropologists. We watched them. We photographed them.

What we saw was that our employees were passionate and entrepreneurial. They were craftspeople. Everywhere we looked, GE people were innovating at their workbenches. They were inveterate hackers when it came to solving problems. I remember the presentation I gave to our key corporate staff to share what we had found. One of my favorite examples had to do with the handcrafted work from our aviation team. One guy made custom parts by tracing them by hand and then cutting them out with an X-Acto knife to create forms that would be machined into high-tech engine parts.

Another guy told me he had grown frustrated because he couldn't find a way to accurately test the tensile strength of a new metal sheet. After failing with the new equipment we had bought, he had an epiphany: From years of practice shooting at a target range near his house, he knew exactly how fast the bullets traveled, and how much they weighed. The next day, he brought his rifle to work and figured out how to use it to test the strength of the metal in a way that was ten times more accurate than the most sophisticated gear we had. And another guy, just starting out at GE, showed us how the fine welding he was doing inspired him to become a tattoo artist in his spare time. He loved working with his hands, loved the orchestration of man and machine.

After my presentation, our core storytelling team—a mini version of the one in our hotel powwow—frantically worked the conference room whiteboard, adding, editing, and deleting sequences of a new GE equation, one that would replace the one we had created years ago. For hours, we had been shouting, laughing, suggesting, demanding, writing, editing. They are among my favorite memories at work, when the team becomes one, when idea builds on idea. We were finishing one another's sentences even as we interrupted ourselves with a new thought or inspiration. Grabbing markers off the table, out of one another's hands, we were pure energy, in a frenzy to find the words that would unlock the *story*.

What the world needs × *Our employees* + *Belief in a better way and our relentless drive to invent and build things that matter* = *A world that works better.* "We give people electricity that powers their homes, their schools, factories, and economies. We provide medical equipment that peers into the human body and saves lives. And we build jet engines and locomotives that transport people safely."

Then, taking it further we distilled it down to: *We build, power, move, and cure to make the world work better.*

GE was manufacturing, yes, but manufacturing of consequence.

We make big "badass" things—amazing mechanical beasts combining human ingenuity and science. GE could still very much be identified with Imagination at Work, but the times called for us to shift the balance from imagination to work. It was a simple, subtle evolution, but one with powerful repercussions.

Next we created a series of ads to focus on what we were *now*. In the first GE Works commercial, viewers follow several factory workers from GE Healthcare's U.S. headquarters in Wisconsin, as they meet a crew of cancer survivors whose disease was identified at an early stage by the MRI machines they make. "You see somebody who was saved because of this technology," one GE worker says as he tightens bolts on the assembly line. "You know that things you do in your life . . . *matter*."

In another, floor engineers at the GE Aviation manufacturing site in Durham, North Carolina, hand-assemble a jet engine turbine as they talk about how they were fascinated by balsa wood airplanes as kids. "At GE Aviation, we build jet engines that lift people up off the ground," one says with real pride. "It's going to fly people around the world, safely and better than it's ever done before," says another.

It expressed both what we were—and what we aspired to be.

Human to Human

"There's nothing more valuable than a human being talking to a human being," David Plouffe would say. "Nothing."

When David was with the Obama campaign, he created a homemade video of himself describing the campaign's strategy to get to 270 electoral votes, and then they put it out in an online mailing. The letter sent with it was informal—"Frank," not "Dear Frank"— and it was signed, simply, "David."

To make our own campaign human, David helped us build the

equivalent of a door-to-door canvassing team, a cadre of in-house ambassadors for the new GE. It was our grassroots movement. The idea was to empower our employees by offering them a crisp version of our new narrative, along with the freedom to be our ambassadors in their local community and with friends and family.

To start, we asked senior-level GE people to identify candidates—influencers in communities—that ran from GE campus recruiters to "power" retirees. Next we asked these influencers if they would be willing to volunteer as grassroots brand ambassadors.

With these volunteers we created twenty- to twenty-five–person teams led by "captains," each assigned to geographic areas or specific business sectors, and empowered them to be GE's representatives by giving them online stories, infographics, and talking points, and offering them direct contact with top-level execs—including conference calls with Jeff.

The idea was to teach them how to solicit great GE stories from their teams and return them to us to distribute and amplify. Soon our ambassadors were spreading GE's narrative of big-iron passion around the country, and returning with stories that illustrated it. At GE, some of the best storytellers are engineers.

One story we got back, for example, came from Mark, a lab manager at GE Global Research. Mark saw firsthand the effect his work had on real-world patients when his young son, Adam, was diagnosed with cancer. The treatment Adam received at the Dana-Farber Cancer Institute included advanced imaging technology developed at High Energy Physics Lab GE Global Research. After Adam completed his treatments, Mark created a video of his story and the role imaging-technology played.

When you make big, intimidating, world-shifting products like a jet engine or an MRI machine, it is easy to take for granted the individuals behind it. And those who make the machines may not see the full force of the product in action. But if you reconnect them with story, then you can make the impact of what they do come to life.

This grassroots story brigade continues today through the robust "GE Voices" outreach effort, enlisting nearly 100,000 GE employees and suppliers to share messages—in person and digitally—about innovation and the economic value of jobs.

Make the Invisible Visible

The only time people think about their electricity is when their power goes out or when they have to pay the bill. Yet without it, the very latest technologies, like their iPhone, wouldn't be possible. People often don't see the amazing feats of science and engineering behind everyday progress. In that sense, people—inside and outside GE—weren't *seeing* GE. To get them to do so, we needed to give people X-ray vision into GE places and spaces they didn't know existed, where we were doing cool feats of science they didn't know about.

But how do you encourage that kind of communication? How do you *make the invisible visible*? We invited people in via programs like #GEInstaWalk, in which superfans got to share photos via Instagram of their visits to our aviation facilities. There is a big community of people who love manufacturing and seeing how stuff is made, and another community of people who love aviation. With #SpringBreakIt, we created a social media campaign in which science enthusiasts and lovers of the science of materials could see how pressure applied in industrial applications would break things—ranging from baseballs to some of the strongest materials on earth.

Not only were these events engaging and fun, but the media they produced was almost impossible not to share. Making stuff became cool. Science became cool.

There was also a lucky and surprising by-product that spun out of the "visibility" initiatives: they led to "horizontal"—cross division—communications, which directly inspired innovation. Appliance engineers discussed how to make appliances with, say, physicians, chemists, and anthropologists. Silos were broken down. People doing different things met and formed clusters, networks, and joint ventures. Spreading our stories outside each silo acted as a catalyst that allowed people in different divisions—or in India, China, wherever—to use the newly visible to figure out and generate actions and, ultimately, innovations. It spurred discovery.

We jumped headfirst into our storytelling as a way to reinforce GE's renewed strategy focusing on industrial might. And GE doubled down on investments in these businesses, new products, and technologies at a time when others were not. Even so, 50 percent of GE's business was still made up of financial services. And that was a challenge for our company, and our story. We told ourselves, "GE

Being Always in Beta

Never being done is part of the inherent experience of sensemaking in digital life. In an analog world of books and paper memos and clocks that chimed at five to release us from the world of work, we had deeply satisfying periods of being "done." But, of course, the flow of life and of events was never as organized as all that. Turning the last page of a newspaper didn't mean that the news stopped happening. Now that we have the tools that have caught up to the endless flow of our thoughts and actions, we're at our best when we let go of the expectation of being "done." A digital innovator's motto is that everything's "always in beta." You're also never done improving. There's always more time to get better.

Capital is a builder—they help build (small to medium-size) busi-nesses." But it nagged at me, and the team.

Investors grew increasingly tired of the financial-services cat-egory, with its lowered returns and market valuation. Regulators had entered the business with their SIFI due diligence, adding more complexity and questions: "Do we need to be here?" became a louder question as we made GE a more focused science and engi-neering company.

In 2009, Jeff agreed to sell much of NBC to Comcast (and all of it by 2014), believing we'd be much better off funding GE's indus-trial future than funding NBC's uncertain digital future. Investors criticized the sale as a low price at the bottom of the market. Yet in the following decade, most of the big media companies sought mergers to survive digital disruption (21st Century Fox to Disney, Time Warner to AT&T, AOL/Yahoo to Verizon).

Could GE have exited Capital sooner, accelerating progress faster? What would happen to the earnings it generated? Could we make up the lost revenues fast enough to suit investors? These ques-tions would haunt GE for years, even after Jeff announced the dives-titure of GE Capital in 2015 and exited all but industrial finance by the end of 2016. It's easy to second-guess Jeff's decision not to sell off assets sooner or at all, as investors would do, with little bandwidth to imagine forward new scenarios. CEOs travel lonely paths where they have to take input from many sources as well as in consideration of the now and the future, often in conflict, to satisfy differing con-stituencies. It's little wonder that some CEOs opt for near-term wins for which returns are more certain and the numbers are the story.

Story can't be what you do afterward. We struggled with this over GE Capital. The ability to harness story is what differentiates a good leader from a great one. It takes courage to connect to the broader trajectory of a business, not just be reduced to what you can see. That's why I am such an advocate of linking strategy and story early in the business cycle. Strategy is the story. The story has to

Write It as a Press Release

The surest test of a sound strategy is that it can be written as a press announcement. I often test my new business ideas, company initiatives, and partnerships this way.

Press releases in and of themselves are an artifact of the past. But the purpose (to alert the world to your news) and the structure (how it is composed) stand the test of time:

HEADLINE: What is happening

SUB-HEADLINE BULLETS: List the two or three most compelling points.

BODY COPY: Restate what is happening in the first two paragraphs, list the anticipated outcomes and benefits, and then quote the leaders of the effort to summarize the strategy. End with supporting points.

END: Summarize in one sentence the benefits, and in another the bridges to what's next.

Ask, Is the strategy and rationale clear? Do the quotes make sense? If they are filled with clichés and empty words, then the strategy isn't clear yet. If you make the release about yourself or your business, nobody's going to care. If you make it about what the reader might want to hear, then you've got a shot at capturing people's attention.

I use this approach after an ideation session with teams. Once we've summarized our best ideas and then agreed to a course of action, I'll assign someone to write a press release. When we get back together again, we review the press release as a way to revisit and test our ideas. Do they make sense? Are we united in the vision? What's missing?

This is also a good way to summarize an idea—to imagine it forward—for your boss, or for a customer, to sell your vision and strategy. When you make it announceable, it becomes more real.

bring to life the strategy. They are two sides of a coin. If you can't do one, then maybe you don't have the other.

Becoming a Content Factory

We were finding digital was a critical component in our marketing and publicity outreach—in targeting the right audience, in sharing the content, in creating new kinds of content. Sensemaking itself was an inherently digital process. Could we digitize GE's marketing more substantially and use it as a proving ground to eventually digitalize more of GE's operation? I focused first on our brand communications, as media was an easy place to test digital, and my experience at NBC had given me the confidence that we could innovate here.

When I returned to GE, I asked Judy Hu, our head of advertising, to lead what we came to call the Content Factory. I had hired Judy years before from the auto industry; she was a solid professional, talented and smart.

In retrospect, Judy was a good brand marketer who was especially good overseeing advertising from BBDO. She did the "digital" basics of the time—a YouTube channel with videos of executives giving speeches, online banner ads, search marketing, the same things others were doing. Essentially she applied traditional models to new media. But I was impatient, and I was eager to distinguish ourselves digitally.

By early 2009, I decided that I would need to create an in-house digital challenger. I brought my old colleague Linda Boff back from NBC to launch a scrappy team of digital innovators to internally attack the digitizing effort with greater creativity and without preconceptions. I carved out 15 percent of the advertising budget for her and instructed her to hire a small team of people who could help her do that.

My eyes were open this time, though. I knew that being ahead of the pack could be dangerous for the challenger. I told myself to live with the tension for now between Judy's ad team, who didn't want to relinquish digital, and protect Linda's team from the politics. In a meeting with me about marketing campaigns, both teams would show up with separate and conflicting ideas on how to use digital media, spending time and money we didn't have. Judy would bring in the BBDO team to present work, and they would present dozens of ideas for digital. And while I love new ideas, BBDO hadn't yet mastered digital. They didn't have the skills of the small digital independents. BBDO thought that lobbying me about their scale, rather than the quality of their capability, would win the day. Or the challenger team would stay in stealth mode too long, not sharing ideas with the ad or PR teams, leaving them out and feeling frustrated. Or the PR team would take sides, depending on what the issue was. Someone was inevitably ganging up on the other. As a team leader, I had to allow a certain amount of tension to exist, yet keep it in check. I spent time coaching Judy and Linda separately and together. I joked, I ignored them, I even lost my temper, but mostly I persisted. Seeding challengers tests your resolve—it's much easier when things aren't changed, especially deliberately.

Once Andrew Robertson, the CEO of BBDO, hosted an intervention, disguised as a lunch, with the purpose of asking me to resolve the tension between teams at GE. He said it was time I dealt with it. I acknowledged the difficulty and asked for patience, explaining, "We're testing new methods. BBDO can't do everything, neither can our brand marketing team. I'm seeding new capabilities. There is a purpose to the madness. It will get better, I promise." And it did.

With Linda pushing us, we signed up for digital, deploying campaigns on Twitter, Facebook, and so on. Consumer brands had begun to use social media more often, but B2B companies like GE hadn't taken the plunge yet. We launched the "GE Tweet Squad," social media experts inside GE who could help others in the company get comfortable with Twitter and encourage more GE people to use social media. (We did this despite the fact that the IT departments at the time in many GE businesses forbade employees to go to social media, which was seen as spam-filled and a frivolous drain of productivity.) It was an uphill fight every day; as we were launching GE Reports, one of the first corporate news blogs, the head of GE.com—a digital "leader," in theory—sent me an *Ad Age* story titled "Top 10 Reasons Companies should NEVER Blog."

My goal at GE was to "shout louder than we spend"—to employ new communications tools to steer our message, repeat it, and flood the zone in order to drive brand position with efficiency. Social and digital media was the big amplifier that would allow us to tell our story and get attention in ways that added value with much less budget.

Linda's team went well beyond the social media and blogging basics. We were one of the first businesses to use new platforms such as Instagram and Twitter's Vine. Linda led our #6SecondScience video project of community-created mini-videos about science, and created moments like Pi Day (to celebrate pi by giving out pies on social media).

I called our new virtual shouting place the Amp Room (or Amplification Room). The purpose of the Amp Room was to use every media tactic possible to amplify our messages (combined with the efforts of our PR teams). We hired former journalists to write and edit content—setting the standard for "branded content." Some of the methods at first seemed silly: A video game to explain how a hospital manages patient flow? (It worked!) Some believed we'd embarrass ourselves. Or that we were wasting money. I always brought it back to our purpose and mission, to connect people to what we did: *We are a company that makes things—through amazing feats of science—that make the world work better. We build, power, move, and cure.* After all, I said, customers, employees, and investors are people first. This is how you win their mindshare and influence buying and hiring decisions. They aren't just interested in GE in a transactional way; they want to connect with GE where they are. Our job is to get their attention in unexpected, even delightful ways. Digital was the way to do that, less expensively and with more engagement.

The digital efforts were gaining traction, but not everyone embraced the change. Some people are eager to change and are just waiting to be given the permission; others are undecided and need proof, permission, and skills; and others still can never get there—either they don't want to change, they don't like it, or they don't have the skills to change and ultimately they leave. Judy eventually did just that.

Years later, Linda told me, this was one of the hardest periods in her career. She's a natural collaborator, and being asked to challenge the status quo meant that she had to get used to tension, often of her making. But it made her better at what she did. She gives the most helpful "no" I've ever heard; she is firm but offers alternatives that people might consider, beyond just "No, we can't do that." She went on to distinguish herself as a digital marketing innovator and eventually was named GE's chief marketing officer.

Moreover, we created something new that worked, and that scaled and differentiated GE's conversation with the world. Here's what we learned about how to transform a company into a "content factory":

1. STAFF THE STUDIO

For a content factory to work, you have to staff it with a mix of narrators and data nerds who are digital natives. You can't outsource this work to an agency.

While your in-house team has to steer the content factory, you need outside perspectives and sparks as well, especially in times of rapid change. In our case, we created what I called a "farm team" of outside creators that could be called upon when needed. One of the sparks was Benjamin Palmer, the head of the creative digital media lab The Barbarian Group. They were given access to go almost anywhere within GE to explore various parts of our business, from wind turbines to jet engines. Partnering with them, we created the GEAdventure.com site, explaining how science happens at GE.

One of the earliest videos they produced was filmed at a wind farm on Jiminy Peak in Massachusetts. They videotaped themselves climbing to the top of the turbine, showing how they got there the way our technicians would. They went on to demonstrate how hugely tall these giants are by tying a small camera to a toy soldier and launching it from the top. Over the years, they created a range of edgy content that connected GE's science to new audiences.

2. BE FIRST

No one remembers who won the silver medal at an Olympic event, and that's as true in storytelling.

At GE, for example, we were the first big company to partner with new outlets like BuzzFeed. This allowed us to spend less money because the platform was smaller and the model not yet fully developed. That gave birth to media interest about the partnership as well.

3. MICRO-TARGET YOUR AUDIENCE

A digital content factory allows you to micro-target new consumers. In other words, you can use digital tools to parse audiences by interests instead of blunt demographics. Sometimes you want to connect with five million people. But many times you really only want to be in contact with the five thousand you've specifically targeted.

For example, in telling stories about the wonders of railroads, we targeted what the rail industry calls "foamers"—people who foam at the mouth over trains—with "The Juice Train," a two-and-a-half-minute time-lapse video that follows the Tropicana/CSX Juice Train, powered by two 4,400-horsepower GE Evolution Series Tier 3 Locomotives, as it hauls Tropicana orange juice up the eastern seaboard. What's the point if they're not buying locomotives? you ask. We were going after the hearts of rail enthusiasts with the knowledge that many of them influence the purchase decision, some of them may one day work for us, and more than a few hopefully have GE stock in their portfolio. Micro-targeting takes pressure off feeling like you have to achieve Super Bowl or World Cup reach and spend all the time.

4. CREATE A SMORGASBORD

Building and running a content factory requires constant experimentation rather than giant, one-off campaigns. Essentially what you are doing is laying out a smorgasbord of content to see what is most desired. Shareability is the key: if something is getting shared, it has struck a chord.

Take a bit we called GE Flyovers. We created a behind-the-scenes experience at GE factories, for which we captured aerial footage from the factory floor and let viewers vote on what they wanted to learn more about. People voted across all of the channels in our digital ecosystem: GE.com, Facebook, Twitter, Instagram, and BuzzFeed. By the end, the four videos earned over 500,000 total views. And those views, in turn, led to a flood of ideas from people outside the division—and the company—about how we could improve, change, and imagine forward what we did. This turned into GE Drone Week—think Shark Week for science and engineering geeks—a recurring series that features live-streaming videos from drones flying over test beds for aircraft engines, deep sea oil exploration, wind farms, and even the Rio Olympics. It has gotten millions of views now. And GE recently joined with Vice to spread Drone Week globally on its video channels.

5. CONVENE CONVERSATIONS

Marketing is a conversation. Invite others in, and give them opportunities to talk back, as we did with #GEInstaWalk and GE Flyovers.

We did versions of "Ask Anything," teeing up scientists on platforms ranging from Facebook to Reddit, to talk about environmental science or 3-D printing.

GE had a prominent role in the 1969 moon landing. To retell that story on the occasion of the forty-fifth anniversary, we introduced on Snapchat our revision of the original moon boots—metallic sneakers designed with some of GE's most advanced materials. One hundred boots, termed Missions, went on sale on the anniversary day for the price of $196.90. Buzz Aldrin helped with the launch by posting a photo of himself on Snapchat wearing a pair. The conversation continued as DJs and comedians showed up wearing Missions. The shoes ended up on eBay for thousands of dollars and have been worn by celebrities and featured in the Brooklyn Museum of Art.

6. MAKE THE INVISIBLE VISIBLE

Generally, we tend not to appreciate inventions that came about before we were born or came of age. We take that technology for granted. That's a challenge for companies like GE, whose technologies provide some of the fundamental pillars of progress, such as electricity. Part of our challenge was to make the invisible visible. These are often complex technologies, so the stories about them need to be simple.

In one of my favorites, we turned our R&D center over to the Slow Mo Guys, YouTube filmmakers who created amazing slow-motion videos, such as the one of superhydrophobic and magnetic liquids (which has generated over twelve million video views). And another time, we convinced Ron Howard and Brian Grazer of Imagine Entertainment to coproduce a series with us for National Geographic television on stories behind modern science breakthroughs, including some of GE's.

7. BRING DATA TO LIFE

Increasingly, all companies struggle with the huge streams of data they generate. Early on, we teamed with designers to create visual stories around the data. One great example of this was an excursion led by GE brand innovator Sam Olstein to accompany explorer Sam Cossman to the edge of a volcano and to create a series of videos and digital experiences on the Internet that combined data with science as part of GE's efforts to increasingly digitize big things.

Soon after we launched our content factory, we were noticed by the business community for our embrace of digital, winning us yet more attention. The *Wall Street Journal* called us a "surprising experimenter." *Entrepreneur* said, "GE is killing it in social media."

My point here is that "big brand" doesn't necessarily mean "big budget." A lot of these new media initiatives were inexpensive: A

2017 Interbrand study estimated our brand value at $44.2 billion, on an annual media spend of less than $200 million. IBM and Mercedes had similar brand values but spent over $3 billion each to get there. We calculated that for every $1 spent via our content factory, we got $1.41 of value through amplification.

When I launched the content factory, no one else was doing this. But frankly, not enough companies are doing it even now, because they are sometimes afraid of risking any of their spend on new methods. I continue to get calls from CEOs who want to know how to shout louder than they spend.

What I tell them is that it really comes down to a (relatively) simple equation: great content + the right time, right place, right audience + amplification through conversation + shout louder than we spend = massive brand ROI. You have to grab shares of people's hearts and minds before you can hope to grab shares of their wallets or loyalty. And you always have to make room in your budget—and mind-set—to challenge and experiment.

CHAPTER 10

MINDS, MACHINES, AND MARKET SHARE

When I was first introduced to Thomas Edison in grade school in Winchester, Virginia, he was presented as the quintessential American inventor. But that description does his wide-ranging mind a disservice. In fact, he didn't actually invent the lightbulb— British inventors had demonstrated electric light forty-five years before. Rather, he invented a way to communicate about it, and commercialize it (his carbon filament dramatically extended durability and reliability). And finally make it scale. In other words, he made the invention *real*.

In 1878, when Edison was ready to launch his version of electric lighting, he faced a daunting obstacle: people were deathly afraid of electricity. In a world grown accustomed to candles and gaslight, they had no reason to believe they needed incandescent light.

Edison saw what many people miss—that getting people to adopt

Getting people to adopt
a new way of doing
things, mobilizing them
around a new story,
is the hard stuff of
innovation.

a new way of doing things, mobilizing them around a new story, is the hard stuff of innovation. A lot of innovators put their focus on coming up with new ideas, which involves creativity and the ability to ignore constraints. But the harder part, the especially hard, big slog, is inspiring the enthusiastic embrace of change among people who aren't that interested in changing—i.e., most of us. As Ralph Waldo Emerson said, "Ideas must work through the brains and the arms of good and brave men or they are no better than dreams."

To build public support for his grand project and demonstrate it was safe, Edison organized an "Electric Torch Light Parade," in which four hundred men wore lightbulbs on their heads—connected via wires that ran up their shirts to a steam generator that rolled behind them. Through the vehicle of the parade, Edison invented an idea that people could rally around: safe, reliable, 24/7 electric light. Once he created *that* idea, the lightbulb quickly became one of the most disruptive technologies the world had ever seen.

In the weeks following the financial collapse, I thought back on Edison's parade and Emerson's quote. GE was facing a new definition. We were an industrial company, built on mechanical engineering, that had reinvented itself as a financial juggernaut. And now we needed to redefine ourselves again. Again? Didn't we already do this? That was on the minds of most everyone I spoke with. I had to remind them: if you want to stay relevant—reinvention is a continual act.

The digital world was beginning to change everything, from how we communicated to the movies we watched to the books we read, touching the entire product chain from design and manufacturing to sales and customer service. I believed that it was just a matter of time before digital—meaning the Internet and mobile versions of our technologies—would impact more parts of the business world in new ways. It seemed inevitable to me, although I had no idea how it would unfold. I had come to know this feeling—the feeling that says to me, "Pay attention."

I may have sensed the coming change overtaking us in the oncoming digital age more clearly than most because of my time working on digital media inside NBC. But that didn't mean it was clear to me what the emerging digital world would mean for GE—only that it would be breathtakingly complex, given our range of industries. What I did see at NBC was the way that data was coming into our homes. We talked about Microsoft's Xbox as a Trojan horse in our living rooms, capturing not just how we fought battles in "Call of Duty" or rocked the band in "Guitar Hero," but that potentially recorded data about the patterns of our lives. Same for the cable set-top box. Start-ups emerged on our radar that saw the cable set-top box as a way to target in-home users with advertising by knowing who was watching what. You could imagine forward all kinds of future scenarios from there. We saw the rise of home health devices that allowed patients to go home from the hospital early and upload data for their doctors to see. With mobile phones, and the emergence of location data, technology was untethering us physically but holding us more tightly together digitally. The sheer pace of digitization was dizzying. Data collected by companies telling them how consumers used electricity, or what the wear and tear on appliances was, was clearly going to have great value in gauging what people wanted and how to reach them.

Of course, in 2008, this was a far-off opportunity. In the early days of an inflection point, all you have to hold on to are little fragments. But I knew that if we could harness data from our machines and from the work patterns of our people (sales, marketing, manufacturing, operations), GE could make a huge leap forward; we could radically remake how we work, and even what we work on. How far from the Xbox collecting data in our living room was it to monitoring when your washer's spin cycle ends, or monitoring patients' vital signs remotely? If we could figure this out quickly, we could lead. But if we hesitated, I feared we might well become Kodak, an industry giant that had stumbled and fallen. A faded photograph of past glory.

I was convinced that we needed to fully embrace the digital world and change how and what we sold—even if it just meant engaging our customers online so that they could find GE solutions, pay their bills, or order parts. But how to prove it?

How many times have we heard the cliché "I'll believe it when I see it?" But that isn't necessarily true. Sometimes even when you see it, or hear it, if it is at odds with what you've always thought to be true, your beliefs and behaviors won't change one iota.

In part, I was haunted by a story I had heard about a nineteenth-century Austrian doctor named Ignaz Semmelweis. To me, it was a cautionary tale of what could happen to our business if we failed. In 1847, Dr. Semmelweis was working in a Viennese maternity hospital with two separate clinics: doctors delivered the babies in one clinic, and midwives delivered the babies in the other. And yet in the doctors' clinic, mothers and their babies were dying at triple the rate of those in the midwives' clinic.

By observing the different processes in the two clinics, Semmelweis discovered what he thought was the reason: The doctors were coming to the deliveries straight from the autopsy ward, where they had been examining the previous day's cadavers, many of whom were mothers and babies who had died as the result of a devastating bacterial disease called childbed fever. These doctors would promptly infect the living mother and newborn infant with the same bacteria, repeating the cycle. Once Semmelweis had these doctors wash their hands before attending to the births, the mortality rate at the doctors' clinic plummeted.

But when he presented his discovery to colleagues three years later at a medical conference, he was met with rejection, derision, and mockery. His colleagues, and even his wife, thought he was going crazy and had him committed to a mental institution. He died shortly thereafter.

Why had he failed? What had gone wrong?

As I replayed the story of Semmelweis's failure to convince doctors and medical institutions to adopt the practice of washing their hands, I came to the realization that to change what people think, sometimes you have to change *how* they think. Semmelweis's observations and experiences conflicted with conventional medical thinking of the time—that disease was the result of an imbalance of the four humors of the body (this was more than a decade before the work of microbiologist and chemist Louis Pasteur). That was the mental model under which the doctors in that lecture hall operated. And neither Semmelweis's accounts from the clinics nor the concrete data he presented could sway them from it.

Our mental models are *deeply ingrained habits of mind*. Those habits are useful in filtering out what is important from what is not in day-to-day life. But they can be hard to break when they turn out to be wrong. Changing our mental models requires much more than a single lecture, no matter how convincing the evidence; it requires an ongoing presentation of experiences, discussions, provocations.

To change how people think, you need to go at people in full surround sound. They need to see how new models work in specific contexts. The really revolutionary innovations—the ones that change the world—need to be *explained* before they can be accepted. They need to be *experienced* before they can be believed. And they need to be communicated *repeatedly*. Just when you think, "Surely they are sick of me saying this," you find you need to explain it again. Shifts in how we think don't happen overnight, any more than eating a single lettuce leaf will make you thin.

Transforming people's mental model of how business works— *shaping* the new market—is almost infinitely complex. But my experience at GE and NBC has taught me that people can't just be told change is coming and be expected to spring into action. They have to work through it. Your job is to create the environment, actions, and coaching to shape opportunity before others even see it.

Galvanizing others to make a new vision of the future come true is risky, sometimes very risky, yet most necessary in times of rapid change when you are trying to grab opportunity. After the financial meltdown, I sensed it was time for grabbing GE's digital future. But first we needed to figure out what it was.

Survivor

As GE began to emerge from the financial crisis in late 2009, I cast around for a market in which I could test my ambitions to shape GE's digital future. The first call I made was to Jean-Michel Cossery, then the chief marketing officer at GE Healthcare. I had worked with Jean-Michel before I went to NBC; he was our most imaginative CMO from a business-making perspective. Supersmart (two PhDs in life sciences, plus an MBA), dynamic, and full of optimism and charm.

A slim Frenchman with a heavy accent, Jean-Michel had a fearless approach to life and work. In fact, at the time, he was into horseback archery, having been the French university show-jumping champion in his youth. I could not think of a better ally in my quest to shape the future.

Finding champions at work—true allies—is necessary for anyone who wants to transform an organization. You need a network of people who take up new ideas critically but honestly (and with passion). Change and innovation are team sports. They require internal allies against the relentless and inevitable nay-saying that will take place.

I could see the consumerization of health care taking place through digital media—from WebMD to the rapid acceleration of health content on the Internet from customers like the Cleveland Clinic and GlaxoSmithKline. They were fledgling efforts to connect more directly with consumers. In periodic strategy reviews, we would get our teams together to plot the future. These reviews were ostensibly about something like how GE could better serve the Cleveland Clinic, for example, but then we'd end up brainstorming future opportunities, like connecting the patients to the hospital remotely, through their mobile phones or small devices not yet commercialized.

In a more connected world, consumers would have all kinds of digital data about their health that they could use to take more control of their care. The health industry was looking closely at digital because one of President Obama's stimulus packages gave doctors incentives to use electronic medical records. Certainly GE customers would be impacted, and eventually GE. What was the opportunity for us to get ahead of it?

Jean-Michel and our R&D center were incubating an Imagination Breakthrough about home medical devices with sensors—in-home tracking of elderly people—while I was trying to link NBC health media initiatives with home appliances and electronic medical records. Our efforts were still very vague, but we could see the outlines of what was being shaped by digital.

This lack of clarity at this early stage is a typical obstacle for the change-maker. You have to act boldly on instinct and not wait for the data to tell you what to do, rather than the other way around. You have to respect the data but love imagination more. As a change-maker, you need to engage in what author Amy Whitaker calls "art thinking." That is, not getting from point A to point B but inventing a point B and then determining if it is possible to get there.

The need for imagination and courage is why shaping the future is a communal endeavor that requires a safe space full of allies. New ideas and observations are far from perfect on their day of birth. Often, you can't even put the concept into words. That's why I firmly believe in running a fitness test for them—and those tests require a place where people feel free to speak, make mistakes, argue, and iterate.

Act boldly on instinct;
do not wait for the data
to tell you what to do.
You have to respect
the data but love
imagination more.

Jean-Michel and I created a shared team for discovery, comprised of two marketers plus one from our MBA program. Each of us went off to uncover where digital was already taking place in health care. We met with giants such as Google and Microsoft, and with consumer companies such as Walmart and CVS who were toying with in-store care beyond pharmacy (there once was a time when you couldn't get a flu shot at CVS). We also reached out to start-ups like PatientsLikeMe and MedHelp that were growing communities of patients who were sharing health data.

We started to map out our vision for consumer health—centered on a totally connected person who could take action early and proactively, given all the personal medical data available.

"Appliances could become a digital health care business," I stated. "Water becomes a health care business, because access to clean water is essential. Power becomes a health care business when you really think about it—by giving access to power that can create new medical centers and health care in remote parts of the world. Generating power with clean technology, reducing pollution and health diseases like asthma. Doctors can be beamed in via videoconference to do telemedicine."

Jean-Michel shook his head.

"First, we need to worry about all of the data that is coming in—from consumers, doctors, hospitals, the Internet. It's random and not connected," he insisted.

Jean-Michel and I had enormous trust in each other. We could challenge each other freely, loudly, and dramatically—in fact, with Jean-Michael, everything was dramatic! And our teams felt the same way. Our meetings were physically draining and yet mentally invigorating at the same time.

"We need to create the data backbone," Jean-Michel would exclaim, jumping up and drawing a primitive train track on one of the huge notepads I had placed on easels around the room. Then I would get up and grab the marker out of his hand. "And here is the locomotive on top," I'd say, drawing a dreadful train, the kind more worthy of a first-grader. "What's in this locomotive?"

And off we would go on this riff, in a state of pure give and take. It was workflow Zen.

To ground ourselves, we'd return to two key questions: What problem are we trying to solve? And, what's the simplest, fastest way to test a solution?

"Health care costs too much, it's not good enough for most people who need it, and too many people cannot get access to it—whether they are living in a developing country like India or in parts of the United States," Jean-Michel said. "People everywhere want first-world health care at third-world cost."

"Digitization should allow us to capture the data that proves we can improve quality and access, and lower health costs." I said. "Those are three things that we are going after—cost, quality, and access."

"But people and institutions won't willingly give up their personal data," Jean-Michel argued.

"They will, Jean-Michel," I responded. "Look at what's happening with consumer sites like PatientsLikeMe—users are sharing their diabetes data and identifying themselves to the community because they believe in the power of the community to help them. Some hospitals are already using electronic medical records, and start-ups are preparing to capture data from mobile devices."

Next, we were off to discover. The key to our discovery is encapsulated by the Japanese phrase *genchi gembutso*, go and see for yourself. It's a management principle developed by Toyota and based on the importance of going to where the action is and observing it directly. This is a fundamental aspect of meeting change early.

That's why, not long after we launched our health discovery, I found myself walking through the lobby of a hotel in Riyadh, Saudi

Arabia, the smell of sandalwood wafting through the air. I was fully covered in the required Middle East uniform: a black head scarf and a heavy black abaya that covered the fact that I was lightly dressed underneath to survive what seemed like 1,000-degree August heat. (It was 115 degrees Fahrenheit.) Out of the corner of my eye, I spied Mike Tyson, the boxer, seated on a sofa.

"What is he doing here?" I wondered. A better question might have been, "What am I doing here?" I had never been to Saudi Arabia; at the time, few from GE had been there, especially women. As I was preparing for my trip, one of my female colleagues said to me, "Why would you go to Saudi Arabia? I don't support how they treat women there. I always have Saudi customers meet me in Dubai."

I would come to find Saudi Arabia one of the most interesting places I've ever been in terms of a business setting. We had convened a lunch with a group of female doctors, investors, and professors, some of the most intelligent and forceful women I've ever met. Our goal was to understand how they used technology, their views on the state of health, and their aspirations for their daughters, their families, and themselves.

When we learned that Saudi Arabia's minister of health was looking for a systematic approach to improving health care, including investing in data analytics, we thought this might be our proving ground. Once the minister was convinced that GE could help, he invited us to visit, asking us to look first at the vexing challenge of preventing women from dying from Stage 4 breast cancer. Cancer was considered a curse to many in Saudi Arabia, something to be ashamed of. Because of their customs, privacy issues, and the lack of mobility for women, cancerous breast tumors were often ignored until they became dangerous and ultimately fatal.

Jean-Michel and I had extended our teams to include two local colleagues in the Middle East, Rania Rostom and Ali Sala, and we went to work to better understand the problem. That meant looking at the narratives behind these women's actions. The solution wasn't as easy as saying to them, "Get your exam." It was about testing our image of a digital future against Saudi cultural norms, health narratives, and behaviors.

We worked with doctors, nurses, and their patients. And most of all we listened. In the course of our work, we discovered the cultural issue behind the health care failure. Screening rates were low because of the stigma and difficulty of having to go to a hospital combined with a potential diagnosis of deadly cancer.

By being in Saudi, I learned firsthand the importance of meeting face-to-face, immersing myself in someone else's culture, and seeing the world through their eyes. The women were not what I expected. "Ask us anything," one said, "but just don't waste our time talking about why we can't drive cars [a restriction that was rescinded in 2017]. We have more important things to solve." Like staying alive longer, I realized.

Ultimately we created a mobile mammography screening van designed for maximum privacy and that went *to* the women in their neighborhoods. The technology uploaded test data wirelessly to personal health records and to a Saudi national database. We developed a digital media site where women could ask questions of doctors and nurses anonymously, cloaked as a digital avatar, a virtual self that gave them a new identity and, with it, a boldness to pose questions they previously would have felt ashamed to ask. This was a big breakthrough for the health ministry—so big that they asked us to create a nationwide advertising and digital media campaign on health and wellness. Only by embedding ourselves in the kingdom and observing behaviors were we able to know that Saudi women were both privacy-obsessed and digitally savvy.

Once we addressed our product design with these discoveries, we began to reinforce our digital health narrative's scaffolding with emotionally evocative data. We found that a shocking fifteen million years of "healthy life" were lost worldwide in 2008 because of women who died early or who were incapacitated by breast cancer.

In Saudi Arabia alone, some 28,000 years of healthy life were lost. The data coming increasingly from digital health records unlocked powerful insights.

How to provide access to better, more affordable health care came into focus even more while working with our professor in residence, VG Govindarajan. He helped us to see that our products were not always aligned to emerging regions. Most of our technology was too high-end for us to take advantage of global market growth—for example, health monitors that didn't withstand being moved over rugged roads to local health centers in rural India or CT scanners that were developed for research and tier-one hospitals but proved too expensive for, and with features not needed in, rural Chinese hospitals. No wonder we weren't growing overseas.

As in Saudi Arabia, we immersed ourselves in other developing markets, and in doing so, we discovered new digital product ideas at the edge of our vision. One case in point: GE Healthcare had a $50,000 electrocardiogram (EKG) machine that was used to diagnose patients with heart problems. But when we went to India, we realized that a huge, expensive machine that plugged into the country's unreliable electricity grid was about the last thing the country needed. With the unique constraints of rural India in mind, GE created a $500 version of the EKG machine called the Mac I. It runs on batteries and weighs as much as a laptop. It's simple to use and small enough to transport, which is a critical feature for those in rural areas who can't get to a hospital.

The best thing about the Mac I—what made it "reverse" innovation—is that it created a new product from the grassroots up, the way it should be. The Mac I became such a success that it spawned an entire GE line of value-based health care products and a fast-growing business unit that target emerging markets. My favorite from this effort is the VScan, a handheld ultrasound that looks like a smartphone with a probe. Applications range from emergency care in ambulances to maternal care, putting it into the hands of midwives who can use it in areas where doctors are scarce. VScan became a symbol of GE's accessible, mobile technology intended to shape the future. And I was able to visit midwives in Indonesia and hospital administrators in Vietnam. I sat with doctors in rural China to understand how digital X-ray would help them help patients. While in some cases, they visited patients on bike, even horseback, most doctors and health care workers had mobile phones and sophisticated means of communications. You have to see it for yourself. (China and India would prove to be the most fertile ground for market-back innovation. China is home to GE's first innovation center, built in Sichuan province, to focus on rural health care; it is the birthplace of dozens of accessible health technologies, such as telemedicine and remote diagnostics.)

At the same time, GE was investing more in health care IT to provide workflow solutions for doctors who were expanding into electronic medical records. This would prove to be challenging for GE in the coming years, especially as start-up companies saw opportunity to make an impact financially and socially.

By May 2009, Jean-Michel and I had worked our strategy into the story we came to call Healthymagination, a $6 billion commitment to invest in technology and programs that focused on cost, quality, and access. And in turn, we believed GE could be a force in transforming health care. Like Ecomagination, this was about profit and purpose; it was a story about our relevance in the world, told via actions and measurable impact. We were packaging GE around health outcomes, investing in new products, aiming to boost revenues, and, most significantly, sparking better health for more people.

Our employees, especially, loved this. We created a comprehensive workplace health certification for six hundred GE sites that gave employees incentives and programs to improve their health, ranging from nutrition to on-site fitness to reduced insurance costs and digital fitness trackers. We turned many of our employees into health consumers, giving them access to their data, improving their health and wallet in the form of insurance discounts, and reducing costs for GE. This expanded to a HealthyCities program—in dozens of U.S. cities—that had us partner with other companies and local health providers to build a systematic approach, giving consumers access to health-behavior change and data, and, in turn, improving health outcomes in a way that was measurable and repeatable. We created a high-powered advisory board; engaged with key NGOs on rural health care in places ranging from New Orleans to Nairobi; and contracted with Oxford Analytica, an independent research and consultancy firm, to document product usage that lowered cost and improved quality and access—we kept a set of impact metrics, just as we did with Ecomagination. Our first set of products included GE Capital financing for U.S. physicians to install electronic medical records—from GE and various providers.

Healthymagination quickly started showing returns—brand increase, a richer sales pipeline, reduced health costs. But among the more traditional managers, it seemed unnecessary. Unfortunately, one of those was Jean-Michel's boss, the new business CEO who had been minted in GE's love of process through a series of manufacturing assignments. A short-term-numbers guy set loose in the health care industry at a time of critical change, he didn't want marketing involved in a strategy role—he wanted to direct it.

The customers and business models of home health and electronic patient records weren't clear to the new boss, and that caused friction with Jean-Michel's team. GE had joined with Intel to form a home-health joint venture, featuring tracking devices that captured vital data of the elderly and chronic health patients in home. It was an outgrowth of the digital health Imagination Breakthrough. Unfortunately, it never got the right level of championship or traction, even though it was well funded (and because of this, resented). As the effort struggled to come up to speed, the new CEO employed it as a virtual noose over the heads of Jean-Michel and me. He blamed Jean-Michel for getting GE into this new and complicated area.

I fought like crazy to keep Jean-Michel involved and regularly talked him up to Jeff, because I knew that our health care business needed a strategist and market-maker more than ever. And Jeff was a fan. For eighteen months we held back the old guard. But eventually the lack of support from his boss broke Jean-Michel, and he resigned.

"We have to expect this, Beth," he told me when he left in 2012. "We can see things that others can't. And it makes us a joke sometimes—for daring to imagine what will be."

Jean-Michel's departure was a loss for me professionally and personally. It frustrates me that established companies don't protect and develop these people who are good at seeding innovation and nurturing the tender, early stages of its development. Not everyone can or should be scaled operators. As a team leader, you have to

Champion vs. Mentor?

A mentor is someone who's willing to give you their time, expertise, and wisdom to help you develop your career. A champion, on the other hand, is someone who talks you up to others, someone who actively *promotes* your good work. Champions understand the impact you wish to make, support your work, and want to see you and people like you do well. I think it's important to have, and be, both.

Do you know what the people who champion you are saying about you? Do you take time to tell them your story? It's important to check in with them regularly to make sure they have an up-to-date version of your accomplishments and your goals. The same is true for people you're championing. The more able you are to champion other people's good stories, the better leader you become.

champion the innovators like Jean-Michel who can generate ideas, navigate ambiguity, and still take action toward a new future. As a change-maker, you need to find the champions who will do the same for you.

While we lost Jean-Michel, with the launch of Healthymagination we had achieved viable proof points for GE's push into digital technology—accessible technology made more so with digital connection and mobility, home health, and digital records. Digital was far from taking shape, but we could hear it rumbling in the distance. We had to convince the rest of GE, and the world, that it was a necessary, valuable—and unavoidable—future, even if we couldn't clearly describe it yet.

Rolling Thunder

When I first began carving a digital future from the rock of possibilities, my team took every opportunity to "educate" Jeff and the functional leaders (like our CFO) on digital concepts. Early on, I went into one of those meetings with Steve Liguori, our executive director of global marketing. Steve was a trusted deputy—together we wrote a treatise on the "4Is" of marketing for *Harvard Business Review*—and even though he wasn't a digital person per se, he just *got* how digital could help us work more closely with customers.

We had been trying to convince Jeff that "business model" innovation—new ways to generate revenue—was as important as technological invention. In health care, a business-model change could come about from selling ownership of an MRI machine differently—from a model where the hospital owns it outright to a new model that allows hospitals to pay by the scan and not own the MRI. Digital connectivity was becoming more of a differentiator in making these models easier, through better data capture, tracking, and ability to layer on additional services.

It was already happening in dramatic fashion with the iPhone and its app platform, which offered benefits for everyone from users to app makers to Apple.

For the meeting, we prepared a presentation. Now we take for granted the Apple application platform, but then it was still new. With great confidence, Steve began:

"Platforms are changing business. They are a means to aggregate data and then use that data to create new products," Steve said.

Click. Next slide.

"The Apple App Store is a good example of a platform we can learn from. Apple creates a technology backbone, a tech stack, for the iPhone. They create their own applications. But they realized that they could get more apps faster if they opened up their platform."

Click.

"What it meant for new app developers is that they could use Apple's platform and have access to users they could never get on their own. In return, they have to give Apple 30 percent of their revenues."

Click.

"To make sure the experience is a good one for the consumer, Apple becomes a gatekeeper, setting up guidelines. And they get to keep all of the data that flows from the app."

Click.

Steve handed off to me, and I explained how a platform sets in motion network effects: the more people in the network, the faster the network grows and the more value it creates.

We thought our pages were blindingly clear. But the rest of the executives at the table seemed to have heard another language. As I began to launch into the second half of the presentation—"how we might do this"—Jeff couldn't stop himself from breaking in.

"Apple is about consumers, Beth. They don't apply to us. We make complicated infrastructure tech. Not mobile phones and apps," he says. "I get what you are saying—I do. But I just don't think it applies. They are apples to our oranges."

Steve jumped up and responded, "Think of the iPhone as the small version of what GE could do," he said, pausing for effect. "Take the framework of an open software platform muscled up with data and analytics and imagine—*imagine*—what happens when you apply that to our big iron. Health care, jets, turbines—an energy platform where outside experts publish programs that improve the efficiency of our wind farms!"

Steve's the kind of guy who barely takes a breath when he is excited. And that could make for tense meetings with Jeff, who wasn't always as enthusiastic. This was one of those times. Steve's passionate *A Few Good Men* riff was met with annoyed silence.

Looking back, I can see that we didn't yet have the language to translate our ideas in a way that Jeff and our fellow GE leaders could understand. There was a gap between our vision of the future we had been describing—the value in Apple's ecosystem, data, and platform—and how it applied to GE's future.

This moment is where the evangelizing process stops for most companies. But I saw that Jeff's response wasn't a no. It was just a failure of language. If Jeff understood what we saw in digital and he was still dismissive, okay. But that wasn't the case. *He just didn't see it. Yet.* And we weren't hearing Jeff well either. He was making a point that perhaps industry is different, with different competitive issues relating to data. We were stuck on our iPhone analogy.

We kept going back and going back, improving our presentation, poking, prodding, refining. Every time we dared to bring up the App Store or Apple, we'd get shut down. "Don't talk to me about the iPhone again," Jeff or the finance guys would moan. But we persevered.

These education sessions, demos, sparks, translators, proof points, and whispers—the tools of the change-maker's trade—are little moments of metaphorical dialogue that taken together, over time, become the basis of a major Broadway production that acts on the collective psyche of the organization's leaders and workforce.

Corporate America has been going on about out-of-the-box thinking for decades—but the thing is, we still seem to love the box. Anything outside of it is irrelevant, or a fanciful "cartoon." The GE team's inability to see how a seemingly unrelated example could inform what GE does is the result of a common cognitive bias that psychologists call *functional fixedness*.

The German psychologist Karl Duncker defined functional fixedness as a "mental block against using an object in a new way that is required to solve a problem." In a famous study, Duncker created something called the Candle Problem: subjects are given a box of tacks, a candle, and a match and told to affix the candle to the wall so that it doesn't drip wax on the floor. Most people try to stick the candle to the wall with wax or tacks and fail, instead of rethinking the problem, which is to dump out the tacks, connect the box to the wall, and put the candle in the box—because they cannot see the box as anything but a container for tacks.

The good news is that this bias can be overcome. Repeated exposure to different views and novel experiences can prime us to question our assumptions and consider alternatives—that is, to see the box holding the tacks as a candleholder. The repeated exposure does something else that's critical: it creates discomfort—the discomfort that comes from being stuck on a problem. Studies in creativity show that it is an important early stage in the process of people generating an insight, creating those *aha* moments. It's a subconscious signal to the brain that a problem exists and a solution must be found.

Our brain tends to grasp for easy answers to solve the problem and end the tension. And organizations behave similarly. At first, they deny a problem exists. Then they admit that a problem exists—but it's not theirs. Then they say that it's their problem, but it can be solved by the tried and tested pathways.

In advocating for change, the change-maker's job is to maintain the discomfort. Necessity may be the mother of invention, but I've

Necessity may be the mother of invention, but I've found irritation works pretty well, too.

found irritation works pretty well, too. Yours and theirs. They call your idea a cartoon? Become a cartoon artist, making it clearer and clearer until it makes sense. (As a sketch artist, Michelangelo gave his figures extra-dark outlines, a defining characteristic of his work.) Keep coming back. That persistence ultimately triggers new ways of thinking as people get exposed to the notion and interpret it in a new context. You have to keep communicating these examples and finding translators and sparks to get attention.

One key to giving these constant provocations organizational weight is to insinuate them into the organizational events at which the company's future is decided. At GE, these took two major forms: Growth Days and the Commercial Council.

Growth Days, which I set up with Jeff, grew out of the Imagination Breakthrough reviews we held, in which we would spend one Friday a month looking at growth ideas and new technologies. These get-togethers are important for any company, as they inculcate a disciplined approach to seeking out new ideas for growth, forcing leadership to focus forward in an organized way.

These were often debate-filled meetings, especially between our good-natured CTO Mark Little and me. In tech-based companies, the battle between marketing and tech can be described as Should versus Can. The technology folks often want the most advanced, sophisticated features, no matter how overengineered or expensive they might be—they are pushing the limits of what's possible. Marketing helps interpret what is valuable in the market—not what could be made but what *should* be made. Jeff's job was to navigate the tension and make the tough calls based on input from both areas.

While Mark and I (and Jeff) had good debates about the future of health care, we had especially tense battles over the future of solar energy. And the tension usually arose around changing or improving the technology versus changing the business model.

Mark was focused on the solar PV panel. "The photovoltaic panel is the gateway into the building. We're engineering dramatically improved efficiency, and in time, it will be cheaper. Why would someone want an inferior PV panel?" he asked.

"Because the PV panel is good enough. There is a different way into the market," I would argue. "That's what we're seeing in start-up companies like Solar City and Sunrun. Basically, they offer the consumer less-costly electricity, they finance the solution for its life-time, and they take over the pain of installation and upgrades. And they are able to knit the system together with software, making it easier for consumers to sign up, easier for installers to be part of the network, and are capturing customer data along the way. As the panels commoditize and get better, their cost of the system de-creases. It's a different way to solve the problem, by controlling the whole system."

Solar continued to be a point of violent debate and various at-tempts and stops. Because we were functionally fixed, GE teams didn't confront the most existential questions of all: What happens when someone figures out how to make money with solar? What happens when fuel is essentially free from the sun? What happens when our turbines are replaced by electronics and digital tech, and no longer the power behind the power system?

I debated the issues at our monthly Growth Days, and again at our quarterly Commercial Council meetings, when we focused on how to sell in new ways. This was the meeting at which we opera-tionalized the growth ideas we cultivated on Growth Days. That meant getting salespeople comfortable with new products and new ways to generate revenue.

Commercial Council had become increasingly frustrating to me. Jeff seemed less patient with the marketing side; he felt he needed to focus more attention on global deals and big customer wins as we scaled global growth. And because Jeff felt comfortable working with me, he'd often bring his freewheeling style of discussion—the "cartoon-shaming"—to the council.

I remember one meeting in particular: We met in the Lyceum, a tiered lecture hall in Crotonville styled like a gladiator pit. I sat up front, next to Jeff, with Jean-Michel and my colleagues behind us. When it was my turn to present, I squeezed behind Jeff's chair to go into the "pit" to be challenged. I stared up into the crowd, gathered my breath, and explained how a new focus on harnessing consumer interest in health care, via the Internet, could be helpful in getting us closer to our customers—to doctors and hospitals. Health, I said, could be the new "green" for GE.

Jeff scrunched up his face and shook his head.

"Digital consumer health care? That sounds like a cartoon, Beth," he said. "What you've painted is too far off to talk about. You're at step 40. What do we need to do to focus on step 5? How about EMR [electronic medical record] financing, how's that going?"

Jeff wanted to know how to sell something now.

One of the sales leaders, Jim, was even more combative. "What are they supposed to do with this, really?" he said, waving me off. "Consumer health? Beth, we don't sell directly to consumers."

"No, not now," I said. "But imagine it forward." Your customers have customers. Your customers are doctors and hospital administrators. They serve patients. Our utilities serve home and business owners. At the end point, these are consumer businesses.

Then other GMs piled on, and the point of the conversation was lost and we moved on to the next thing.

Once the interrogation was over, I squeezed back behind Jeff's seat to mine and held my chair arm with an iron grip. It was only when I got back to my room at the Crotonville guesthouse that I allowed myself a cry of frustration. This happened often after meetings in this forum. I wasn't able to get through to those guys. I felt I had been too surprised and intimidated to fight back.

"They don't want to listen," I complained to Jean-Michel in frustration.

After pushing digital without success at a few Commercial Council meetings, I decided I needed to bring in an expert—a spark, a

Lost in Translation

"They just don't get it, do they?!" Watch out for those moments when you are frustrated enough to think this way, or worse, say it. We've all been there; it's so tempting to dismiss those who don't get it as thick-headed or worse. Even if you don't explicitly say it, remember that your tone and body language speak much louder than words. I have a bad habit of looking at a teammate and rolling my eyes when the conversation becomes frustrating. It's the sort of thing that makes everyone look bad.

Avoid phrases like "It's really simple" or "As most people know." For one thing, maybe they don't know. Most people don't want to admit when they don't know something, especially in a group setting. It's helpful to send a simple overview in advance and offer digital links for people to explore further. I once asked what I thought was a reasonable question in an investor-relations meeting. One person retorted, "Well, anyone who knows how investing works wouldn't need to ask that question." And he never answered my question. I felt like an idiot for the rest of the meeting. Most industries have specific terms and acronyms, and knowing them proves your insider status. Sometimes, industry language is wielded as a barrier to keep away neophytes. Good leadership focuses on making concepts easy to understand, and inviting people to engage.

Challenge yourself to truly engage others:

- First, don't assume everyone has the same level of understanding that you have.

- Ask questions. I'll often start a meeting in which we're introducing a new concept by asking questions to engage the room. What do you know about this subject? What kinds of questions do you have?
- Don't get lost in translation. We may use the same words but interpret them differently. I've learned to focus on a few words, stating something like "Here's what I mean by this," and then ask, "Does this mesh with your interpretation?"

translator—who had been validated by the market. That's when we happened upon Aaron Dignan. Linda Boff had hired Aaron to help develop ideas with the digital brand team. Aaron had cofounded a consultancy called Undercurrent that billed itself as the McKinsey of digital and that came recommended by a former colleague who was now at Pepsi. Aaron's work expertise had been validated by people we knew on the team at American Express, and he helped us create a digital advisory board, which continues to this day. Our goal was to convene a group of digital makers who could inspire us with their insights and advise us on our strategy, especially in marketing and community building. The advisors have included Chris Poole, aka moot of 4chan (who himself became a valued spark to Linda and me), Scott Heffernan of Meetup, Bennett Foddy of the NYU Game Center, and Amanda Kelso of Facebook. They helped create confidence about the digital strategies we were building and gave us early insights and access to emerging platforms. This kind of advisory board can be effective in any change initiative a company is leading.

Linda and I decided that Aaron's work on the digital brand deserved to be promoted to the Commercial Council. So we threw him to the lions and asked him to appear at the next council. Outsiders are usually greeted with some skepticism.

But Aaron dived in, using the most consumer focused of all technology products: Google search. We take it for granted now, but in 2010, this was still surprisingly difficult for industry to engage with. After explaining the various algorithms on which Google search worked, with plenty of bored shifting in the tiered seats, Aaron pivoted.

"Now, Google search isn't just about finding cake recipes and cat food," he said. "Large companies are using customer data gleaned from Google search to generate targeted leads that turn into real sales—with 10, 20 percent conversion. And they are uploading videos about products to YouTube, creating an earlier moment of discovery for customers. Maybe you don't need as many salespeople if customers know about your product before you show up."

"Wait, wait a minute," one GE executive said. "More leads, fewer salespeople? I don't get it."

"They can find your products and information themselves—in fact, you can steer them to it by buying keywords in Google search. Look, your industrial competitors are already doing it." He pulled up a video of a small power-generation unit from a competitor. "See, customers can see your competitor's product in action. And there are hundreds more like this. Do you think they are asking 'Where's GE?' Look at how Caterpillar is using mobile technology so their distributors can order inventory and monitor the status of shipments via applications."

Yep, consumer-modeled applications were being used in enterprise businesses. Aaron, the spark, had broken through. GE's leadership continued to challenge him, but they did it with better manners, and they listened, or at least pretended to.

Behind all of the various tools I use to create the "rolling thunder"—the gradual announcement of the arrival of something new, until it is too loud to ignore—there is a scaffolding of psychological theory. You need to create an emotional pull and push; you need to balance paranoia and possibility.

. . .

Here is my rolling thunder rollout:

1. GET PEOPLE EXCITED

In the early days, as I continued to push digital, Jeff kept saying, "I know it's important, but what is it for *us*?"

We kept putting ourselves in Jeff's shoes and asking, "What does digital and software look like at GE? Data from our machines? Wind turbines that chat? What does that look like?" This iterative process helps to hone the story, making it more believable, relevant, and saleable. Eventually, your audience will start to interpret the digital future in their own ways and add to the narrative.

2. LOOK FORWARD; STRESS FUTURE UTILITY

I invited Marc Benioff, the head of the groundbreaking (at the time) cloud software company Salesforce, in to talk to us. Marc was a few stanzas ahead of GE, and his vision of a cloud-based world was infectious. I had him talk to GE's business leaders about how he managed his entire business using data in the cloud.

Marc's marketing strategy was to hit constantly on the idea of a world without installed software on its computers—hence the "No Software" stickers he took everywhere. He knew that people would only gravitate to his products once they accepted the utility of the concept.

3. TEST THE SCARY STUFF AWAY FROM HOME

You can create proof points that convince leadership by trying riskier stuff far from headquarters.

We brought in one of our marketers, Ipsita Dasgupta, who was leading growth for GE in India and had been hired from Cisco and IBM, to speak at the Commercial Council. Working with our GE Energy teams, she had mapped out a way to incorporate digital services into our power generation and wind offerings in India. She could explain how software was working in energy, what we could do with more data, and how to monetize it. Having worked for software firms, she could translate how data could be used in examples GE's leadership could relate to.

4. LOOK, WE'RE ALREADY DOING IT!

As with Ecomagination, we looked first to those parts of GE where digital was already a part of our business. The big *aha*: GE's revenue from its existing software products—largely in manufacturing automation—qualified us as one of the world's top twenty software firms.

With this insight, people inside GE almost became less afraid of digital. In fact, employees began to go around bragging about our ranking (number fourteen at that time). It helped turn the mind-set inside GE. We could now concentrate on the fact that we needed scale, alignment, and momentum to compete.

5. PARANOIA WORKS

A good part of the innovator's job is to scare people. Tell them what might happen to them if they *don't* jump on the train. To instill in my team a fear of inaction during the early days of Healthymagination, I took them to the Consumer Electronics Show in Las Vegas, which I attended every year to keep my thumb on the market. I walked Jean-Michel and the other key members to one of the exhibition halls and pointed.

"What do you see?" I asked.

"Booths and booths of health industry start-ups," Jean-Michel said.

"And do you know how many booths were here last year?" I asked. *"Four."*

By the time I'd finished my sentence, Jean-Michel was dragging his colleagues over to the closest booth.

"Oh my god, there's somebody here with a heart monitor tethered to a smartphone. That's so great . . ." he said. "Wait a minute. That's going to disrupt our ECG business."

6. CREATE COMPANY-WIDE FEAR OF MISSING OUT

As your change-making initiative begins to gain momentum, shout your successes far and wide. No one wants to fall behind their peers inside the company.

During the early years of our digital discovery, I sent out repeated e-mails to our sales and marketing leaders to incite them to jump on the train. "We're getting our digital groove going at GE, and it's good to see," I wrote in one e-mail. Then I launched into a laundry list of digital successes, from examples of finding new value for customers to a mention of GE Genius, an iPad app that delivered real-time data to sales teams.

Proof point, proof point, proof point. The e-mail pep rallies went on to create a din of positivity. We flooded the zone with so much data and storytelling that we made people paranoid that they would miss the future.

Eventually, things started to click. Those who doubted us, even the most negative voices on the Commercial Council, began to doubt themselves. As several digital-related Imagination Breakthroughs (such as Dose Watch, a digital gauge for hospitals; Fuel Tracker for airlines; Grid IQ digital monitoring for electricity grids; and Rail Network Optimization) began to show results, more people in the company began to shift from neutral to positive.

Jeff agreed that the future was digital. What GE needed was a more concentrated effort, he said. So he established a digital initiative that would put it on the level with our past initiatives, like new growth and our global expansion. In other words, the "cartoon" was real. Now we had to make the rest of the world believe it.

Mindshare Before Market Share

Despite some progress, GE was missing a keystone of market-shaping: a new, shared language. If you are to have any success pulling the world to a new market before you have actual products—what I call *mindshare before market share*—you have to introduce a language with which you can talk about it. This new shared language allows your teams (and others) to work together and create new things.

The essence of innovation is not technology or business but the connections between them. Once you have a language, you can tell the story of the product and, in doing so, help to evolve and grow the product. The tough part is getting the story right, and spreading it far and wide.

For GE, the breakthrough came in late 2011, in a meeting between Jeff, Mark Little, Steve Liguori, Bill Ruh, and me in Jeff's office. Mark and I were enthusiastic champions for a digital future, but for different reasons. Mark saw the capability to embed more sensors into our big machines, and I saw new end-user markets.

As we tried to define our new language, I continued to bring our story back to consumer examples, which would make Jeff crazy. "Imagine if your jet engine tweeted to you. What would it say?" Jeff made his "cartoon" face again.

"You know, Beth, I really don't care what a jet engine would tweet. I care what my daughter tweets. Stop bringing me cute consumer examples, talking milk boxes, the 'Internet of Things,'" he said, throwing up his hands. "This is industry, not the Internet."

Without a second's thought, Steve said the first thing that popped into his mind: "No, Jeff—it's the 'Industrial Internet.'"

Jeff often complained that Steve talked too much—but he didn't complain this time.

"That's so right!" I said.

"Yes it is, Steve! Yes it is!" Jeff said.

The Industrial Internet perfectly captured what we were doing. It was simple, and it gave us a way to explain to people inside and out that we weren't selling to consumers on the Internet or marketing enterprise software like Oracle. We were capturing data from machines to give our customers better insights about the performance of machines and the equipment we made. It offered the kind of clarity that a new language needs to spread our message.

It may not have been sexy or clever, but it *was* practical and easy to understand. We are a digital industrial company building the Industrial Internet. We work with sensors, data, and intelligent machines, combined with big data, analytics, and predictive algorithms.

Next, we needed a way to spell out what the value proposition would be for the Industrial Internet. In other words, we needed to offer a simple and easily repeatable business model. We had to answer the question: What would it mean to a customer to have access to data from our machines?

That's how Steve and Linda and I developed what we called the *power of 1%* effort—it was a way to talk to customers and, equally important, share the potential impact of the digital world—the world of software and zeros and ones—on our industry with media and investors. We picked a simple paradigm: What if going digital could increase industry productivity by 1 percent? How much would we save? How much would customers save? In aviation, a 1 percent savings on fuel would offer $30 billion over fifteen years; in health care, a 1 percent increase in productivity would return $63 billion in fifteen years; and in rail, a 1 mph increase in train speed would have a $200 million impact per year on one of our big customers.

These became jumping-off points for simple stories that could be shared and repeated across the company. For example: Did you know that the average train goes 21 mph? It's not because GE can't make them go faster—they do, much faster. It's just that there is so much congestion of rail cars and other trains that rail transport gets slowed. By connecting sensors to parts of the locomotive and rail cars, operators know where they are and how to ease congestion faster. Same for a hospital. Did you know that a nurse spends an average of twenty minutes per day looking for misplaced equipment? With sensors and mobile devices, nurses can find things more easily and be more productive.

As we were developing the language of our business case, I realized I was going to have to make a concerted effort to get our business plan accepted in Silicon Valley. The Valley has a history of being both wildly open to new thinkers and every culture, and insular and elitist when it comes to "old" technology firms doing things differently. It helped that Mark had hired a longtime Cisco strategy exec named Bill Ruh. A global digital leader, Bill had heard the distant thunder of the future and came to GE with a longstanding passion for the "Internet of Things." He quickly hired software engineers at a new GE Software Center of Excellence (COE) facility in the East Bay across from Silicon Valley, increasing our credibility in the Valley.

Next, I set up a kind of digital coming-out party for GE. Along with Alex Constantinople (who had left GE and was running the OutCast Agency communications firm, which had a roster of Silicon Valley tech clients from Facebook to Salesforce), we mapped out a view of the Valley that illustrated key influencers across a spectrum of organizations.

Soon, I had set up dinners for Jeff and me to meet tech-world stars such as Reid Hoffman of LinkedIn, start-up CEOs like Aaron Levie of Box and Lynn Jurich of Sunrun, *Wired* editor Chris Anderson, Stanford professor and Lean Startup architect Steve Blank, and venture capitalists like "The Godfather of Silicon Valley," Ron Conway. Marc Benioff came to one of the dinners as did Netscape founder and famed venture capitalist Marc Andreessen. At each one, Jeff and I evangelized the Industrial Internet platform, selling it with possibility, mutual benefit, and a bit of fear of missing out on top.

One of those we reached out to was Tim O'Reilly, founder of O'Reilly Media, a technology publisher and convener who brought together thinkers and then propagated ideas that shaped the future. The term "open source" was coined at one of his conferences, as was the term and concept "Web 2.0."

When I first suggested to Tim that we could team up to do original content around the Industrial Internet, he was dubious. "That sounds like something really commercial meant to benefit GE. And we don't endorse products, you know," he said.

But I flew out with Steve and Linda, and we laid out the story of the Industrial Internet: yes, it would benefit us, but it would also serve as a platform that would benefit everyone, like Marc Benioff's propagation of Software as a Service.

We talked through a long dinner and a series of phone calls, and Tim came around to our image of the Industrial Internet as a real opportunity, as something bigger than the Internet of Things, which he now saw as the consumer subset of our project. You have to name it to claim it.

Like all major events, the Industrial Internet needed a launch party to make an irreversible grab on mindshare. In August 2011, Andreessen wrote an article in the *Wall Street Journal* that went viral, declaring that software would "eat the world." He claimed that we were in the midst of a major technological and economic shift in which software companies would take over huge parts of the economy. As more products were made smart and connected, software would be the connective tissue for creating value, even at companies that sell physical goods; think Amazon, a software company that's taken over retail offering vast arrays of products and free shipping from your couch. We agreed—to a point. But the physical world was not going away anytime soon. The race was now on for us to define value at the intersection of the physical and digital world. It was a way for GE to enter the debate with a splash, announcing, "The race is on."

We planned our big event for November 2012 at San Francisco's hot Dogpatch start-up hub, and we dubbed this "name it to claim it" shindig Minds + Machines. The guest list included scores of venture capitalists, entrepreneurs, tech thinkers (such as Andrew McAfee of MIT), media (of course), and customers, with the guest star being Andreessen himself.

The opening of the event caused a collective gasp from the audience, as we unveiled on the stage an actual shell of a GEnx jet engine, huge and beautiful in all its formidable big iron power. And then we kicked off.

Before introducing Andrew McAfee, Jeff gave his intro, hitting hard on GE's five thousand software engineers, the 1 percent story, and the announcement of Industrial Internet products we had twisted our business leaders into agreeing to.

After McAfee had blessed the idea, and Bill Ruh and I and an Alaska Airlines VP had dived down into the specifics of the information a jet engine could report, we moved to our big moment. Sitting in blocky white-leather chairs dwarfed by the GEnx, *Wired*'s Chris Anderson chaired a panel with Jeff Immelt and Marc Andreessen.

Andreessen expanded on the theme of his famous *Wall Street Journal* column about how the value in the economy was migrating to software—and would continue doing so inexorably—and that the best software companies would win the economy. His theory felt bulletproof, and for one moment I wondered if we would ever digitize that big jet engine. But Jeff seemed, in fact, to welcome Marc's words. His response was magnanimous, and in almost total agreement.

"What we've learned is that there's another 5 percent of productivity, 5 percent of fuel burnt, 10 percent of maintenance, to be saved by modeling the analytics around those products," he said. "I've been CEO for eleven years, and eleven years ago I might have said, 'Let somebody else do the analytics.'"

The new GE would make that market, though, he said. And to hit that point home, Jeff looked over at the giant GEnx engine, lit in a deep-sea blue, with something resembling love, like fathers look at sons, the way Steve Jobs looked at the first iPhone.

With twenty sensors, Jeff explained, the engine could generate a terabyte of flight data every day; GE's latest locomotives are rigged with over 250 sensors that measure 150,000 data points per minute. GE had 250,000 pieces of intelligent hardware in other industries, Jeff said, from medical scanners to wind turbines. GE would gather and crunch that data. We would be an industrial platform player.

Jeff stood in front of the engine and said in closing, "Marc, eat this." What he meant was, you still need jet engines and gas turbines to make the modern world go around. It was said in a friendly way, but with intent: there was a new Internet, an Industrial Internet, and we were at its center.

Discovery is an ongoing, never-done project in every company, but especially in a company as large as GE. Jeff formed a Software Council as a way to bring together GE's various businesses around a common goal of creating more software and digital engagement.

Bringing together such communities gives birth to creative abrasion that radiates energy. Outsiders sometimes underestimate the power of going horizontal in breaking down silos to get an entire organization focused on a few core initiatives like digital.

Together, these communities constituted a classic sensemaking operation, tasked with seeing where things are more alike than different—for example, where solar energy technology meets societal desires for clean energy, or ultrasound technology that can be used to monitor and inspect oil pipelines or jet engines.

How to Get *Your* POV Out There

In the Middle Ages, wandering troubadours brought news of wars, royal marriages, and religious pronouncements. In ancient Greece, troupes of actors did the same thing. In the modern world, professional media organizations reported the big stories, first in print and then over the airwaves. Today, digital technology has opened up the field to just about anybody. When companies use digital channels to tell stories on their behalf, it's referred to as branded content or brand journalism.

I believe that everyone—every organization—has the ability and the responsibility to tell the merits of their own story. Moreover, they have an obligation to do so. If you don't tell your story to the people who are interested, somebody else is bound to do it for you.

We were an early pioneer of branded content. Telling our own story daily with GE Reports helped different parts of GE that might otherwise have rarely been in touch talk to one another. It uncovered assets that we didn't know we had. It helped GE learn how to move forward faster and innovate as a company.

As more brands tell their stories, the quality of branded content has proven to be uneven, causing some to question the entire practice. But a few bad company stories have not lessened my faith in the process. The risk of running a less-than-optimal story is the price of sharing your point of view.

To get our storytelling capacity up to speed, we worked closely with Alexander Jutkowitz, cofounder of Group SJR, one of the agencies that pioneered brand journalism.

Here are his tips on branded storytelling:

- Digital storytelling is in some senses a race. Speed matters.
- Serialize and atomize. In an age of ephemeral content and short attention spans, the ability to serialize a story and tell it in small pieces over time determines its staying power. It's essential to tell stories that can live anywhere and respect the rules and quirks of a particular platform (i.e., Twitter, Facebook, LinkedIn).
- Too many companies assume that what they do is too boring for anybody to care about. That's not true. Whether you are involved in infrastructure, tech, food service, consumer packaged goods, or financial services, you are supporting the basics of civilization. To you, it might be a daily grind; to somebody who doesn't know your business, it is often a source of magic, wonder, wisdom, and fascination.

Platform Power: The Age of Brilliant Machines

Mind + Machines put us on the digital map; people started to believe we were serious. But we had also drawn attention. Our competitors now saw the opportunity. Digital-first companies like Amazon were opening up their cloud services to industry, and software giants like SAP and IBM followed. Even GE competitors like Siemens were turning their focus to data analytics.

The very public launch allowed (or forced) me to turn to my

new role building models for ways we would commercialize digital. I used our new bona fides to hire Kate Johnson to lead digital commercial. A driven, good-humored Oracle sales executive who wanted to become part of the next wave of digital, Kate was charged with building a software solutions team that would include highly technical software architects who could translate customer data needs into products, not to sell the jet engine, per se, but to sell the technology and the software that would help make that jet engine more productive—i.e., run longer, burn less fuel, connect directly to the service team.

With Kate and me in the lead, our efforts shifted away from products to discovering new revenue models for GE digital. We created a center of expertise for digital sales and marketing—we needed to seed new capabilities with experts, especially as the need impacted every GE business. It was becoming clear that our contractual service agreement (CSA) model of selling a service contract for the life of the machine, with maintenance commitments and parts replacements, was reaching its limits. New technology innovations were happening faster, and the technology was better, meaning less need for service. And services are high margin with customers eager to take back profits. Digital would add new opportunities to upgrade machine output and create additional revenue streams. By embedding software, the machines could be upgraded remotely with new offers—for example, determine the wind speed affecting a turbine blade—as a subscription or à la carte (just like your smartphone after all!). This was also potentially disruptive, meaning remote software could replace in-shop repairs in many cases. If we didn't offer this, someone else could. This made everyone nervous, especially as our customers wanted more integrated systems—products plus software. They wanted to buy "outcomes"—i.e., productivity or savings—not just a jet engine. In some ways, Ecomagination was our first outcome-driven initiative—delivering energy efficiency and economic impact. Now we were poised to take this big with data.

Much of the heavy lifting of these major organizational pivots has to do with bringing in the right outside agitators, sparks, and translators. We almost didn't find Kate. Frustrated that we had few women among the senior ranks of GE sales leaders, I could hardly complain if I wasn't addressing this directly when I hired new people. I called up the recruiter and asked, "Why are you not giving us more women candidates?"

"There just aren't many women available," he said. "Try, as we do, I can't find many women in software."

"What?" I countered. "There are no women selling software? I don't believe it. We're not going to move forward until we have female candidates to consider."

We found Kate and three other women who could be candidates for other roles. Kate hired sales and marketing leaders from software companies and embedded them into the business units to model the kind of market development and selling required. Sales leaders were increasingly required to be more consultative, helping customers operate better, not just sell them a product. Value propositions were changing—sales and marketing would have to work more closely together. Business unit CEOs had a hard time at first understanding all of the changes that digital was bringing, and progress was slow. As I had seen at NBC, the fight between digital and big iron represented the *haves* and the *have nots*—the cool kids and the legacy. Digital moved from R&D to become an official GE business unit, making the tension even more pronounced. Kate grew to lead all digital sales; and while she accelerated revenues and hired great people, the tension of all that change took its toll. Sadly, after four years with GE, Kate left for a big role at Microsoft.

Simultaneously, we developed a series of ad campaigns to explain the benefits of industrial data and our role in it.

The moment that put us in the center of the conversation—a breakthrough storycraft moment that seeded our Industrial Internet identity with the public—came a little later, with a nerdy kid named

Owen. Bespectacled Owen starred in a series of GE ads about a college grad who has to break the news to his friends that he isn't going to work for his buddy's cool app company, which makes playful GIFs, but for GE. "I'm going to transform the world," he says, as his friend interrupts with a GIF of a cat costumed with fruit: "I can do casaba melons!" In a second ad, Owen's father waxes proud that his son will be manufacturing at GE, and passes on "Grandpappy's" sledgehammer. "But I'll be writing the code that will allow those machines to share information," Owen says, to which his father answers, "Pick up the hammer. I bet you can't pick it up," a line that became a small sensation.

Those ads fundamentally changed GE's perception. We had reached our goal of being recognized as the science and engineering nerd, proudly laughing at ourselves, winning mindshare, and changing the world. Within a month of airing the commercials, visits to GE's online recruitment site jumped 66 percent.

GE would go on to hire thousands of coders and data analysts, including a horde of people who gave up high-tech jobs at Google, Apple, and Amazon because they believed in our mission and were excited about the industrial scale of data and its power in addressing the world's problems.

The digital and physical worlds were converging, even if we didn't know exactly how it would all turn out. In the coming years, the Internet of Things is going to put fifty billion machines online, each shipping off a continuous stream of data. Our machines are telling us about their inner lives and how they can make our own lives better.

The Industrial Internet story continues to evolve, as digital technologies such as wearable devices are increasingly monitoring and interacting with the physical world.

For the first time in history, intelligence is spreading not only from person to person—but from human to machine, and back again. Jet engines, for example, will be outfitted with more sensors to gather data on the environments through which they fly. We'll be able to fix engines before they break and extend their useful life. If an average airline with one hundred 777 aircraft extends its engines' time on wing by just 1 percent, it saves approximately $100 million over the lifetime of the fleet.

In the end, data, machine sensing, and enhanced human understanding will fuel a virtual cycle of productivity: gather-analyze-adjust. And this new, mashed-up operating system is going to fundamentally change how we work and live.

Challenges

CONSIDER THE UNEXPECTED

The next time a result that isn't supposed to be there pops up on a report, don't dismiss it. Take a close look at it. It might be the first bit of evidence, the first drop of rain in a coming storm you need to weather—or the first sign of a trend you can take advantage of. Management guru Peter Drucker identified "unexpected occurrences" as one of the major drivers of innovation. When someone says, "That is an outlier. Don't pay attention to it," this is your chance to ask, "What if it's not? How can we see if there is something here?"

ERASABLE ZEN

I find a whiteboard to be an essential tool for real-time collaboration. I also keep a stack of blank, white paper at my desk and in conference rooms, along with a full jar of colored markers (I travel with a smaller set). When I'm in a discussion, I'll map out the conversation in a series of illustrations or key phrases. I find keeping these pages as a record of my free associations helpful when I synthesize the points to share later.

INCORPORATE STORYTELLING INTO YOUR DAY

I once bought an expensive basket of berries despite the fact that they were twice the price of the others. The proprietor told me that a young Amish girl had just picked the berries that morning. I imagined a sweet, hardworking girl in the morning sun tenderly picking the fruit and then gingerly placing each berry into the basket. I was sold. A good story sells—always has and always will. That is its power. Perhaps good stories are the only things that ever sell—with the great product or experience required to make the story stick.

THE STORYTELLING CHALLENGE

Take a set of routine work activities, and weave a tale around them that infuses insight, humor, collaboration, failure, and success.

- Come up with stories about a person on your plane, train, subway, or bus. What is his story? Where is he going and why? Can you tell his story in a sentence? What about the people who work on and in support of the bus or plane?
- Do the same after a meeting. Do it for a colleague or a competitor or an important customer. Share it with a colleague. Can they top it?
- Try ending every meeting with a story summing up the project at hand. Can you use the story in selling the idea to clients or management?
- Turn story into an ongoing team challenge. Put it on a whiteboard or collaborative digital space. Encourage teams to challenge one another with humor, with impact, with valor. Offer gold stars to the most concise story.

Legend has it that Ernest Hemingway won a bet over whether or not he could create a compelling six-word story with this: "For sale: baby shoes. Never worn."

What's your story today?

Creating a New OS

CHAPTER 11

OPENING UP

New Power Trumps Old

*O*pen is the ethos of the digital era. Easy access to ideas and information—and the informality, immediacy, and autonomy that creates—has instigated a shift from hierarchy to networks, from centralized bureaucracies to decentralized platforms, where sharing and transparency are the standards. From around 2007 onward, all this openness began to speak a language that those in GE could understand: growth, revenues, and profits that scale exponentially. It was unprecedented. Apple, Alibaba, Amazon, Facebook, Google were embracing this new open, boundary-less reality to orchestrate people and resources in entirely new ways, rapidly scaling at low cost by enabling a self-governing ecosystem of buyers and sellers and developers and even competitors to share information, perform transactions, and create value. It was unprecedented.

The nature of these open economic exchanges—the relationships they created, the business models around which they were built—was entirely new. And it introduced a level of messy complexity that

I knew would terrify those within GE. "Who's in charge?" we'd ask. "How will we protect our secrets? How will we know who's working on what, when?"

GE's questions were borne out of a culture and processes built for an industrial age, when a premium was placed on productivity, certainty, and top-down control. To GE, the hypercollaborative endeavors of this new networked age came across, then, as free-spirit dot-com insanity. GE and the best of corporate America—think of them as Old Power—had always won by developing proprietary knowledge and then ferociously guarding that knowledge as a valuable asset.

In the past, partnerships with GE, like much of the corporate world, went something like this: do it my way. The goal was always to get 51 percent ownership interest in any joint venture. Someone had to be in charge. The idea of working collaboratively with other businesses and individuals in order to increase returns for everyone was highly suspect. Old Power worked like cash. There was only so much, and you tried to hoard it for yourself.

In the digital age, power functions quite differently. The problems we need to solve (the environment, health care, access to technology) are increasingly too complicated for any single organization—even one as big as GE—to go it alone. As authors Jeremy Heimans and Henry Timms wrote, "New power is open, participatory and peer driven. Like water or electricity, it is most forceful when it surges."

The dynamic of Old Power meeting New Power was on the top of my mind as I sat on stage in January 2013 at the beginning of a panel at GE's annual Global Leadership Meeting in Boca Raton. New Power players were on stage with me, and they weren't a very "GE" group: a confident boyish man, dressed all in black and barely into his twenties, named Ben Kaufman; a perpetually upbeat man named David Kidder, just flown in from the Bahamas and completely underdressed because his luggage had been lost, but still wearing his signature blue Buddy Holly glasses; and Phin Barnes, an approachable guy who, with khakis and a polo shirt, was the most "GE normal" of the three, save for his fluorescent-orange sneakers.

Facing us was a sea of people raised on Old Power: a seven-hundred-strong audience of GE execs, a corps of mostly men in golf shirts. It was a delightful powder keg, this combination of established gatekeepers with my ragtag crew of underdressed foreigners, because each inherently did not value the other. My merry lunatics thought the Six Sigma posse was a group of dinosaurs, while the execs who made GE purr didn't value the network power the three misfits represented. They couldn't fathom the one million inventors Ben Kaufman had brought together on his virtual innovation platform, Quirky; nor the community of hugely successful entrepreneurs who had provided the wisdom David had just published in his book *The Startup Playbook*; nor the VC world that stood with Phin as a partner at First Round Capital.

Old Power. New Power. The challenge was not to reject one for the other but to blend new and old, combining more openness and transparency with the kind of leadership and structured mechanisms that create action and accountability. The goal was equal fluency in both. I would come to call people who became "bilingual" *emergent leaders*, and such "bilingual" businesses *adaptive organizations*. It would take some time, and a dose of heartbreak, before I understood exactly what that meant.

I looked into the light at the familiar execs before me. They didn't know the surprise my friends on stage had in store.

I had met David earlier in my career, when we had had lunch at the TED conference. He was running a media technology start-up called Clickable and had published a bestselling series of *Intellectual Devotional* books, and our conversations that year and going forward were just total creator energy. He told me he felt so passionately obliged to share what he and others knew about seeding businesses that he had decided to write *The Startup Playbook*, in which he asked the world's best entrepreneurs two questions: First, What are your selection criteria for picking great ideas? And second—and this one really spoke to me in the context of a big company—What do you do in the first five years so that those ideas don't die? I was so excited, I just blurted out, "I need this knowledge in GE."

Ben was something else entirely.

Ben is incredibly infectious, a great salesperson full of energy. There was something so appealing about his excitement, even when he bragged, "Yeah, I did that in two days." Ben was one of the few people I had ever met who seemed to have a purpose he was trying to deliver on in the world, something that mattered more to him than money. When he would give his impassioned speech about innovation and improving the world with ideas, you could tell he meant it. When someone's authentic, people can just smell it.

The basis of his crowdsourced invention company, Quirky, was that its community of small-time inventors submitted ideas, voted on them, and the winners were turned into products by Quirky's industrial designers and marketers. It epitomized the openness and ecosystem mentality—the "open innovation"—that I wanted inside GE.

In the days after we first met, a year before, Ben just bombarded GE with ideas—Quirky had meticulously aggregated thousands of ideas from its community, including hundreds that related to dishwashers and refrigerators. So not long after, I sent him out to the Appliances division in Louisville, Kentucky. Around that time, Jeff had declared that Appliances was GE's lab for new manufacturing methods.

For Ben's tour of Appliances Park, we paired him with the head of product, a traditional manufacturing exec named Brett. Brett was a good GE guy, talented at getting products out the door, but he and Ben were not a good fit.

"We've got to show you the coolest new thing. We're going to have a sideways hinge on the oven door—something we've been

testing for over a year now. We should have it in production some-
time next year," Brett told Ben.

Ben's response, cocky and rapid-fire as always, was, "Why would
it take that long to test? And now it's going to take almost another
year to go into production? I don't get it."

Brett replied that it would take thirty-six months, and the plant
had been optimized to ship ovens that fit neatly in traditional oven
boxes. "If you can innovate *inside* that 24x46-inch box, I'm all yours,"
he said. "But don't give me anything else. We have constraints, and
it takes time. That's the way you do it at scale."

Ben, who developed products from idea to shelf in twenty-eight
days, lost it. "That's innovation? That's *lame*," he said. "Come on.
You're GE. I'm embarrassed for you."

To start off the Boca panel, Phin spoke eloquently about the need
for investors such as GE to start with early-stage funding as part of
their venture capital (VC) model. He might as well have been speaking Martian.

Then I turned to David.

"So, David, if you could ask our leaders one question," I said,
"what would it be?"

David smiled and squinted, like a parachutist at the plane door.

"Well, the question I'd ask is, 'Jeff, how many $50 million com-
panies did GE launch last year?' I bet the answer is zero. If that's true,
you should be terrified. How is that possible if you have 300,000
people and billions in the bank? How come you're not using GE as a
platform to embed and launch start-ups on a regular basis?"

The room went dead silent as I imagined their collective fury at
me for bringing David there. I had told him to be fearless, but I was
expecting some limits. "Oh well," I told myself, "this is how you
seed change."

"Why don't you tell us how you really feel, David?" I joked, to
lessen the tension.

After we had had a thoughtful chat about the importance of innovating inside the organization—and learning to become *creators*, not just operators—it was Ben's turn. I had told him what I wanted to discuss, so when I nodded to him, he smiled his cockiest grin.

"One of the great pluses of tapping into a community of innovators is speed," I said. "More heads, more ideas, more innovation. But that's hard at scale. So, Ben, let's talk about that: You visited Appliances Park recently. Give me your impression."

"Appliances is innovating, all right. How about those new hinges that will be ready to ship in three years on the same ovens in the same boxes! *Sorry, but there's nothing innovative about that,*" Ben said.

There was a surprised group inhalation from the crowd.

"You might not fear Quirky now, but be afraid," Ben said. "If you think *that* is innovation—'New hinges in 2016!'—I'm going to eventually beat you. Why can't you do a hinge *now*? Hell, why can't you do a new smart oven in a new box a year from now? The whole situation screams opportunity."

We were the last panel of the morning, and after Ben's edgy appearance, we moved to lunch.

"Oh, I hope I didn't offend people," Ben said to me as we unhooked our microphones.

"No, Ben, it was great. Mission accomplished."

As we were walking through the crowd, the head of Appliances, Chip Blankenship, pulled me aside. He was not happy. "That was really rude, totally inappropriate. That little smart-ass doesn't know what he's talking about," he told me, face flushed, well within earshot of Ben. "What was your goal in bringing him here? He doesn't know anything about how to make appliances. Have you seen the stuff he puts out? A five-year-old could make that stuff."

At the same time, there were people in Appliances who instantly loved Ben. One was Kevin Nolan, the CTO, who found me to say, "You know, I like the way that guy thinks; we need more of that."

One of the lessons of that panel was that provocateurs like Ben and David serve as a way to filter who's in from who's not. When pressed like that, people have to choose a side.

The tension continued into the evening. I had placed Ben next to Jeff Immelt at dinner, because I knew Ben would not shy from planting new ideas in Jeff's head.

Ben did not disappoint. Over appetizers, Ben starting filling Jeff's ear about his big plans: "I'm going to launch bigger, more complex products. You look at this stuff today, it's plastic, simple gadgets, but tomorrow it'll be dishwashers. And eventually MRI machines. Get on board, Jeff, or get left behind!"

As bombastic as Ben was, Jeff liked his full dose of the guy: "I just wanted to squeeze his cheeks," Jeff told me afterward, charmed by his boyish pluck. Ben's just immensely passionate, and Jeff was predisposed to listen.

Later, as the event was winding down, Jeff got on stage to say that David's question about $50 million businesses was one of the most important questions he had heard in Boca. A month later, he wrote to all GE shareholders to mention the two most important books he had read in the last year—one was David's *The Startup Playbook* (the other was *The Lean Startup*, as I'll talk about later).

The seeds of change were planted.

When David Kidder shouted his $50 million business query, it forced us to reconcile something very basic—and very scary: Why was new growth still so elusive at GE, a company overloaded with talent, money, expertise, international reach, and scalable leverage? And Ben Kaufman's mockery of our new oven doors made us question our basic standards for innovation: How could the size of an appliance box inhibit new ideas?

We—all of us: GE, the corporate world, the government—were slow, organized into strict hierarchies and silos, and so beset with complicated rules and minimal feedback loops that everybody inside was largely disconnected from everyone outside. There was something in the way we were organized that inherently limited our

In change, people have to find their own path. You can't mandate how that happens. But you can create the right conditions.

agility to respond to our rapidly evolving environment. That limited our ability to adapt.

We had an operating system that produced order—that celebrated and enshrined a way of doing things that had enjoyed a stunning run of century-long economic success based on the industrial operating system (OS)—getting bigger and bigger by optimizing, well, *everything*, and mitigating risk. But we had lost the capacity to create and grow to entrepreneurs, VCs, and the tech-driven agents of New Power. We had misguidedly given up on the new, attempting to buy our way to greatness, by what I call R&D-by-M&A (research and development by merger and acquisition).

Could we become more agile, creative, and adaptive while retaining the very hierarchy and bureaucracy that inhibit such capacities? We needed to upgrade our OS. But how? I wasn't sure. But I knew the first step involved opening GE up and exposing it to more New Power, driven by open, peer-dominated communities.

It would require GE to understand a radically different mind-set based on informal decision-making and self-organization, open-source collaboration, transparency, do-it-yourself "maker" culture, and tolerance for risk-taking and variability.

For 120 years, GE had functioned as a medieval castle with high walls, jealously guarding its talent, resources, and knowledge, and treating outsiders (people, companies, ideas) with deep suspicion. The job I'd assigned myself now was to get GE to not only allow these strangers entry into the castle but to invite them to help tear down the walls, pave over the moats, and connect the castle to a diverse flow of goods and people from other villages the world over.

Party at GE . . . and Everyone's Invited

It started with a simple invitation: "Hello World! We need your help."

In the aftermath of the financial crisis, the venture capitalists who had backed the soaring clean-technology industry had gobs of investments in clean tech that were going south. There was a collective realization in Silicon Valley that new models of energy generation, such as solar, battery storage, and biofuels, would require a lot of capital to scale—and that returns would come much farther down the line than past investments.

While that was true, we knew that clean tech remained essential both for the future of humanity and the future of our business. Those certified products generated $20 billion in annual revenues for us by 2010. In this fervid moment, we created our own high-profile open-innovation event—the GE Ecomagination Challenge.

Along with VC firms Kleiner Perkins, RockPort Capital, Foundation Capital, Emerald Technology Ventures, and Carbon Trust, we launched a contest for outside inventors to submit clean-energy innovations and committed a combined $200 million to fund those picked by our selection committee.

As a stab at open innovation, the challenge was a great success. We had expected a few hundred ideas, but we found ourselves swimming in proposals from entrepreneurs around the world—over four thousand ideas from 150 countries. While not all were good, many were. It forced GE to make the humbling admission that it didn't have all the answers.

We ended up investing $140 million in twenty-three of the startups, and we gave out grants and awards to many more. Some went on to good success—such as Opower, a cloud-based service that tracked residential power usage and created data visualizations for utilities and consumers to save energy; others seemed a bit far out but really captured people's attention, like a plan to pave roadways with solar generating material.

And yet, we struggled with what to do with all the good ideas submitted. Take the solar refrigerator for Africa. Now, it didn't get the temperature very cold, but it really helped reduce food spoilage. It was a lifesaver. But we didn't know how to gauge need or launch a low-cost consumer product in Africa, so no one was willing to invest.

There were hundreds of good ideas like this that made me see the limits of how companies and VCs measure start-ups as investments. Venture investors ask one basic question: How will we exit?— meaning, How will we make a return on the company as it gets sold or acquired in a defined period of time? With that guiding them, VCs, like many people, favor models, people, and outcomes with which they are experienced. I think this is one of the reasons it has been so hard to seed diversity in Silicon Valley.

As the eco challenge went on, it became clear that the real power of the community we were building was not its offerings to us but its ability to collaborate inside itself. Why not connect the solar roadways to a water extraction invention or electric signage? By not

Dabbling

One of the labels I fought at GE was that of "The Dabbler." Jeff would say, "Yes, but that's just dabbling," when we'd talk about one of our open challenges. In other words, "Tell me why this isn't a waste of time." But dabbling is an essential part of the innovation process. It is that early pretesting phase that helps you refine what you seek to experiment with, a way of filtering ideas.

As psychologist Dean Simonton argues, the difference between Bach and his mediocre colleagues is not that he struck out less often, but that he had many more ideas. More ideas, more innovation, and more contact between people lead to more insights, theories, observations, and unplanned connections. To head off the naysayers, however, you have to show that the "dabbles" are part of a broader strategy.

focusing our efforts on harnessing that power, however, we failed the community. As soon as the challenge was over, the agglomeration of big organization and start-up entrepreneurs went away.

Still, I saw real promise in these challenges as cultural catalysts and strategic mechanisms to see things earlier, to generate new ideas, to partner for speed and access, and to share the risk and reward of moving fast into new spaces.

Directed dabbling is what led me to Bre Pettis, a former art teacher from Seattle who started NYC Resistor, a Brooklyn maker space, and also launched the 3-D printing company MakerBot next door. I had been tracking Bre as part of our digital development effort.

I e-mailed Bre to ask if I could simply hang out and watch what he was doing: "I want to understand the new wave of micro-manufacturing, and especially what you are doing with 3-D printing."

Resistor was a higgledy-piggledy series of rooms on the fourth floor of a run-down factory. There Bre introduced me to his "makers" as we walked between workbenches covered with bits of sheet metal and wires and boxes of odds and ends. I saw people making a miniature wind turbine and a portable water purification system. That is, GE kinds of things. One guy was building his own miniature gas turbine, because, well, he could. "Why not?" he said. "People want to live off the grid."

"We could use this ingenuity inside GE," I said out loud.

After NYC Resistor and MakerBot, I met with Shapeways, in Queens, an advanced contract manufacturer where people submitted designs to be 3-D printed for a fee. As we toured the space and talked about the jewelry they made, I saw printed object parts arrayed in a bed of powder—part of the 3-D printing process. I reached in; the first thing I grabbed was a blue, croissant-shaped sex toy.

I laughed, but the point is that what's next always comes from the edge. It's like streaming video: its first use was for porn, not *House of*

Cards. It's easy to let yourself think, "This isn't important." But the center always gets its innovations from the edge.

Sensors, 3-D printers, data science, the melding of physical and digital—I didn't know how it all would work together then, but I knew in my gut that it would lead to a leaner, smarter manufacturing environment.

Now, how would I translate this for GE? How would I bring makers and their networks back to the organization? That is the critical step for the market innovator. The explorer has to make it real for the people back home.

Amid a flurry of activity, along with the help of spark Aaron Dignan (who would go on to serve as a spark for GE for nearly a decade), we initiated two threads of activities: First was to offer engineering teams across GE a 3-D printing machine for each workspace to see what they could do with it. The idea was to enable new creation and provoke new interactions by putting the machines in every department, without any threats or instructions. Just play with it. Use it.

Second, we needed a symbolic maker product as a proof point to capture GE's collective imagination. To this end, Steve Liguori and I set up one more challenge—one that also challenged the expertise of GE's engineers and scientists. (I recall one scientist calling us some version of "the village idiots.")

Until this time, GE had been using 4.5-pound brackets to hold 727 jet engines in place. We had been trying for years to design a lighter bracket to make planes that used our engines more fuel efficient, saving millions in fuel every year. Our engineers and suppliers had gone as far as physics would allow—or so they thought.

So we turned to GrabCAD, an online community of over a million engineers and designers, and laid down another challenge: whoever designed the bracket that cut the most weight while still safely supporting the engine would get a cash prize of $7,000.

It was small money, but the entries poured in, some seven hundred in all. The winner? Arie Kurniawan, a twenty-year-old

Indonesian engineering student who cut the weight by 84 percent, to just under twelve ounces, by using what they call a genetic algorithm. It creates a virtual block of material and then (again, virtually) scrapes out a little bit, and then tests it, and then scrapes out another random bit, and tests it again. It does that a couple of million times, and each time creates a finished bracket based on random scrapes that is tested against the specs for high strength and low weight. It repeats the process over and over again until you end up with a perfect part.

That's the genius of digital manufacturing: we could iterate the most complex products for virtually no cost. As Luana Iorio, who oversaw our research on 3-D printing, told *New York Times* columnist Thomas Friedman, "Complexity is [now] free."

Getting Quirky

Call it intuition, call it pattern recognition, call it a hunch, but I knew that whatever new form of management needed to arise inside GE would at least, in part, be based on cultivating the experiences, skills, and knowledge of entrepreneurship. I didn't know what to call it then. I just went in pursuit of it, starting first in Silicon Valley, then the epicenter of start-up culture.

What I learned about Silicon Valley is that its success does not arise from the genius of a few individuals but from a connected collective that integrates technologies, funding, and ideas from across the spectrum. That requires resisting the pull of rigid, hierarchical order and capitalizing on the collective, chaotic, self-governing intelligence of groups and networks.

That's what we needed to discover as we sought to digitize GE. First I needed to connect, and build GE's and my personal network in Silicon Valley, so I enlisted my old friend Alex Constantinople. After our days working together at NBC and GE, Alex had moved to San Francisco and was now running a communications agency called OutCast. Alex helped me create a map of the key influencers in the Valley. We printed the "map" on poster-sized paper and sat around an OutCast conference table talking about the influencers and the interconnections and the conflicts among them. I can't say enough about the value of such a process to understand an ecosystem. I kept the map on a wall near my desk for a year afterward, and it was instrumental in helping me understand dynamics and helped me set up meetings with the people I'd need to know.

To do this, we grouped key players in areas ranging from venture capital to enterprise software, consumer start-ups, and big tech companies (like Google). We listed media, thought leaders, and upcoming founders of interest, as well as key events as a timeline going forward. We mapped them geographically, by influence (not scientific, more directional) and also to show how they overlapped. For example, who funded whom and where founders previously worked.

I was in search of the innovation magic that happens when you leave your castle and engage with the broader system. It makes way for more collisions of ideas and capabilities, even serendipity. But was there a name for the kind of structure or set of rules that enables such adaptability? And could we engineer our own ecosystem to create more innovation magic and serendipity at scale?

I found answers not in management guides but in the biology books of my college years. Unfortunately, the answer isn't simple. In fact, it is so large that it has become difficult to see. Yet I believe it has urgent implications for everything we do. As our planet-wide digital nervous system grows, it is causing a mass reorganization of people, money, information, and things. That digital information flow has become the main driver of change. And we need new frameworks to understand and anticipate what comes next.

One of those frameworks is known as *emergence*, a term that until recently has been used primarily to explain natural systems—what biologists call complex adaptive systems, systems that can adapt and evolve within a changing environment. Colonies of insects such as

Emergence

Emergence describes how, when individual cells, or birds, or elements interact en masse according to a set of simple rules, highly complex structures and behaviors emerge. The billions of neurons that join together in a brain to create the wonders of consciousness; a flock of ten thousand starlings flying at 40 mph making hairpin turns in an instant; the clusters of tiny circuits on chipboards from which staggering computational power arises—all are examples of simple agents working in concert to become more than the sum of their parts.

In nature, the classic example is ants, which have the most complex social structures after humans. Even though an ant queen doesn't actually give orders and individual ants aren't that intelligent, these creatures manage to build massive structures, dispose of trash, bury their dead, and conduct coordinated maneuvers against their enemies. How? Each individual ant is programmed to respond to changes in its environment by releasing a few simple chemical signals that other ants can sense and to which they can respond.

In both markets and anthills, these patterns of organization are examples of what economist Thomas Schelling called "macrobehavior originating from micromotives." But here's the key point: As more and more human activities flow through digital systems, those activities also take on the properties of adaptive emergent systems. *We are collectively and spontaneously reorganizing around the flow of our digital information.*

The collective micromotives of connected humans are growing new macrostructures. The notion of emer-

gence helped me to understand the extraordinary
growth of the tech titans in Silicon Valley like Google
and Facebook, and the growing power of networks and
communities.

From the micromotives of tens of thousands of entrepreneurs and VCs, a small region in Northern California
has emerged as a world-changing innovation hub. In the
world of organizations, Google, for example, was designed to harness emergence. Its products were released
unfinished and exposed to its vast community of users
whose continual feedback allowed those products to
evolve and grow, and the company to quickly learn and
adapt. There were open-source coding projects, without
any centralized governing body, cocreating the world's
largest knowledge repository, Wikipedia.

Suddenly I could see emergence at work everywhere.
Technology and the digital flow were allowing unimag-
inably large numbers of interactions around common
goals and shared purposes, where serendipity flourished
and human energy (without top-down human control)
drove all kinds of activities, making the kind of innovative and imaginative leaps that were once the sole
province of well-financed corporate and government
laboratories.

Emergence to me is a way to make sense of the new
dynamics of change in a digital world.

ants and bees, for example, use simple rules and networks to produce
adaptive behavior.

How could GE tap into this emergent knowledge and these diverse skills? How could we experience the power of emergence?

Emergent change seems impossible until it happens, at which point it becomes inevitable.

Ben Kaufman and his ant army of inventors seemed like emergence incarnate, and exactly what GE needed.

I had first met Ben through Aaron Dignan. I brought Aaron on one of our committees at the Cooper Hewitt, Smithsonian Design Museum on whose board I served. During one meeting at which we couldn't hear people on the speakerphone, I turned to Aaron and said, "We need a base for the speakerphone, something to stop the vibration." And Aaron replied, "I have a friend who's got this crowdsourced invention company he just started. I'm going to get him to prototype it."

A few weeks later at our next meeting, Aaron showed up with the phone pillow from Ben Kaufman's company. And it worked really well. I hadn't even met Ben, and I was smitten. Here was this guy who was inventing, designing, and *producing* products with fearlessness and speed. I had to get to know him.

So Linda Boff and the marketing team held a contest with Ben's company, Quirky, for products that could be improved by adding software. The product Quirky came up with—Milkmaid, a connected milk jug that told you when your milk was going bad or running out—was fun and grabbed a lot of attention (TechCrunch called it "gorgeous"). This guy had figured out how to innovate faster using crowdsourcing! He had so much to teach GE, I was convinced.

That's how I found myself in Quirky's Chelsea warehouse offices in New York City in late 2012. Ben had taken over an old storage space on Twenty-Eighth Street and Eleventh Avenue. He and I hit it off right away as we walked the floor and saw his team. And Ben had been a fan of GE since he was a kid.

"I love Thomas Edison, Beth. If he were around today, he'd have founded Quirky," Ben said.

From that moment forward, I knew that Ben Kaufman was on to something that we needed, especially in our Appliances division. He was rapidly prototyping and crowdsourcing and turning out new products in a matter of weeks. His company was organized around his network of thousands of amateur inventors, which he had transformed through his passion and oversight into a cohesive community. Quirky's MO was to democratize invention; I felt he was ushering in a new era of innovation. He was the embodiment of what I would come to call an emergent leader. I felt that finding a way to partner and fuse all that he and Quirky represented into GE's industrial operating system, without destroying them in the process, was the massive challenge GE had to solve in order to thrive for the next one hundred years.

Appliances seemed like the perfect starting point. A consumer business that produced refrigerators, washers and dryers, and stoves, the unit was an outlier for industrial GE. Jeff had tried to sell Appliances, but the sale fell through, and we needed a new plan. The consumer brand was solid, but the quality and product set needed an upgrade. And it was a poor fit for the high-tech digital industrial we were becoming. (The Appliances team had tried for nearly five years to figure out a smart home play, where appliances are connected to the Internet, but got mired in technical details.) Realizing that Appliances would have to become better at product quality and manufacturing if it were going to turn a real profit, Jeff committed $1 billion to make it our test bed for advanced manufacturing.

"I need some good ideas for this business," Jeff said to me, and anyone who would listen.

I kept coming back to Ben. Linda and I were talking to him every few weeks, trying to figure out how we could work with Quirky to inject new ideas into GE. At one point, Ben suggested we hire them on a $300,000/month consulting contract. Ben liked to talk crazy money.

I had taken over responsibility for GE's licensing business. I wanted our GE-branded consumer products to be higher quality. I believed products sold under our brand needed to enhance GE's position as a digital innovator. Cheap electric can openers, blenders, and computer cables weren't doing it.

The licensing team's great asset was its access to thousands of patents from our research lab that either weren't being used by GE or had additional potential. So we set on the idea of sharing our patent portfolio with Ben's community.

In April 2013, we announced a partnership with Quirky in which GE would open up two hundred patents to Quirky's community of inventors to create new products or businesses. It was also a good testing ground for a bigger GE/Quirky partnership. Brad Irvine, then president of GE Licensing, was taken with how fast Quirky worked—and with Ben himself. Brad would call me once a week saying, "You're not going to believe what Ben did today." The "amazing Ben Kaufman" would lead an all-nighter with his team and spit out dozens of potential GE-licensed products the next day. Brad sent the sketches to me—and they *were* good!

I found myself thrilled by the energy Ben was bringing. He wasn't perfect—he could be a brash punk who rubbed some people the wrong way. But he was breaking things that needed breaking, something we desperately required.

So I suggested our efforts needed to have a bigger connection to GE's digital future for the products to make sense. We were building the Industrial Internet, but that wasn't relevant or tangible yet to a consumer. Consumers would never see firsthand a GE jet engine that reports its status to an airline's headquarters. "Could we do connected products with Quirky?" I asked. "That might make our digital story more understandable."

"Funny," said Brad. "Ben just sent us some ideas about that."

Brad went to work on a licensed-product agreement. Linda and I were the brand and design champions. And Ben was the Captain of Speed. "We'll have six products in the market by Christmas. It's the only way to make this work," Ben said. "I'll see that we distribute them in Home Depot."

It was summer, and we didn't have even one product. And yet we knew somehow Ben would do it.

I was using Quirky as Exhibit A of what it meant to work within a fast-moving, community-driven culture. Every Thursday night, Quirky held Inventors Night, an Internet product fair with Ben as master of ceremonies. The community would vote on ideas they wanted to see commercialized. The Quirky product team then selected the ones they thought could best be designed and sold, and a panel of judges weighed in. Ben exuded a cocky charm that the community just loved.

All of the Quirky employees attended, and the evening was punctuated with takeout and beer. I brought in any GE leader I could wrangle to watch the show. Mark Little, head of R&D, loved being a judge and helped pave the way for his researchers and Ben to collaborate on a host of possible new products, such as how to redesign a home fuse box or a home generator.

A few months after Quirky and GE inked our connected-product licensing deal, Home Depot agreed to be our exclusive retail outlet. We were on track to deliver our six connected devices in time for Black Friday, the opening of the holiday sales season. Some of the six Home Depot devices ended up being hugely popular, such as the Pivot Power Genius, a smart version of the Pivot Power bendable power strip, and the Spotter, a multipurpose sensor that could signal a range of remote actions, such as if water were leaking in your basement or your baby were waking up in the bassinet.

Others, like the Egg Minder, an egg tray that lets you check the freshness of the eggs in your fridge from your smartphone, were frivolous. We tried to convince ourselves that preventing salmonella was a worthy cause, but it was a dud—and worthy of the ridicule it received. The community had voted that one up, but the community was wrong. What was worse, Ben ordered the production of thousands of the Egg Minders. Everything had to be ten times bigger for him. Those egg trays sat idle in a warehouse. Ultimately you have to have somebody with market and product skills to manage the portfolio.

In these inevitable moments of what seems like "failure" is when the learning happens, and indeed, experiments like the Egg Minders set the stage for GE and Quirky to create something truly innovative: one of the first consumer software platforms for the smart home.

Not long into our partnership, Ben needed to raise another round of investment for Quirky and asked GE to invest. By then, we were already at work on the smart home platform, called Wink, which was far more ambitious than the Egg Minder and other "Quirky by GE" doodads at Home Depot. Ben wanted GE to invest $50 million. I could only get Jeff to agree to $30 million, on the theory that a closer partnership could usher in a new future for GE Appliances.

I brought Jeff to Quirky to seal the deal. He said to Ben, "If you can deliver on the small appliances, then hell, maybe you can run the whole Appliances division."

That was just what Edison Jr. wanted to hear.

There was a madcap burst of activity at the last minute as I led a team to do financial due diligence on Quirky, which had already raised over $100 million. I contacted Scott Weiss, a partner at Andreessen Horowitz—the "hot" VC in Silicon Valley—who headed the Quirky investment. Scott told me Ben was a genius: "He reminds me of a young Steve Jobs." (I should have asked if he knew the young Steve Jobs.)

Appliances CEO Chip Blankenship, as expected, was not a fan of the idea.

"It was bad enough we've had to hang around him. But now we're going to give him money?" he said.

Chip thought Ben was clever, but he also thought that because Quirky only made small consumer items, Ben had little ability to scale big appliances GE-style.

Jeff called the two of us together. "Chip, I think you can learn from Quirky. I like what they're doing," he said. "And frankly, it's the freshest idea we've had for Appliances in a long time. Let's give it a shot."

While Chip hated the idea of joining with Quirky, many others at Appliances were eager to partner on something new. Ben and CTO Kevin Nolan dove in on the small appliances challenge, choosing an air conditioner as the first product. Kevin wanted to work fast and with the community; he loved the new methods he was learning from Ben. He was a good teacher for Quirky as well, helping them understand supply-chain management, and engineering sophisticated technologies at scale. I remember watching Kevin draw out how air conditioners were made—from sheet metal to showroom. Ben, who never went to college but had launched his third start-up by age twenty-one, was soaking it up.

The Aros air conditioner Kevin and Ben began to work on was the first of its kind, an Internet-connected unit that allowed users to control it from a smartphone app that tracked energy usage and made economizing suggestions. It was the perfect encapsulation of what we hoped for from the partnership: the marriage of an algorithm from a Quirky community member—a former U.S. Energy department employee—GE technology and production know-how, and Ben's product-development process. It was a fleeting glimpse of an upgraded OS, an exhilarating validation that GE could become the kind of adaptive organization found in Silicon Valley.

But partnerships are messy. Even the best of them take a lot of work.

Early on, we had assigned a GE Appliances product marketer named Jon as project manager for Quirky, to align expectations and processes. Jon questioned Ben on administrative mistakes—Quirky was not an orderly process-driven organization—and Ben *hated* the oversight. "Jon is hurting us. He is manipulating, unhelpful, and incredibly time-consuming. He adds no value to our process, and requires a ton of babysitting."

Now, I knew none of this to be true in an objective sense, but I had no doubt that, to Ben, Jon's questions seemed like Orwellian surveillance. We asked Jon to be a bit less intrusive but also made it clear to Ben that he would have to accept Jon's presence.

While Ben was the provocateur we needed, it started to become clear that Ben's passion and authenticity and belief in his perpetual rightness would undercut even those who most supported him—like me. For example, there was the Local Motors spat. Eager to continue discovering new models of community-based innovation, I introduced our Appliances team to the founder of Local Motors, a start-up that made open-sourced automobiles. I thought that their community of engineers—many who had worked for major manufacturers—could help Appliances solve their bigger engineering challenges, things outside the Quirky consumer and digital wheelhouse.

A Local Motors partnership was also a way to calm the waters inside Appliances. The Local Motors CEO and cofounder, Jay Rogers, was a veteran of an elite group in the U.S. Marines, and his military sensibility appealed to Chip Blankenship's engineering and process-driven perspective.

We announced in March that we were going to partner with Local Motors to launch a micro-factory to do limited-run manufacturing, and join with Local Motors to build an online community platform called FirstBuild where engineers could contribute to designing new machine-based products faster.

FirstBuild admittedly sounded a lot like Quirky, but its foundation was different, a successful way to merge the "maker" movement I had been pushing with the GE product challenges. It brought together the networks we had experimented with in those open innovation challenges, the flow of product ideas coming in from outside GE's walls, and the fail-fast iterative speed of low-volume manufacturing inherent in 3-D printing.

Of course, Quirky was my bet. But Ben didn't take kindly to my decision to allow Chip to partner with other challengers. "Wonderful!!!" he barked at me sarcastically.

We were partners, working together to make something great; the negativity was frustrating. I could see Ben's point, but I also knew that Quirky's strengths were not in heavy manufacturing—they were in product design, commercialization, and digitization. But Ben was convinced he could do it all. We wanted Quirky's start-up DNA inside our walls, and we were happy to invest in it. But at the same time, we needed to make multiple bets across many industries and sectors.

As a scout and translator of what's next, I couldn't force Chip (or anyone) to embrace a new way. I can surround them with change-makers, harass and harangue them, and call in the boss, but ultimately they have to *want* to change. And to do so, they have to find their own path. You can't mandate how that happens.

The tension with Ben was made even worse by the fact that he wanted to spend a lot of money, especially to launch a new advertising campaign. It became a huge issue, in part because as part of our investment in Quirky, we offered them access to our advertising inventory on NBC, as well as access to our ad agency, BBDO. But Ben wouldn't take any advice. The ad ideas he was getting from the GE team were "NOT CREATIVE!" he said. "Too corporate!"

He finally decided on a campaign from Partners and Spade about how Ben was the "Least Important CEO in the World" because he worked for the community of inventors. But despite the title, it was really all about him. The ads did okay, aided in part by Ben deciding to spend Quirky cash on the creative and asking us to use all $10 million of the media time we had committed (and planned to use over three years). I let him, though I regretted my decision. I'm incredibly disciplined about myself, but ultimately, it was Ben's company.

Despite the friction, however, Quirky's network was offering GE the kind of open innovation it needed. The Aros air conditioner had been successful (although not as much as Ben had hoped, when, after our teams put in the production order, he secretly went back in and tripled it). We expanded the GE scope. Our Lighting group had been trying for a long time to develop an Internet-connected light-bulb, a consumer-grade LED bulb that users could manage with their smartphones and connect to other smart devices. But after five years of work, we had nothing to take to market. Yet within just five months, Ben and his Quirky team had the Link Bulb ready. It was another proof point for Quirky-style rapid prototyping as a way for us to do things cheaper and faster.

The bulb was marvelous, and it, along with Ben's enthusiastic personality, helped us reestablish a relationship with Home Depot, which had dramatically downsized GE Lighting's presence fourteen years earlier in a pricing dispute. They loved Quirky.

Home Depot's embrace of the Internet-connected bulb also helped Quirky and GE push the Wink platform, the smart home system that had spun out of the connective software system we had built for our Egg Minder and which now tied together con-nected appliances—light sensors, the Aros, and a security system we planned—with a kind of central control panel. (This was the kind of connected home platform we had envisioned in the early days of digital health.)

There had been some bumps, but Quirky seemed to be hot. We were creating products, they were getting noticed, Wink was taking off, and people were starting to see the smart, connected home as a coming reality. And then we got a piece of news that made me feel as if we had hit the jackpot.

Quirky was spending a lot making its way forward, so Ben was looking to raise money again. He had done the rounds with a num-ber of VCs and had gotten a term sheet from Japan's SoftBank that defied belief: the terms SoftBank offered would've doubled the val-uation at which we had invested in Quirky less than a year before.

I was feeling incredibly positive about our investment and part-nership, and proud of my decisions. That tingling childlike thrill had converted itself into soaring optimism. I rarely outwardly cel-ebrate successes or show much pride—it went against my nature and, besides, I had seen plenty of "successes" fail. But this time was different. After the SoftBank numbers came in, I went around the halls of GE, virtually high-fiving people. I had a lot of skin in the game on this one. I had particularly felt challenged by the business development VP I had to go through to get the investment done, who was skeptical of Quirky because, as he said, "I don't invest in things I don't understand." (That VP happened to be John Flannery, who took over for Jeff Immelt in 2017 as CEO.)

And then it all started to fall apart.

GE had been trying to sell the Appliances business for five years or so, but we had paused when Jeff decided that we would use it as a laboratory for new manufacturing. Now Appliances looked attractive again. Quite suddenly, our ugly duckling looked more date-worthy, and appliance companies that had turned us down were again looking the unit over.

Ben got wind of Jeff's intentions to sell, so he rifled an e-mail off to Jeff telling him he'd put together a deal and buy the division himself. No matter that he was under thirty and had no major management experience or money of his own. He was Ben Kaufman, dammit.

I talked to Jeff, who was bemused as always at Ben's audacity, and he put a call in to the bankers he knew at J.P. Morgan. It was the longest of long shots, but we knew Ben wouldn't let that bother him. And not long after, in mid-July, Ben's offer actually did come in: J.P. Morgan and some new investors were ready to pay $2.5–3 billion to buy GE Appliances.

A lot of us, Linda and I and Kevin and even Jeff, were rooting for him. But we also knew it was a long shot. Jeff had to make a choice based on the best interests of our shareholders, not what felt right, and a coalition of investors with a twentysomething CEO candidate who wanted to take on loads of debt and leave GE with a minority stake was nothing if not shaky.

So we were prepared for the worst.

In September, Jeff announced that GE was selling Appliances to Electrolux for $3.3 billion. Jeff felt it had become a distraction for GE, and now it seemed like the investments we had made had boosted the division's value. The time was right. The money was right. The buyer was right (though in the end the deal would fall apart on antitrust grounds, and we'd end up selling to Chinese manufacturer Haier for more money).

Ben was crestfallen. We had always said that the Quirky investment was a bet on a model that would help Appliances, giving us a faster, leaner footprint and a new, community-based manufacturing model. Ben had dreamed of being the new face of GE's invention machine. While we understood the numbers behind the deal, the announcement put into question the partnership's entire reason for being.

I had to call Ben to tell him about the sale. There was an eerie silence from him, the guy who always had something to say. It was only when he called me back ten minutes later that he said, "I'm pissed. What does this *mean*? It's all gone? Everything we were building together?"

The announcement of the Appliances sale felt like the beginning of the end. The original investors, including GE, had long questioned Quirky's financial rigor, which was sloppy but not unusual for a company of that stage. To calm them, Ben brought in a new CFO in advance of the SoftBank investment, but the news was worse than we could have expected. Quirky had to restate its financials because they had recorded some of the Wink development funding they got from GE Licensing as revenue, and it turned out that they only had a few months of funding left. Worse, the summer hadn't been as strong as expected and Ben's stealth tripling of the Aros order was now a burden.

SoftBank went away. To stop bleeding money, Ben decided that Quirky had to pivot, which meant closing down the manufacturing bit and concentrating on open-innovation design and consulting.

That's when the board decided to sell the Wink business and use that money to execute the pivot. The existing investors, including GE, were not up for putting in more cash. There was no way I was going to be able to convince anyone to put more in, but I was going to try my damnedest to find enough money to keep Quirky alive.

The good news was that a company called Smart Things, which was one-fifth the size of Wink, had just been sold to Samsung for $200 million. We could trade on the valuation of Wink to capitalize Quirky. Lucky for us, the Wink connected platform had really taken off publicly, and Amazon, Google, and Samsung all began to sniff around. It felt like we had a way out.

Then, suddenly, on a Saturday morning in April 2015, in the midst of the sale negotiations, the Wink software broke. A programmer had typed a 1 instead of a 10 into the security certificate, meaning it would only last for one year instead of ten, and Wink Hubs crashed fifty thousand connected homes. We eventually got most of them back online by creating a self-service fix for customers, but it was a mess. When they heard what happened, the brands that were thinking about buying Wink backed away.

I called our "good buddies" at Home Depot to ask if we could codevelop Wink with them. "We never invest in our suppliers," they said.

I got Jeff to call Jeff Bezos—Ben had been summoned there recently to make a presentation—but Bezos told Immelt that while he liked Ben, he had gotten Quirky too far in debt. His excess optimism had left him deeply in the hole. Most of the venture capitalists were soon to follow. In VC investing, if something is not a sure huge winner, it's a loser.

While Ben kept saying that they were close to a new round of funding and he probably believed it, he was pretty honest in public: at the Fortune Brainstorm conference in June he admitted onstage that Quirky, which had raised some $185 million, was basically out of money. A few weeks later Ben was pushed out, and the company declared bankruptcy.

Most of the VCs never looked back. But for us it was always about more than money. We wanted to do something unique in the world. And we had come close. That's why the pain of failing was so intense, the sadness for people who were losing their jobs so visceral. In the good days, I'd occasionally see a young Quirky designer in my kickboxing class. She'd regularly tell me how much she loved being part of the Quirky brigade. And then she was gone.

The Quirky experience hurt even more than iVillage, because this time I had put the partnership together, I convinced GE to join, I led the initiative. And now it had turned into a fireball. *My* fireball.

The GE finance guys were tough on me. Jeff Bornstein, our CFO, said, "This is a tough hit. We hadn't planned for this this quarter." Neither had I, for any quarter. "This is the problem with these risky ventures, we can't plan on them. We can't have you losing money," Bornstein added. When you've had to tussle with these guys your whole career, that's the last thing you want to hear. It was, in GE terms, a small stumble. But I still felt terrible.

Jeff Immelt was fantastic, though: "We need to try things. And if it fails, we keep moving. Forward." Jeff was beginning to focus more on GE's culture and how to get people to try more things.

Still, I was heartbroken.

Such is the path of the emergent leader. This all can't be done without unrelenting passion and humility. You need the passion to try new things and take great risks, enabling others to do the same. But you also need the humility to realize failure is part of your job and you will be unable to know the answer or predict the outcome. You need, most of all, a kind of faith that amidst all this uncertainty and ambiguity, the next new thing will emerge, eventually.

There were so many lessons in Quirky's demise that it took a long time for me to come to terms with them. I had to face up to the perils of overoptimism for an idea or a person. You can't let your heart get ahead of your brain.

I learned what happens in companies—small or big—when you throw too much money at something before it has the capacity and capability to use it well. It's something we now call *premature scaling*, something we determined to fix. My colleagues hate when I say this, but companies often throw too much money at ideas too early. And teams ask for everything for fear they won't get funding later.

I also learned to think hard about timing. With innovation, we race to be first, but being early is not always a good thing, especially if you're not ready or if you oversell the future. Timing is the difference between being successful and being close.

A final lesson is that good comes out of the bad. There is a return on "failure." First Build has become a much-admired and studied model for new methods of manufacturing, with open-source and small-batch at the core. Kevin Nolan went on to become the president and CEO of GE Appliances (succeeding Chip Blankenship). As for Quirky, while there was less value than we expected in the open community in terms of ideas that could scale, there was good reason to have a community to build early feedback and support. Ben's emergent, fast approach had changed us.

Ben himself regrouped. He and his wife, Nikki, gave birth to a baby, Rocco, and he joined BuzzFeed, creating new products with founder Jonah Peretti. Knowing them both, I think that's a mighty mash-up of brainpower. I know I would work with Ben again. He's good.

Mostly, I learned what it means to be a partner in good times and bad. Partnerships are a necessary part of business and will become even more so. Partners share reward and risk. But partnerships are hard.

One thought gave me real solace: I had set a process in motion to open up to collaboration—and change.

CHAPTER 12

ILLUMINATING THE DARKNESS: A FAINT AND FLICKERING LIGHT

G E's Nela Park campus in East Cleveland, Ohio, was the country's first industrial park. And it must have been a beautiful place in its heyday. Walking through the campus today, you'd think you were visiting a small liberal arts college, with its green lawns and strings of brick-faced buildings that seem like metaphors for higher education. A beautiful fountain sits in the center of the campus, offering the 1,200 engineers and product managers that worked here in its glory days a moment to appreciate the broad, pastoral views.

Inside, the original Norman Rockwell paintings from the 1930s that adorn the walls of the Lighting & Electrical Institute spin stories of the majesty of light and the central role it has played in our culture and the economy. Those paintings always remind me of the light-bulb's powerful symbolism, of the notion of the incandescent bulb as the universal symbol of a bright idea—the "lightbulb moment," the *aha* of discovery. On the industrial park's 125th anniversary, GE dug up one of many time capsules that were planted around the campus, and when one of the hundred-year-old tungsten filament bulbs they retrieved was screwed into a socket, it flickered to life!

Nela Park is the symbolic heart of GE's industrial past; this was the place that made the foundational technology of the era, performing gargantuan-scale feats of engineering on which the conveniences of twentieth-century life depended. Standing in the Lighting In-stitute and closing my eyes, I can almost hear the building whisper, "Progress."

Today, though, Nela Park is a faded artifact of the glory that was. That it abuts one of the most destitute parts of Ohio, East Cleveland, only adds to the somberness of visiting there. East Cleveland is now rampant with neglect, poverty, and crime. It's not unusual for em-ployees to run through red stoplights on their way home, because they fear stopping long enough to get caught in the crossfire. At least one dead body has been found outside our security gate.

GE's tagline in the mid-twentieth century had been "Progress is our most important product," but somewhere along the line, when maximizing shareholder value became the scorecard for success, the game became almost exclusively about how we could make more of what we have today for less. Progress became synonymous with the perpetuation of what we've always done, just a little bit bet-ter, cheaper, faster. These mighty industrial parks, once symbols of infinite American inventiveness, became houses of worship to op-timization. Call it the Optimize Today Operating System, or what David Kidder calls Big-to-Bigger O/S—an entire machine built to grow earnings per share.

Layoffs, spin-offs, outsourcing, off-shoring, reengineering, TQM,

Six Sigma—all these manifestations of the optimize-today approach delivered incredible gains to shareholders, but without always changing a company's long-term earning potential. But, wow, for a time, did GE and its stockholders make money! Until we didn't. Until yesterday's success mattered less and less and tomorrow became more and more uncertain.

This is American enterprise at a crossroads. Having for too long replaced innovation with optimization, tighter financial targets, and efficiencies, this is what it looks like when business dangerously loses touch with the process—and joy—of imagination and discovery. GE had long been the lighting innovator, a market leader. As more companies entered the lightbulb industry, GE lost pricing power and margins shrunk. In optimization, GE got comfortable with a fast-follow strategy, which turned out to be costly in terms of share and long-term profitability. Once it became harder to make a profit at GE Lighting, less money was put into innovation.

GE managers put their efforts into what I call "kicking the can"—squeezing every penny they could out of it, putting all their efforts into cutting costs including by moving factories to China. Let the next guy take on the tough investment challenges. And investors and Wall Street were fine with milking the cash cow until it dried up.

By the time Jeff tried to bundle Appliances and Lighting and sell them together in 2008, no one would touch the pair because Lighting was toxic, the ugly underbelly of an industrial company, with old factories filled with legacy issues, including old equipment and chemicals no longer used today. Whoever bought it would have to pay huge bills for cleaning up mercury used to make the filaments and for closing an international web of factories, some of which were operating at 30 percent capacity. Lighting had, ironically, become a dark place.

Clearly, the all-consuming mastery achieved at optimization came at a substantial cost: a diminishing ability to create and grow new assets. That was clear when David Kidder asked GE's leadership, "How many $50 million companies did you launch last year?" and the audience went silent. We needed to reacquire that capacity we would come to call New-to-Big, and quickly.

I knew where I'd find our teachers. Another framework of mindsets for identifying, validating, and growing ideas had emerged out of that primordial soup of entrepreneurs and venture capitalists in the start-up world. I had experienced firsthand the iterative speed and validated learning that was possible, even when neither the product nor customers were known, with New-to-Big master practitioners like Jason Kilar of Hulu. But did I really feel, in my heart of hearts, that there was a chance the organizational beast could be reborn?

In fact, I very much did.

As elusive as innovation was, I knew it permeated every corner of GE. Every day I was inspired by someone at GE who was working—often against the longest of odds—to create something new. There was a parallel reality inside GE—Edison's reality. And no matter how much we had turned away from our messy laboratory beginnings, there were thousands of people inside GE committing defiant acts of imagination. That was the true flickering light, like that hundred-year-old bulb, and if you looked hard enough, you were destined to find it.

Maybe that's why I felt such a passionate attachment to Lighting. That attachment was made even stronger by the 2012 closing of the GE factory in my hometown of Winchester, Virginia, which was once considered one of the most advanced factories in the company. As I began to poke through the many onion layers of Lighting, looking for these areas of imaginative defiance, I discovered a way forward, a flickering ray of light that could guide us to the future.

In 1962, GE scientist Dr. Nick Holonyak Jr. invented the first practical visible-spectrum LED, a device that GE colleagues at the time called "the magic one," because its light, unlike infrared lasers, was visible to the human eye. In the thirty years that followed, a lot of people tried to crack the code on a white-light LED, without success. Then in the 1990s, having seen progress elsewhere, some clear-minded GE soul realized that LED was the future, offering dramatic energy savings and new opportunities to connect and communicate. So he grabbed permission to make the future happen.

Under his oversight, the LED incubations team moved into a tiny office thirty minutes outside of Nela Park and created a hidden skunk works away from Lighting headquarters. As successive GE executives squeezed as much as possible out of Lighting, they either looked the other way or never knew about the stealth team. This little group kept going—protected by a small core of rebel managers who found a way to stealthily seed the business, hiding it from the hungry GE earnings machine. It was as if these leaders had taken a secret oath to defy "the man" and make the future. They not only developed innovative products but carved out new markets along the way—traffic, signage, display—and put LEDs in places where customers saw (and paid for) value. This team was scrappy, operated with small budgets, and failed fast. Along with their successes, they experienced failures in places they thought they'd win—an LED dock light, an LED jewelry case. But they continued to apply what they learned to new products. By 2009, the GELcore team (as it was now called) was successful enough that it moved back to Nela Park.

I saw the seeds of GE's regeneration in this imaginatively disobedient group, in these rebel engineers who saw the future in LED and wouldn't give up on it.

FastWorks

During my discovery pilgrimages to Silicon Valley and various "maker" spaces, I started hearing a growing buzz about lean innovation methods almost six months before Eric Ries published his book *The Lean Startup*. Eric was a software entrepreneur who, along with

Steve Blank of Stanford, his former teacher, had begun to proselytize that start-ups could be much more successful by taking a lesson from lean manufacturing methods. They created simplified offerings called minimum viable products, or MVPs, that would elicit customer responses quickly, thus offering truly useful information to iterate the offering in what he called a "build-measure-learn" loop.

When I found myself at a party for Eric's book launch in New York, I discovered firsthand what *lean start-up* meant, and I was intrigued. Perhaps this could help us launch more internal start-ups—a quest I had not given up on since launching Imagination Breakthroughs.

In the years since we had begun the Imagination Breakthroughs process, we had continued to coach and help GE teams develop "breakthroughs" by bringing in outside innovators as advisors. I thought Eric's code might be just the thing to evolve our GE DNA forward. And so, after Eric's talk wound down, I introduced myself and asked if he'd be interested in serving as one of those "innovation accelerators." His ideas might just work at GE, I said.

Eric blanched a little when I uttered the letters "GE" and took a thoughtful pause before he replied.

"I'm superskeptical," Eric said. "Does GE have the patience for start-ups? You're hardly what I'd call *lean*."

"We're trying to make GE more entrepreneurial and adaptable—especially as digital starts to come into industry," I said. "And you're going to bring that infection in."

Eric smiled. "Will I have to wear a suit?" he asked.

I knew I had found my spark. I sensed that despite Eric's Silicon Valley roots, GE would eventually take to him because he is, at heart, an engineer. Pre–Silicon Valley he would have gravitated to large firms like GE or Xerox Park, because his response to innovation was that of an engineer. Entrepreneurialism involves imagination and creativity, and his process was putting a framework around imagination in a way that engineers could grasp. To me, *lean* is about iterating imagination—you can start small and scale from a place of strength.

We asked him to take a look at some of our imagination break-throughs, and then in August 2012, I invited Eric to speak at our corporate officers meeting—this is GE's annual "partners meeting," where about 175 of us gather to look at the strategic blueprint for the year. My job was to expose these leaders to new people and thoughts. So I asked Eric to lay out the lean start-up principles to this group, a much different audience from that at the Soho book launch.

Eric is an engaging, approachable speaker who can break down complex theory into bite-sized nuggets, but I could tell he was nervous (he even wore a suit!). He had reason to be, as I could practically see the skeptical thought bubbles over the heads of the GE crowd as Eric talked about lean methods in the context of rewriting fifty lines of software code in a day. The face of the Aviation group's engineering leader was practically shouting, "Okay, Mr. Start-up Smarty Pants, you can do that with software, but you can't do that with complex hardware like a jet engine. We're lucky to get one change order in a year!"

I had known beforehand that there would be immediate resistance, as many GE execs would instinctively doubt Eric's methods could work outside of software. So I had asked Eric to run an in-depth lean start-up session on one GE product after his presentation, a proof point to make "lean" real.

With agreement from then Transportation CEO Lorenzo Simonelli, Power CEO Steve Bolze, and Mark Little, the CTO and head of our Global Research Center, we picked the Series X. The X was a diesel engine project (an Imagination Breakthrough) that was frustrating us because our competition was ahead, and our teams declared they couldn't get a new product out into the market for five more years. The lack of speed was killing us.

We took over a meeting room at Crotonville and filled it with a cross section of engineers, and sales and marketing people from the rail and energy businesses. And with the presence of both their business unit chiefs and a few corporate people, they were nervous.

Eric kicked off the workshop with the first step of his lean process—the leap of faith assumptions.

"What do we actually know versus what have we guessed?" he asked. "What do we know about how this product will work? Who are the customers, and how do we know they will want it? What aspects of the timeline are determined by the laws of physics versus our internal processes?"

The Series X team leaders almost licked their lips as they loaded in the PowerPoint deck. And they presented the approved business case for the Series X, including a revenue forecast showing the engine would make billions a year for GE stretching twenty to thirty years into the future. Like many GE business plans, it represented a hockey-stick graph of revenue growth that climbs to the moon in five years. It's easy to *forecast* exponential growth.

"Raise your hand if you believe this forecast," said Eric.

Everybody raised their hands.

Eric smiled.

"Seriously, who really believes that in the year 2030, you're going to make exactly $16 billion from this engine?"

This time no one raised their hands.

"So, what do we actually know?"

One of the presenters cleared his throat and began to speak, more timid this time. There of course was some uncertainty, he said, because the plan was to build a Series X that was 20 to 30 percent more energy efficient and then use that superiority to convince customers to switch.

"Anything else we should know? Anything else unknown?"

Well, our biggest competitor had a network of franchises that had served as a very successful support system, generating loyal customer relationships.

"Ah," Eric said. "So what's your plan for distribution?"

"Well, we're going to build our own distribution network."

"Do you know how to do that? Have you done it before? And when are you going to do it?"

"After the product is done," the rail presenter said, the absurdity of that claim hitting him as he spoke.

"So, you'll spend five years building a product, and then more time setting up a distribution network, all for a product that by then might have been designed nearly a decade earlier," Eric prodded.

The team didn't have many assumptions by the end of Eric's questioning. But Eric helped break things down by asking the kinds of questions he did, by going after the crazy projections without insulting those who gave them. I could see the team having their *aha* moment: they'd spent all their time focused on technical risks (i.e., "Can this product be built?") and zero on commercial risks (i.e., "*Should* this product be built?").

At this point, Eric made a radical suggestion. "The team has been trying to design for multiple contexts and no single target customer, which creates incredible complexity, and thus gets caught up in budgeting and political constraints," he said. "Right?"

Murmured assents came from around the room.

"So, let's pivot to something else," he said. "Let's target one user and radically simplify the engineering problem. Let's do a minimally viable product, an MVP diesel engine."

The room went wild. "That can't be done!" said one. "You mean, an engine that would crash and burn?" said another. "We're not talking model trains here." Then one made a joke: "Not literally impossible. I could do it by going to our competitor, buying one of their engines, and painting 'GE' over their logo."

Laughter at the silly software boy.

Eric laughed, too. I could tell he was used to this. Not once did he get angry at the mockery and resistance. This is one of the values of a good spark. They can say things that people inside the company couldn't or wouldn't.

"Just listen to me. Let's scrap the multiple contexts and concurrent problems. What part of energy saving is the simplest to solve technically?"

A junior engineer in the corner spoke up when the silence began to elongate. "The power generation. I mean, not the moving parts to the wheels and so forth. Just the power generation."

"Good. And if we were to just concentrate on that," Eric asked, "how much time would we shave off?"

"My guess is we could drop from five years to two," the engineer said.

"That's pretty good. But let's keep going. How long to build the first engine?"

Irritated grumbling rose from the group. "This guy doesn't know the economics of mass production," a production VP said. It was Ben Kaufman and the oven hinges all over again.

"I'm not asking about building a line of engines. I want to know how long to build a single unit."

"A year," the production VP said. "But what's the point?"

"Anyone know a customer who'd buy such a unit, if we solved that technical problem?"

The grumbling about Eric's ignorance of the manufacturing process boiled stronger now, but Eric's new thinking was giving confidence to those who were willing to think in new ways, and a VP spoke up.

"Actually, I've got someone coming into my office every month asking for that, a guy in the marine sector. I'm pretty sure they'd buy it and let us test it with them."

With that, the energy shifted in the room. Now we're going from five years to one year for putting a real product into the hands of a real customer. Momentum started to push the team inexorably forward.

"You know, if you just want to sell one engine, to that one specific customer," said one engineer, "we don't even need to build anything new. We could modify one of our existing products."

Jaws dropped. Everyone stared in disbelief.

It turned out that GE had an engine called the 616 that, with a few adjustments, would meet the specs for power generation called for by the original project. Instantly, this new MVP was an order-of-magnitude faster than the original plan: from five years to six months. In the course of four hours—by asking just a few deceptively simple questions—we had cut a project's cycle time and found a way for the team to learn quickly.

As the workshop began to wind down, a manager who had remained mostly silent decided to speak up: "What is the point," he asked, "of selling just one engine to one customer? We had a project worth billions, and now this tech boy talks for a few hours and we've got a project worth nothing."

Instead of irritation or anger, Eric's face displayed a weird kind of joy, that of a teacher who has gotten his student to understand one side of the coin—perhaps the wrong side, but at least one of them.

"You're right," Eric said. "If we don't need to learn anything, if you believe in this plan and the attendant forecast that we looked at earlier, then what I'm describing is a waste of time. Testing is a distraction from the real work of executing to plan."

The exec looked satisfied. But suddenly others at the meeting spoke up, the executive's peers. "We all agreed we weren't certain about our plan or forecast," they said. They began to discuss all the critical but unanswered questions that could kill the project: What if the customer wants something different than we assumed? What if service and support needs are more difficult to establish? What if . . . ?

"Well, wouldn't it be better to know sooner than later? To test, verify, and iterate?" Eric said.

As we shifted from the hard questioning to insider chatter, the most senior technical leader in the entire company and the most admired among the engineers, research chief Mark Little, spoke up with a comment that startled the entire room.

"I get it now. I am the problem."

He was right. It was not that he was literally the one man impeding GE's progress. But rather, he courageously realized from Eric's questions and the recalcitrant replies they inspired, that he along with every other GE leader would need to acknowledge and embrace their own process of unlearning and renewal if the company was to move faster, learn quicker, and get closer to its customers.

From that day forward, the lesson we used from that session was this: It wasn't that we didn't have the technology or the budget. It was that we had too many internal obstacles that were slowing us down. Some obstacles were just approvals and the need to get many people engaged in the process. And some were mental ones that made people feel they had to do things a certain way. As Mark Little told me as we were walking out of the room that day, what was really important was that it changed the attitude of the team from one of being really scared about making a mistake to being engaged and thoughtful and willing to take a risk, shifting our mental model from fear of creating failures to thinking through how to test our assumptions.

It was emergent management at its best. Once we got Eric into the room and the team of engineers had the right framework for re-thinking assumptions, neither Eric nor I really intervened. We were invisible. The team had to own it and work through it, and they did. One step at a time. Let's get something out there, learn, pivot. It's not going to be a straight line. There is going to be failure. Have faith that together we'll get there.

Maybe the most profound genius of "lean" was that the assumptions people once used as excuses for inertia—i.e., it's not profitable enough—could quickly be dismissed by focusing on a much smaller step. "Let's just test this part of it first." The Big Company mind-set meant GE teams only dreamed in scale. They couldn't imagine that something small could eventually get them to big. But now we were taking the first step toward getting them to dream in a new way by breaking things down into smaller activities, to build, test, and learn as we went forward.

A week later, when we shared this example in our monthly growth review with Jeff, he got excited and we agreed to move those sessions company-wide in an initiative we named FastWorks. We created a cross-functional team of executives to oversee the expansion of the program across disciplines, from engineering to IT, but we especially focused on having marketing and HR lead it, realizing this was about culture change.

"We can do something here," Jeff said, almost giddy. "Can we

Taking Up Residence

As our workplaces become more adaptable, increasingly we will hire practitioners based on finite missions, projects—in other words, for specific "gigs" or what I think of as "residencies" as more of a practitioner than a consultant. The range of expertise, skills, knowledge, and capabilities you can capture is vast. Think in terms of entrepreneurs in residence as well as designers, storytellers, coaches, scientists, activists, and so on.

Give your resident experts wide access. Make them a working part of your team and organization. Set expectations, metrics, intellectual property, and term limits in advance. Be realistic about what the residents can accomplish; give them time to discover and incubate ideas. Encourage your residents to share stories about their experiences inside and outside of the company.

go beyond product scope? Can we use this to go after bureaucracy?" He had been increasingly frustrated at how long it took to get things launched.

We used the diesel engine project as a rallying cry. That it had so many engineers and multiple business leaders extolling the virtues of "lean" gave us confidence we could get the attention of GE's leaders, and soon the business unit heads agreed to tee up other projects. In GE's annual employee survey, a disappointing number of people said we were not responsive to customers, that we had become too inwardly focused, that we reverted to old processes and layered on other processes. We had developed even less appetite for risk and had created "checkers to check checkers."

I tapped Steve Liguori and Viv Goldstein, who had been leading the innovation accelerator, to start training with "lean," one team at a time. Each project was chosen intentionally. We wanted as many early successes as possible and with a range of use-cases, or examples, from IT deployment to new products to legal contracts. It was a new rallying cry for the customer, a huge effort across GE to show that the FastWorks methodology could work company-wide, in any degree of complexity, across any business, and all geographies.

After three months of working with the first group of eight teams, they returned to HQ for an update. It was a disparate group of brave souls, who were doing things that no one in their respective divisions knew about. Their one goal was to see if they could fail fast, fail small, learn, and iterate. And they did.

One of the first eight teams was led by Terri Bresenham in GE Healthcare, who had struggled for years to bring low-cost, high-tech health diagnostics into markets like India, because product decisions were made in Wisconsin. By moving product development from the lab to visits with the mothers of newborns and looking to learn quickly at low cost, Terri switched her unit's focus from "Here's our sophisticated baby warmer and we need to take the cost down," to, "How do we take the typical baby-warmer product into places with

FastWorks

Building on Lean Startup was what we called Fast-Works, a jumping-off point for adaptation across teams, function, and industries. Our goal was to get more innovation faster, but also to get rid of bureaucracy and increase critical thinking across a wider part of the organization. You can tell if a culture is changing by the words people use and the actions they demand. Anytime something became slow or overburdened someone would declare, "Why are you working the old way? We believe in FastWorks here!" Here are the key steps of *Lean Startup* methodology:

1. Name the "leap of faith" assumptions that must be true if a planned product is going to succeed—like, say, that people will accept coffee in a capsule, or a car without a driver. This is a make-or-break question: What must be true for us to continue? What are our riskiest assumptions moving forward? Casting an issue as a HYPOTHESIS gives people a sense of relief from having to have all the answers. Can you challenge yourself to use this standard question often: What is your hypothesis?
   - Among the variations of leap-of-faith assumptions are the *value hypothesis* (Does this deliver value?) and the *growth hypothesis* (Will new customers discover it and buy it?).
2. Create minimum viable product (MVP) experiments to test those assumptions. In other words, create a rough and ready prototype that you try

out on, and develop with, customers. After every one of the hundreds of training sessions we conducted, we gave teams a challenge: What are you going to test and learn when you go to work next Monday? You have to pick ONE project or activity that you think needs a different approach—maybe it's a presentation, product feature, staff meeting. Pick something and experiment a new way.

3. Iterate. That means going through repeated build/test-and-learn cycles with MVPs, asking yourself what's working and what's not. After you validate your learning, use that information and start the loop again. That iterative cycle is called build-measure-learn.

4. Pivot or persevere. You continually use the feedback from the build-measure-learn cycle to assess if your efforts are working. On a regular schedule—every fifteen, thirty, or ninety days—decide whether to pivot from or persevere with the project. It's about adapting the vision to reflect reality. But it also means that if it didn't work, you need to pivot to something else. What can you do that does work? We added digital tools like Survey Monkey for getting feedback, Slack for ongoing team and customer conversations, and consumer 3-D printing for sharing early designs.

5. Beware vanity metrics. These are the numbers teams track that make us feel good and look good, but they don't really indicate sound business traction. Think clicks on a digital ad or positive focus

group feedback that doesn't lead to engagement or sales.

6. Embrace innovation accounting. This concept pushes you to think about measuring what matters most for each stage of development. We had learned this in launching the Imagination Breakthroughs, when managers expected profits and market share before the idea had even been tested by customers. The goal we strived for: learning achieved divided by money spent and resources committed. It can be broken down into a few indicators:

   - Number of products/projects reviewed and in what stage
   - Number of project learnings versus gaps identified
   - Percent of projects with clearly articulated customer value
   - Time to first economic exchange, meaning someone pays something
   - Number of significant pivots based on new customer insights
   - Number of projects canceled and resulting money and time saved. (This became a surprising hit and was a sign that FastWorks was working, as more people sought to kill ideas earlier to redeploy funding on ideas that worked.)

Challenge yourself to see if any of these concepts can be adapted for your team.

no resources—a lightbulb aimed at the baby's skin—and design up from there?" Soon enough, the baby-warmer project scaled and the World Health Organization was coming to Terri for advice.

Another team from Legal found ways to reduce the length of their contracts, in one case cutting two hundred pages down to five, thus shaving weeks off a process. And another, my favorite, was Mike Mahan's Monogram refrigerator team in Appliances. Mike was such a rebel that after the Appliances leadership rejected his project—a French-door refrigerator with no plastic parts—he took it underground. With a team of volunteers who continued to do their day jobs, he decided that they were going to make sixty new fridges to test, using 3-D printed hinges. That project went through eighteen iterations as customers repeatedly rejected it for reasons that ranged from poor lighting to ugly colors. But eventually Mike made enough progress, and the execs were under enough scrutiny to show they were on board with FastWorks, that the fridge was reintroduced as an official project.

There was one commonality among all the participants on the first eight teams—their reaction: "Wow, this is really hard." But it wasn't because of the lean methods; rather, time after time, when they went back into their business, the new ideas were rejected or expelled.

It wasn't any easier at the top of GE. The only thing that was mandated from FastWorks company-wide was that every GE business leadership team had to do a daylong introductory session to it. Eric was on hand for most of those sessions, speaking to teams of GE businesses at Crotonville's "Barn." At one of these, an Appliances executive turned his chair 180 degrees away from the podium and looked out the window to show he wasn't listening. His thought bubble was clear: "Please, not another dopey corporate initiative. We don't have any interest."

It was becoming clear to me that GE needed to redefine and articulate that it was safe for our employees to think and act differently—

What If? (or How to Ask Better Questions)

The best thing to come out of FastWorks was that we brought forward a new way of questioning. Questions that seek to learn, not show how smart the person asking them is. Questions that uncover truths faster. Here are some of my favorite questions that we worked hard to get our leaders to ask.

- Who is the customer and what is the need that you are trying to solve for them?
- What is our strength—i.e., What do we do better than most; our unfair advantage? And if we don't have one, why do we have a shot at winning?
- What did we learn from the experiments we ran?
- What is the business model—i.e., How will we get paid?
- Would you bet your career on this idea/solution/ business?
- Why now?
- Where have you failed? What will you do differently because of it?
- What can I do to help? (This question forces humility as opposed to assuming you already have the answer.)

to iterate, to have hypotheses, to move faster. The focus had to be on how to create the culture that would support this new way of working. We had to rediscover our original entrepreneur's mentality. We were once a start-up. Was it possible to turn GE once again into a 120-plus-year-old start-up?

Until then, the corporate machinery would continue killing ideas—and itself.

Refounding

One year later, twelve months after the Series X first training session, Eric was again called into the annual corporate officers meeting, this time to present our progress with FastWorks.

While FastWorks was sending up green shoots of innovation, Jeff was increasingly impatient. The pressure from investors after years of change and a lethargic stock price was frustrating. He wanted quick results from the initiatives GE was experimenting with—especially one with Fast in its name. In the rollout, we had suffered from a shortage of examples to win people over. The more people were familiar with the concepts—MVP was the one to get the most attention—the more people wanted to engage. But with FastWorks still so small, too many people looked for excuses not to attempt it; I remember one debate with an aviation employee who dismissed the idea by saying, "We don't want our jet engines to be MVP." Fair enough, and rest assured, those engines are honed to top-tier perfection. But certainly you have process and business models beyond the big engines that we can improve, I said.

Eric was taking questions from the audience, offering an honest assessment of our progress and weaknesses, when suddenly Jeff cut him off. "We've got to make this change," he barked. "These problems—our slowness, our checkers checking checkers, our ridiculous development costs—are outrageous and they have to be solved. Now."

He asked for a plan to roll FastWorks out to the entire company. We—FastWorks was now led by a team of marketing and HR—debated him on how systematic to make it. The mandatory Six Sigma training we had everyone go through was still etched in the memories of many. We believed that this time a top-down approach wouldn't work. Employees at the "grassroots" level were aching for more freedom, to test things and move faster. We wanted to change people's mind-sets as much as change the process. So we designed Phase 2 in a more emergent, distributed framework. Sure, we'd go out and train CEOs and senior leaders, but for the most part, we spread this like a virus, building a network of coaches, some from outside GE, but most of them GE managers who had credibility with their peers. They would coach projects and share wins at a local level. What I really was looking for was scalable learning.

Our solution was an internal coaching program that taps into the existing core of people whom the network (*not* the official GE hierarchy) had already identified as hubs of influence and expertise, people who, following the first initial phase of FastWorks, had already expressed a passion and desire for learning and enacting the new way of working. We would *seed* the organization with FastWorks, not drown it with our old style of forced indoctrination.

"But just to be clear, the rollout might take two years," I said.

Jeff shook his head. "Sounds like a great plan, guys," he said. "Only change is, I want it done by the end of this year."

It was already August. To make his impatience clear, Jeff demanded that he be given an ongoing scorecard that showed who hadn't completed the required training. We had a lot of work to do.

There were a lot of problematic projects that could have piqued Jeff's impatience and ire, but there was one that was particularly on his mind: the Durathon battery.

In 2007, we bought a company called Beta R&D, which had a sodium battery that was more durable and could withstand higher temperatures than the current industry standard. And it was longer lasting—five times as long as traditional lithium batteries.

Durathon was reimagined as a storage battery that could replace or supplement backup generators in places with spotty connections, like isolated telecom towers. And that, we learned, would be a huge market: in 2009, when the business group pitched this as an Imagination Breakthrough, they saw the market opportunity at $6 billion by 2020.

So Jeff signed off on it.

"Build it big," Jeff said. "It's like when I was in plastics. The orders will come."

That's why we found ourselves in Schenectady, New York, in July 2012, unveiling a shiny new $100 million Durathon factory, with the promise of a further $70 million investment. To me, it was one of those events that made strikingly clear the GE mentality that anything worth doing was worth doing big, as in *really* big.

We gave tours of the huge factory, showing people how batteries were made and that the factory had plenty of room to grow as this amazing new market developed. But our celebratory demeanor was barely papering over substantial cracks in our plans. A year before, as we had started scouring the world for customers, we realized—oops—that we needed to produce a massive amount of batteries to make this factory economically viable. The problem was, there was no single market segment big enough to accommodate all those batteries. Even in telecom, we had problems. We had failed to consider how long it would take to break the relationships telecom folks had with their old suppliers, even if our technology was superior. They wanted to buy small batches and test, but with our massively scaled factory, small batches weren't economically feasible.

While GE was focused on getting the technology right, we had skipped the larger picture—the system integration, the market, everything—and focused just on our technology. We had invested more than a hundred million dollars thinking the product would solve the problem.

As my concerns spiked, I knew I needed to get outside eyes on Durathon. That's where David Kidder came in. I wanted to get his thoughts over a working lunch of sandwiches and tea. He told me he had been struggling with the bureaucracy of his data-marketing start-up's biggest customer—another hundred-year-old, top-tier company, like GE.

"I could teach big companies a thing or two about doing it the start-up way," he said.

"David, we need what you have. We need a founder's perspective inside GE. We need someone whose first impulse is seeing and proving an opportunity, not executing to scale," I said.

I penciled out a business plan for him to launch a forum to bring start-up wisdom into GE. David wasn't ready to leave his firm, so I managed to sign him up as a coach to help reimagine our operating system, our OS, to be more entrepreneurial. David became Durathon founder Prescott Logan's coach and an advisor to Jeff, Mark Little, and me.

"We should have started smaller—we scaled too much too fast," I said during one of our first Durathon crisis meetings, as David and I huddled with Mark Little and Jeff.

David said out loud, "Premature scaling."

Premature scaling was a common cause of failure at GE. Instead of testing one battery first with one customer to get the use case right, as we had with the Series X, we built a $170 million factory. Worse, we did so on a Beta R&D manufacturing system that had never been operated at scale. It soon broke down, producing defective batteries that underperformed or failed in the field. As Eric Ries often said, you have to "nail it, then scale it." Instead, we went after multiple applications with multiple customers. We had never nailed it with a single customer.

"Don't underestimate our ability to make it right," Jeff said, plainly irritated. "I've been doing this a long time. This is just like when I was in plastics—it's following a similar path. We would build a big factory and then figure out ways to fill it. We can do it."

"But that's the wrong goal," David argued. "The idea isn't to say here's the battery market; we'll take 5 percent of it. A founder has a different view of the world, which is 'How big is the problem?' not 'How big is the market?' Total addressable problem (TAP), not total addressable market (TAM). When you shift a mind-set from TAM to TAP, you're not looking for 5 percent of the marketplace anymore; you want all of it. That's why Uber does so well: They didn't say, 'Can we grab 10 percent of the taxi market?' They said, 'People want an easy way to get things done while they get around.' They saw a mobility and time problem and solved it. Does anyone here actually know what problem the Durathon is supposed to solve?"

David Kidder has a talent for coining catchy terminology. *Total addressable problem* is a powerful way to describe the customer-centric viewpoint I was trying to inculcate inside GE. This was the work of new marketing that I had been pushing for years. Thinking of the problem that needs solving inherently means thinking from the customer's point of view.

"I know the tech is better than anything out there, but do people need these batteries?" I said. "I mean, companies are made of people—and they buy based on what they *need*."

"Like, are the batteries vitamins or painkillers?" David added. "Because if you have to explain why something might help them in the future, it's just a vitamin. Vitamins are nice to have: 'Wouldn't it be great if our customer read our business plan and behaved the way we want them to?' It doesn't happen. But if it stops a pain, if it's a painkiller, that's hugely powerful. That's what they need. And that's what they'll buy."

"We have to sell our way out of this," Jeff said. "Building on Beth's thoughts about the business model, we could partner with that guy from South Africa we talked to. We deliver continuous power—an outcome. Can we charge more for that? Create a service around it?"

"You guys are missing the point," David said, interrupting the discussion. He was able to press issues in a way an insider couldn't. He didn't care about saying the right thing to please the boss.

"We should do that, Jeff, but Durathon has all of its resources focused on selling more batteries," he said. "They are racing to the finish line each quarter. What you are talking about takes time—to test it, get energy usage data, and find a willing customer. On this rapid path to scale, you are out of time." David's words hung in the air.

I knew he was right. We were reverting to the industrial age thinking that had propelled GE for so long.

"We're looking for Durathon—a start-up business—to have the same metrics for success as a hundred-year-old power turbine," I said. "So the team comes in with metrics that look good on paper but make no sense in reality. It's like we're playing at something new, but our roles are from GE's old scripts for success."

"Success theater," David said slowly.

"What kind of theater?" Jeff asked.

"Success theater. Look at how this was set up, how all GE projects get set up," David said, picking up speed. "Some engineer has a great idea. And they're usually great, because GE engineers are the best. Then it goes to the business side, and they do a thousand surveys and make a market estimate. You put those two things together on a PowerPoint, and it becomes the Word of God."

"Come on, it's not that bad," Jeff said.

"Seriously, it is," David answered. "To say, 'This is a failure'— that's dangerous. That's what Elon Musk means when he says that wishful thinking is the enemy."

It was becoming clear as we talked: Success theater, the fear of being wrong, is why big companies like GE are afraid, at some level, to name things as they are. GE saw Durathon as a big business that could only get bigger, but in truth, it was an experimental start-up with significant risks. It was a very GE mentality: we made this commitment, so we have to do it, and if we build it they will come.

With his lean start-up mentality, Eric Ries had helped us create the front half of our new OS, the engineering process of build-measure-learn. But we needed a change in the jury box, in how we chose between freedom and the death penalty when it came to new ideas. It was here that David's experience in the start-up and VC world was helpful, as was that of the venture capitalists I had begun to hire at GE.

During my earlier period of digital discovery, I scouted my way through Silicon Valley, meeting with start-up founders and VCs who might partner with us. VCs are disciplinarians, and I had come to appreciate their laser focus on what would make an idea break out. What I found inspired me to create GE Ventures, and the growth boards we developed to greenlight projects, as a strategic effort. It basically reimagined the VC process for big organizations. It was part venture capital—meaning we'd invest in start-ups to help us get to new ideas earlier—and part growth machine that would work to connect start-ups with the larger GE organization. I called it our *scalerator*, meaning we would be able to scale and accelerate new growth for start-ups, and for us. We used venture investing strategically to see things early and to "de-risk" GE's future with early bets. Start-ups could get money from many sources, but they couldn't get the access to customers and knowledge at the scale that GE had.

By the end of 2017, Ventures had one hundred start-ups in its portfolio, covering everything from software, energy, and health care to advanced manufacturing. Sue Siegel, who had been a venture partner in our Healthymagination open challenge for breast cancer, led and grew the Ventures business for me. She hired impressive VCs—people with experience in companies such as Kleiner Perkins and her old firm Mohr Davidow Ventures—to lead GE's investments. She made sure no next-stage money was allocated before the technology was ready and the start-up leaders were capable of using it wisely to get to the next stage. With her partnership, we would go on to build the growth-acceleration machine I could only imagine in those early days of Imagination Breakthroughs. We would incubate a dozen businesses with outside founders—an immunotherapy business to deliver personalized cancer treatment, an inspection-by-drone business, a consumer-data health company—creating hundreds of millions of dollars of upside for GE. Our biggest leap would be to establish Ventures as market and model R&D. Increasingly, innovation and disruption comes in the form of new business models, not just as a result of new technology.

Sue stood as a strong testament to the value of hiring great, diverse people. For one thing, we rounded each other out. We were both wildly crazy about innovation, and while I tended to go wide in discovery, Sue grounded herself in disciplined questions. She is one of the clearest thinkers I know, and her approach resonated greatly with my GE business-leader colleagues. While I was dramatically imagining it forward, Sue was challenging convention with her questions and offering colleagues clear steps to make it happen. Sue's network of investors and founders was strong in Silicon Valley, and mine was strong in new areas beyond. We worked hard to create incentives and payment structures that would attract entrepreneurs to join GE and to be rewarded for risk taking—giving them a percentage of ownership in a new business or milestone bonuses based on revenue growth. Women and minorities comprised over 60 percent of the staff of GE Ventures, a rare achievement in Silicon Valley and something of which I am very proud. I believed that part of my job was to flood GE with diverse talent, knowing it would not make us just more inventive, but that we would attract more talented people who could see alternate paths of success coming to work for GE.

With the early days of FastWorks, our plan was simple: every ninety days, new projects would be judged by a *growth board* on whether they were meeting their goals, and whether they should be killed, pivoted to a new direction, or given another ninety days to move forward as they were. It was classic VC metered, or milestone-based, funding, in which you fund based on progress. It allows you to kill a project early if you determine it's not succeeding. You are "de-risking" innovation by spending less money on more ideas earlier, and killing off the ones that aren't working. It allows you to move forward with confidence when an idea is ready to scale, and invest accordingly. David Kidder proved particularly helpful as a growth board catalyst—helping us operationalize the process, and as a coach for business leaders, giving them room to test methods and make them their own.

My secondary aim was to remove what I call *entitlement funding*. It's hard to get a project funded in a big company like GE—there are many people who want to weigh in on a seemingly limited funding pool. But it's equally as hard to get it "unfunded." We needed to drop the barrier on both. Innovation without constraints is no blessing. The goal is to think of funding more like an extension of credit—it's only good until you get to the next phase.

With growth boards, we could bankroll more small projects, more "productive failures," to drive a portfolio view of all of GE's products in development. Growth boards are funnels. In the start-up world, only one in fifty ideas makes it; the growth board process makes sure you kill the other forty-nine quickly. If not, they become "zombies"— (another Kidderism)—the walking dead.

Durathon became a zombie. But it didn't have to. It wobbled on for three more years. In 2014, the Durathon plant was idled due to manufacturing trouble; a few months later, GE reassigned most Durathon workers and stopped production. In November 2015, we announced the closure of the Schenectady plant, after investing nearly $200 million.

Durathon was a classic example of what can happen without the lean start-up concepts, the no-idea-before-its-time mentality we were infusing with GE Ventures, and the growth boards' rigor.

Just as we were changing how GE approached innovation, we

How to Organize a Growth Board

A formal growth board serves to deliver discipline around key decisions in funding, testing, allocating resources for projects, and new businesses. I believe growth boards are fundamental to driving innovation in an organization.

Here is the framework for organizing a growth board:

1. Convene a cross-functional group of decision-makers with enough different perspectives to add value; the smaller the group, the better. All decisions are made here; there are no backroom deals.
2. Leverage your core set of questions as projects move through the various stages.
3. Ideas/projects are greenlighted only as they move through each stage, meaning they pass the test for *should versus can*; gaining *traction* is moving from one to many customers; *scale* means that the products work as described and the commercial model is sound and growing.
4. Beware that growth boards don't become overly bureaucratic or that you start adding growth boards beyond where they are useful. In venture capital, Mondays are set aside to convene partners, make funding decisions, and send pitches back for more work or decline them completely. VCs are pitched thousands of ideas a year; only a few dozen are funded.
5. I use this approach for funding any project with my teams, not just for new businesses. For example, when digitizing workflows or our sales

HOW TO RUN A GROWTH BOARD

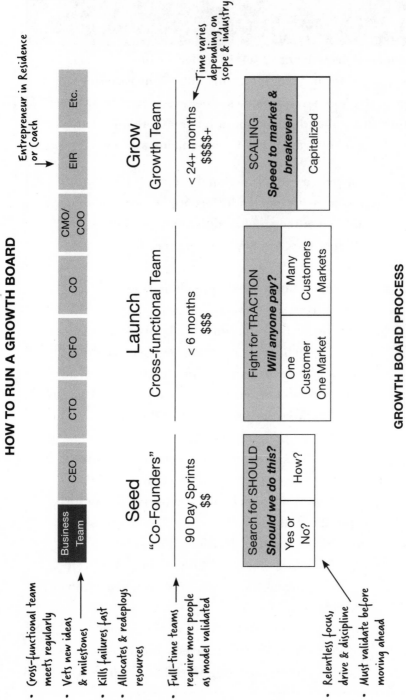

Entrepreneur in Residence or Coach

Business Team	CEO	CTO	CFO	CO	CMO/COO	EIR	Etc.

Seed
"Co-Founders"

90 Day Sprints
$$

- Full-time teams require more people as model validated

Launch
Cross-functional Team

< 6 months
$$$

Grow
Growth Team

< 24+ months
$$$$+

Time varies depending on scope & industry

- Cross-functional team meets regularly
- Vets new ideas & milestones
- Kills failures fast
- Allocates & redeploys resources

Search for SHOULD	
Should we do this?	
Yes or No?	How?

- Relentless focus, drive & discipline
- Must validate before moving ahead

Fight for TRACTION		
Will anyone pay?		
One Customer One Market	Many Customers Markets	

SCALING	
Speed to market & breakeven	
	Capitalized

GROWTH BOARD PROCESS
- Discipline around test & learn
- Capital allocation
- Right people for right stage of development

> teams across GE, I convened a group of com-
> mercial leaders; we agreed to jointly pool our
> resources—budget, people, capabilities—in a way
> that would scale the best ideas fastest. Everyone
> got smarter in the process, and since it was all
> GE's money to begin with, we quickly shed the
> limitations of fighting over budgets and control. I
> wish I could have done this earlier in my career,
> but we needed some examples of success with
> growth boards at GE for people to feel confident it
> would work.

had to change our training and indoctrination system to be something more emergent. The old GE way was command and control,
top down. But we couldn't afford to treat our new OS with the
same mentality, slapping lean start-up and FastWorks and growth
boards in a manual and teaching it only in a classroom. This was
hard stuff, and we needed buy-in. People needed to engage in it to
embrace it.

Certainly, we made sure the top leadership teams in each business
had been immersed in the concepts and understood the critical questions and decision-making processes. We then deputized coaches
within each business unit—sometimes they were people from the
unit who had shown passion and skill at the new OS. Sometimes
they were outside sparks such as Eric, David, and Aaron Dignan and
increasingly other serial founders—entrepreneurs in residence—that
Sue and the Ventures team were able to attract and direct.

Our central teams created a series of communications and best
practice sharing in this community of coaches. Because it was people inside the units teaching one another, it gave those in the process
a sense of agency and a sense of local identity: "This is ours."

The coaches started small, working on the first promising Fast-Works projects with what former President George W. Bush would call the Coalition of the Willing. With every success, we'd further congeal this coalition, and the number of willing would grow. Among the early successes:

- Digital Wind Farm, an effort to maximize wind output via software and no additional capital expenditures. In less than four months, the team created a new business model that was validated by a customer and delivered 20 percent more renewable energy per wind farm and a turnkey solution with a revenue opportunity of $50 billion.
- Circuit-Plus, a global ERP (enterprise resource planning) deployment for GE Lighting that reduced time and money spent.
- GE's Business and General Aviation division's advanced turboprop engine. Developed with FastWorks and an entrepreneurial team, the engine won a big deal from Textron against an incumbent. Time and again, I'd see Aviation as one of the most entrepreneurial divisions in GE.
- Preventing train derailments. Using FastWorks, the GE rail team reached across GE for access to technology that would help prevent storm-related derailments. An MVP was accomplished in ninety days.

In the first year, eighty coaches were trained for almost one hundred global FastWorks projects, exposing almost one thousand GE executives to the methodology. As we expanded FastWorks over the next few years, that number would grow to nearly four hundred coaches and one thousand projects. Eventually, it simply became the way we worked. We even amplifed ways to use FastWorks every day. I loved hearing colleagues say things like, "What's your hypothesis?" or "Let's just MVP this."

The speed and depth of our success with our coaching approach was a major *aha* moment for me. Several simple *tenets* of innovation became clear: First, to build trust you need to stop viewing business units and project teams in terms of hierarchy and more in terms of local guilds or tribes—as communities of practice. Second, the emphasis isn't on providing an answer so much as asking penetrating and probing questions that get people to reflect on the old assumptions and cultural habits that are influencing their thinking.

I wish I had appreciated the role of coaches earlier—master craftsmen and -women who teach their apprentices the craft of imagination-making. Consultants tell you what to do and leave; coaches lean over a business leader's shoulders and advise them: "Good. Good, bad. Right move. Now faster." The coach's role is the essence of emergence—it's about setting a good "mission objective"—giving the teams the freedom to iterate and learn forward. Pretty soon, "mission-based teams" became pervasive across the organizations, with teams shedding hierarchy in pursuit of the outcome.

As we led the rollout of FastWorks, it was clear that GE also needed to get rid of the institutional structures that inhibit these new behaviors. To create new beliefs and encourage new ways to act, we needed to rethink GE's incentives and rewards.

To this end, HR chief Susan Peters and HR FastWorks champion Janice Semper retooled the iconic performance management system—the way success and rewards were measured at GE since the 1970s. People involved in a process that demands productive failure cannot be judged solely by a system that rewards profit margin and punishes imperfection.

Emergent leaders must be rewarded for the productivity of their failures—their idea generation, their pivots, their learnings, their clear-sighted zombie kills—as well as for their major successes. To do this, creating constant feedback loops—and getting rid of annual performance reviews—is absolutely critical. At GE, we moved to ongoing feedback via an app named PD@GE (Performance Development @ GE). Managers now give ongoing feedback to their employees—and vice versa—in a process that holds both account-able to each other and responsible for constant communication and coach-based behavior. Culture needs to be first in mind, not the last thing you do.

By asking the right questions throughout the year, instead of an-nually feeding employees abstract benchmarks to hit, we were piv-oting to an environment that gives permission, encourages candor, and sets up new levels of trust.

I also developed something I called the Culture Club, a multi-level group in my business unit to give me feedback and, more spe-cifically, be a way to drive culture change *together*. I needed our teams to hear directly from me that it was okay to test and learn, and they needed me to hear from them why it wasn't so simple. We met quarterly. I challenged the team to bring me one thing I didn't want to hear—something I or other leaders were doing that stood in the

FailCon: How to Host a Convention of Failure

The Culture Club identified fear of failure as a key issue to tackle. Our employees were good at their jobs, they cared, and they didn't want to let their managers or their teammates down when something went wrong. They were failing at failing forward. So to get over that fear, they created FailCon, a failure convention to cel-ebrate mistakes. Andy Goldberg, our creative director, led the way. We picked one day when everyone, in all of our teams, would share their failures in brown-bag discussions around the globe. I kicked the day off with a video sharing the Quirky failure and saying, "Let this be a testament to successful failure. We tried, we learned. New business got started in GE because of it."

way of meaningful speed and change. I discovered a lot of time and energy was going into keeping reports, meetings, expectations alive that I had long forgotten about. We used these discussions as a way to reset expectations, drive candor, and hold one another accountable for change. Honestly, I wish I had done this much earlier.

It would take years for such ideas to be completely embedded in the company, but by the time the next stage of the rollout had been completed—in time for Jeff's end-of-year deadline—it felt like we were rebooting GE's OS, if not yet its soul. Those who had dismissed my ideas initially now not only accepted that there was value in this shift in our cultural OS—many even embraced it.

Current

In the spring of 2014, I headed west with Jeff for a "deep-dive review" of our digital operations at the GE Software Center in San Ramon. By this point, the home of GE Digital had a team of hundreds of software engineers, coders, and data scientists working on building the software that would surround our big iron machines with data and offer customers new outcomes to run their operations more efficiently.

On the day we arrived, the team was delivering an update on "edge computing"—that is, computing power embedded in sensors and controls that allows computing operations inside industrial hardware as opposed to in the cloud. I got into a lively discussion with one of the center's engineers, Tom DeMaria, who was explaining his excitement about the new wave of computing power that was coming to LED lighting. We were on the same wavelength. I knew it was only a matter of time that we (as in humans) would put amazing computing power anywhere there was a light fixture. Later that year, we planned to launch Link, GE's first Internet-connected LED fixture for the home, developed with Quirky. I was thrilled by the idea of lighting as the connected infrastructure of a home, potentially replacing the need for broadband cable and creating a truly smart home.

"Thank goodness we have a vibrant growing LED business," I said. "The humble lightbulb drives the connected future, right?"

"Sure, that's great," Tom said. "But think about the computing power once the Intels of the world start to focus their computing power on the Internet of Things. I know they're already thinking about it, because we've been sharing our vision with them about the Industrial Internet."

He and I got carried away, riffing about the possibilities in connected buildings and cities.

"With LED-based tech we could report on energy usage and help with energy management."

"Or provide location services. Maybe citywide Wi-Fi. Traffic monitoring and parking optimization."

"And then there's security and safety. It could . . . warn about gas leaks."

"Or look out for terrorism. And that's just the start."

Jeff eyed us with that look of *"Focus here,"* but he also looked intrigued.

I rode with Jeff in the car to Menlo Park, where I asked him to meet with Sue and a few of our portfolio companies. (He always liked those meetings as a place to learn and also as a way to poke the business unit leaders about what they were missing.) "Wouldn't it be funny if the oldest business at GE leads the way for our most advanced effort," I said. "Think about it—we're having a hard time getting people to understand what the Industrial Internet is about. Well, everyone understands lights. Every business and every home. That's why I'm so keen on this connected-home project with Quirky."

"Sure, Beth. But you know we're not a consumer company now," he said.

But Jeff saw enough opportunity here to make me an offer that caught me off guard: Why didn't I oversee GE Lighting?

"I like the spark of imagination you showed with the Quirky connected light project," he said. "You have ideas for what to do with Lighting, and we need to do something different."

In a company as big as GE, Lighting wasn't on many people's minds. It meant a lot emotionally to the brand legacy of the company, but it was relatively small (for GE)—with $3 billion in revenue—and old and declining. But in it, I imagined the future.

In the weeks after, I kept playing thought experiments on how we could put the LED unit on a path to greatness. Despite neglect—and downright hostility early on—the LED had become an almost $1 billion revenue business. Nonetheless, GE wasn't interested in investing in a business that was largely built on a boring commodity, with declining profitability. While LEDs had a much higher price point, they also had a much longer shelf life—years, rather than months. Nonetheless, Lighting had shown the survival instincts of a determined runt. And it had grown the business as if its future lives depended on it.

At the time, I was seeding a skunk works project with the Ventures team to imagine and map the future of energy. We were keen on energy storage as a way to make renewable energy scale—currently there is no affordable way to store excess sun or wind power at night or on cloudy days. But I was obsessed with solar, as we were with software that manages two-way electricity flow from consumers and businesses as they sought to gain more independence by generating their own electricity.

We just knew that a more distributed energy world was going to drive the future, meaning that energy would increasingly be generated not only by centralized utilities, but onsite by businesses and even consumers. This made our utilities customers nervous, especially since their path was fraught with regulation. But we could see the seeds of disruption emerging. A host of start-ups were coming into their own, and with GE Ventures, we were investing and part-nering with many of them—such as STEM, a battery storage start-up run by a former GE marketer.

As our Venture-led incubation took shape, I saw in Lighting's LED-led resurrection a metaphor for reinvention. We would turn Lighting into the next generation energy company for the com-mercial and industrial space. By combining the energy efficiency of LED lighting with solar power and eventually storage capability, we could first save customers 20 to 40 percent on costs. Using software, connected through sensors to the LED fixture—we'd then deliver the future in an "intelligent" network in their stores, factories, and offices onto which other applications could be built and bring all kinds of new value.

The story we created for the new business was simple and reso-nant: deliver unprecedented energy outcomes to our customers and provide them a ubiquitous digital network to run operations more productively. In a large retailer's site, there are towering lampposts throughout the parking lot, and after the sun goes down they light the way for thousands of busy shoppers. But these are no ordinary lamps: they are high-powered LEDs, and embedded inside the lights are dozens of sensors and cameras. These intelligent light posts, well positioned high above the ground, have the ability to monitor and transmit information on available parking spots via a mobile app.

Same for inside the store—hundreds of sensor-embedded LEDs throughout that, in addition to providing energy-efficient lighting, are connected to a larger system that allows the store (from the local manager to the enterprise) to know where inventory is, link consum-ers to available inventory, manage energy usage, track traffic flow in the aisles, and communicate with consumer smartphones for loyalty points and incentives. The store manager may also decide to generate some of his energy with solar panels, and eventually store it on-site.

Best of all, the reinvention of Lighting as an "internal start-up" would allow us to amplify our new OS throughout GE. My dream was to see thousands of employees bringing entrepreneurial skills to work. *Why is this just the domain of Silicon Valley?* It was a new twist on GE's early LED skunk works. Every function needs to be connected to a refounding. It's a continual act. *We could do this.*

We settled on a name for the new Lighting: Current. As in energy. As in what makes light. As in something that was current, now, today. More specifically, it would be "Current, powered by GE." To show that it was a venture, not a division. Its own world. A proud rocket launching off platform GE, with $1 billion of sales as a rocket booster. We thought it was a future-driving name, with a nod to the past. But some employees were skeptical, even scared, as they hadn't yet contemplated a connected, energy future coming from the one-hundred-plus-year-old lighting business.

Now I had to choose a CEO for the business, someone who embodied the emergent, fast, and lean principles of the new GE. That was not going to be simple. What I really wanted to do was to "Hulu" Lighting. I wanted a seasoned entrepreneur with a track record of seeding and launching a new business. I wanted to keep it tethered to Lighting but not constrained by the needs of a company at scale, a legacy company at that.

"Why can't Maryrose lead this?" Jeff asked me.

Maryrose Sylvester was then the CEO of GE Lighting, a skilled operating leader who had grown up in GE. I had watched Maryrose grow her leadership style and impact, from our early days seeding the GE Women's Network, and by now, I had worked with her directly for about a year since taking over responsibility for Lighting in 2014. She had been a champion in growing the LED business to almost $1 billion of annual revenue, but I didn't see her as an entrepreneur; I viewed her as a GE operator.

"One billion dollars in sales! That's what it takes to be a Silicon Valley unicorn," Jeff would say anytime I brought up alternate CEO names from outside of GE. "A unicorn. We have a unicorn right here within GE."

Jeff was right about Maryrose's selling capabilities. I had learned in the year we had worked together that she was a commercial zealot. She also had been steadily transforming the business to LEDs for the past five years, had a good command of the details of the business, and was excellent with customers and channel partners. Maryrose would go *anywhere, anytime* to win a deal.

Maryrose had a more diverse background than many GE business leaders. She had worked in our semiconductor and industrial automation businesses when they were in the portfolio. She had led a global software team. Yet I questioned whether Maryrose had the entrepreneurial tolerance for ambiguity and iteration or the passion to excite her teams toward a new future. Her style was understated, her methods precise. She led her team well and they liked her, but they hadn't been tested beyond what they knew. Selling new LEDs to existing channels was a start, but now we were suggesting more change—a new business that would go beyond light fixtures to include solar and energy storage, along with software so that the LEDs could connect to the Internet and host a range of applications from in-store location positioning to energy efficiency. Eventually, Current could become a virtual power provider and help manage electricity flows between business and utilities. To get business on board, Maryrose and the team would now have to call on new decision-makers—CIOs, CFOs, and CEOs—and not with an existing product or a solution but with untested and unproven offers built on energy savings, shared cost savings, and new applications. In many ways, this mirrored GE's broader challenge with digital.

Now my challenge was even clearer: not just to launch a start-up from GE's oldest business but to encourage an established leader and her tactical operating team to be entrepreneurial. This was a living, breathing FastWorks challenge. At scale. Premature or otherwise, this was now mine.

I broached the idea to her that we were going to separate Current from the consumer business and now she'd be running only the future-proofing business under the Current brand. Her CFO, Bill Lacey, would now be CEO of the old consumer lighting, as a separate division.

"But Current is small," she said. "Look, I believe in the vision. I do. But I know how to run the whole business. And that's what I thought you wanted me to do?"

"Yes, you are a great operator. But we need to focus," I explained. "We need to keep the legacy from getting in the way of Current's future. If we do this well, we're creating a whole new life and value not just for Lighting, but for GE. How can you focus on growing the new if you're worried about old factories and whether we win more share at Home Depot?"

"It's just that there are many synergies and reasons to keep the lighting businesses all together. I need access to the manufacturing plants and the sales from all the global regions—we share talent and technology. Now we're funding Current from the consumer business profits." she said. "All of this works together."

Many of our GE business peers measured their standing in the organization by the size of the P&L statement—by how much revenue and especially by how much profit they gave back to the ever-hungrier operating machine. Now Maryrose had a job where there were no profits to fund the future—in other words, a classic start-up play, where losses are immaterial in the face of the land grab, the installation of a customer base. We were to be dependent on corporate funding and short-term financial scrutiny in addition to taking on something that wasn't proven. This made her nervous.

It made me nervous, too.

You see, the stakes were higher for me now as well. In mid-August 2015, Jeff called me to his office right after our usual two-week vacation break. New staff changes happen then—I called this Jeff's reflective time of the year, because he always came back from vacation with pages of handwritten notes that we had to decipher (he has the worst handwriting), capturing his ideas for projects or areas of focus. And this being August, I went in with my list of the thoughtful things to discuss, knowing that his mind would be particularly open then. (I have finally learned that timing is critical—and often overlooked—in having your ideas understood.) After the usual niceties about vacation, he said something I wasn't expecting.

"I'm making you a vice chairman. I've taken this to the board, and we're good to go."

"Wow. That's a big deal," I said.

Surprised but acting cool, taking it all in. Sometimes I'd get a heads-up from HR about things being considered for me. But not this time, which was odd because earlier that year I had talked seriously to HR head Susan Peters, saying that I thought it was time for me to leave GE at the end of 2015. I was feeling I had reached the end of the road there, and frankly, I was tired of pushing the change and innovation boulder up an ever steeper incline.

But it *is* a big deal, being named a vice chair at GE. It was symbolic in that it represented a capstone to a GE career for me, but also because it symbolized what themes were becoming important to GE. Growth and innovation were being recognized. Marketing—the new kind, the outside in, discovery-minded kind—was being recognized. And I was the first woman to hold the role ever.

"We need the work you do here. I like what you're doing with Ventures and making progress with Lighting. Current is a good idea. We have to do more of these. The GE brand is in great shape. FastWorks is important—we need your help more than ever," Jeff said. "Please help me change the place. Digital industrial and outcome selling—we have to make these real. The culture simply has to move faster. I need you to keep pushing."

There was an urgency to his voice. It was not the laid-back Jeff I knew. There was still work for me to do. Ever loyal, I was back in. Later that night, I sent Jeff an e-mail, now that things were sinking in: "Thanks for the support. This means a lot to me." He responded, "Feel good for a minute. And then help us change! Faster. We need this."

In October 2015, we launched Current with great fanfare. Our oldest business gave birth to our youngest. Maryrose and the team were energized by the market reaction, and big, new leads were coming in. She agreed to locate Current in Boston—a city we chose because of the entrepreneurial talent. Ground zero was a collaborative worktable in a shared workspace where the core leadership team sat—about a dozen of them, with others remaining in Nela Park, San Ramon, and Schenectady (Solar's headquarters).

Sing It

I believe that symbolic acts matter. Whether you are leading a project, a team, or a company, you need to take visible actions to show you are seriously committed to the cause. One of my favorite examples came from Bill Lacey, the CEO of GE Lighting. He was dealt a tough hand in running the simplified consumer business, yet he managed it, while continuing to fund smart-home technologies and pushing for new growth. He wanted to win the Lowe's account badly. Not only would it increase revenues but it would cap a so far unsuccessful, twenty-year effort to gain a major presence in their stores. Bill needed everyone in the organization to work toward this goal. So he enlisted the help of Katy Perry. Bill told his colleagues that Katy Perry's "Fight Song" inspired him to win the deal. So he asked employees to share their favorite fight song, creating a playlist to motivate everyone on the team. Every time someone walked into the building, a new song would play, reminding employees of the goal they were all working toward.

What's your fight song?

Soon after we picked Boston, GE announced it was moving the headquarters out of Connecticut to none other than . . . Boston. With the act of selling off GE Capital, announced in 2015, Boston represented a fresh start and a visible sign that a new GE was emerging—more open and collaborative, one ready to be part of a vibrant ecosystem of universities and start-ups. For the Current team, it was like your parents announcing they are following you to college.

But then 2016 would prove to be a tough year. Tough times always come. These are when you are sorry that you announced an idea to great fanfare—you get customers you desperately need, but you also raise expectations.

We kicked off the year with a team meeting to remind everyone of the vision. We'd had such momentum ending 2015—a GE darling, industry buzz, interest from customers and employees from across GE and the energy sector who wanted to join the Current team. Maryrose took to the front of the room. She was talking fast and softly. Everyone leaned forward to hear her. She was fading away, as if the enormity of what we were trying to do hit her just at that moment. The vision was on mute.

I spent a lot of time talking to her about owning the vision, telling the story, asking what help she needed.

Current had very aggressive sales targets—this was GE, and we had set a stretch target of $5 billion in revenue by 2021. Our confidence was high, and perhaps, we were high on it. We projected 60 percent growth based on continued strong sales in LED (they had grown at over 50 percent over the past few years). We expected that we'd close a big deal with J.P. Morgan Chase. Heck, Jaime, our sales leader, was a West Point grad with the confidence and charisma to lead troops into battle and new markets.

But the targets hadn't been wishful assumption, and a big part of the sales plan—what we called the "whale strategy"—was to spend our time hunting the megadeals like J.P. Morgan Chase that would give us a huge installed LED base in bank branches, and then upsell them on other capabilities like solar and, ultimately, software and services that gave ongoing revenue. The team had little experience selling these deals and assumed they would close more quickly than the twelve to fifteen months it really takes. At one level, it was an issue of split motivations: we still had the LED machine running full on, bringing in sales through channel partners. And this is where the team kept much of their energies, because it was what they knew. It felt good to see revenue flowing in. Big deals required more strategy, planning, partnership, and patience; they were hard.

To follow the new OS, we surrounded Maryrose with aides: David Kidder set up her growth board; Aaron Dignan coached her on culture; and we brought in an entrepreneur in residence, Erik Straser, as the master guildsman. He had run several energy start-ups and been a venture capitalist with Sue.

Despite the help, things started to wobble early on. We were trying to do too much. We still carried some of the "build it big and they will come" mentality—especially for our offering for cities, which in a year had ballooned with hardware feature creep, burning cash that we increasingly didn't have.

For the first year of our new life, we projected about a $35 million loss for the business, with additional new revenue of over $200 million. GE Corporate was covering the loss as part of "growth funding"—a mechanism we had put in place to seed Imagination Breakthroughs and other big bets. I think these mechanisms are important to have as a way of seeding possibility with discipline. By the end of the first quarter, the projections proved wrong. Sales had not moved as fast as we had planned—we needed time to build a pipeline and the sales were complicated. We had hired too many salespeople ahead of developing a clear offer, once again scaling prematurely.

Most worrying, the problems were cultural OS problems, which are the most resistant to change. Here's the thing: people say they want to behave like a start-up, but the old behaviors often return, especially in moments of stress. Erik, as our resident coach, was a sounding board for Maryrose and a commercial sensei for the sales team. He saw his role as helping the team get to a viable commercial model—getting them from one customer to many. Maryrose brought on board Bruce Stewart, a skilled marketer who came with energy and start-up experience. He brought a relentless drive to segment customers and hone value propositions. He led the *test company* and *scale company* approach—first assigning a small team to test and validate new commercial models, and once greenlighted, moving projects to the scale team, which was incentivized to sell and make bigger, faster. But people kept going back to what made them comfortable. Current's new MO demanded open communication, but many people, when asked about their worries, would say, "I got it." They never asked for help, never let anyone see them sweat. This phrase "We've got this" requires special attention—and a good "BS" detector. If it means "We're making progress, give us time to figure it out" or "We'll ask for help when we need it," then encourage the team to keep going. In my experience, "We've got this" can also come laden with arrogance, a way of saying "We don't need help because we know the answers." If that is what is meant, watch out.

Worse, I found out sales was turning down deals because the margins weren't good enough. "We don't take anything under 25 percent," Jaime said, shrugging. He just wasn't interested in going from selling a thing (money now!) to selling a service (more money over time!).

Maryrose panicked. She had violated the first rule of GE: never surprise with financials. I had said to her, "Your job is to grab land, as much as you can; we're measuring you on top line, not profit." But it was hard for her to adjust, as deeply programmed as she was to deliver. Her DNA kicked in: Her first call was to GE's CFO, not to me. She was asking for forgiveness. I was frustrated.

Originally, the agreement was to have limited HQ reviews and instead use our growth board to make big decisions. But behaviors are hard to break, and once we missed our sales forecast, the team was forced into the standard GE operating rhythms for a fully scaled business. This was a bad turn, because we needed to move under the radar and use start-up metrics. The beast again was attempting to eat its young.

Would it even be possible to change GE's OS? And was I cut out for this? I truly believed I was, but at moments like this, my insecurities come out. Had I taken on a losing proposition? Had I pushed a strategy before its time? Were we destined to fail?

The calendar gave us a welcomed respite. During the second quarter, the business rebounded and came closer to meeting our financial plan, meaning that some of the urgency wore off. Maryrose was convinced we would have a strong second-half recovery. There were also some signs that offered optimism. But then, the third quarter brought an August break and weeks of lower intensity. Maryrose called me desperately to say that sales had missed by a long shot and that we were going to have a huge loss.

"We're another $35 million short. I don't know how, but the sales just . . . didn't happen."

It wasn't a huge number for a company like GE, but it was huge in the fact that it was unexpected. We missed; we didn't sell what we had committed to. We also had higher-than-planned costs for developing our storage and solar solutions. Our internal credibility was frayed. I spent the weekend alternating between freaking out, beating myself up, and mapping out an action plan. I created a set of new recommendations for Jeff. I had been planning all along to seek an outside investor for Current as a way to validate our model—and with the added benefit of giving us additional funding, of hedging our risk. And I knew Jeff was keen to sell the consumer-lighting unit, so selling it sooner could present other funding options.

By the end of the weekend, I had beaten myself up enough and was actually now pissed. Here was a 140-year-old business that had been driven to the end of its life, with little additional investment, and we were actually trying to do something with it. So what *exactly* was our fault? Were we the only ones who had been naïve enough or stupid enough to suggest a potential upside? Was I perpetuating magical thinking by endorsing our outrageous targets? No. We were among the GE few who were actually taking the risks needed.

I had asked for time with Jeff on Monday morning to review potential options. As I walked in, I saw the stance he had chosen: staid, impenetrable, tough. It was like being called into the principal's office. As I laid out my suggestions to sell old Lighting and take on investors into new Current, Jeff shrugged, like I was missing the point.

"I'd be thrilled to sell the old consumer lighting business, assuming anyone wants it," he said. "But no for outside investors. We need to project some strength. You need to make this work, Beth. Listen, your business let the company down, and potentially could cause everyone to miss their incentive plan. Keep your eye on the ball. You need to be more in command of the details."

"Jeff, I know," I said. "But I can't change a 140-year-old business overnight. We're all stretched tight, there's little room for error. I can't guarantee predictability with new business models. We didn't lose $35 million we never had. Our assumptions were too aggressive—assumptions everyone signed up for, mind you. We're learning a new space."

"Beth, I just need people to do what they say they will."

"But we've never done this before. Shouldn't we have more wiggle room, a little patience?"

Jeff shook his head. "Just fix it."

And then, when all seemed dark, when the "stink of fail" followed us into every meeting (when people don't sit near you as if you smell bad, when you think they won't look you in the eye, when they virtually stamp "Failure" on your forehead, when you think this isn't going to ever work out), things started to turn. Not immediately, not with sudden clarity, but it began. Rays of light here, a sprout there, and then the realization of undeniable improvement.

The need for clarity and focus seized us. We quickly moved to shed things that stood in our way, getting out of regional markets that were barely big enough to cover costs. Speed and focus became the goal. Our clunky cities play made way for a smart licensed partnership with AT&T, keeping us in the space but with less risk. Solar finally broke even, but storage was too far off and got sent back to the R&D labs for more development. This was disappointing because everyone knew this is what gets us to the final leg of the strategy. What's more, we all had enough evidence now to believe Current could be a virtual power provider one day. But we understood the reality. Focus had to be the mantra.

The team began to convert the projects in our pipeline. There were major sales to J.P. Morgan Chase, Sainsbury's, Simon Property Group, Hilton Hotels, Home Depot, and Walmart. The city of San Diego began to install a smart system. Maryrose was fired up, leading the team through cleaning up the old and launching the new.

We began to set more realistic and less rigid goals. We were pacing well on revenue, marching toward profitability, and proving that there are multiple customers.

Just as important, our leaders transformed, or if they couldn't, they had to leave. Jaime moved on, and Deron Miller, the new head of sales, was blessed with the rare experience of knowing how to sell both hardware and software. He loves coaching salespeople and consulting customers. More new people joined with expertise in developing digital products.

An inner courage came out in Maryrose, giving her a boldness I had not seen before. She owned this. She wanted to be here. She shed the consistent industrial mentality and stepped up as the adaptable leader she likely always was. She opened up to new ways of working. For example, she and her team regularly tested what customers will pay for and didn't just stand beholden to feature creep (light poles with gas leak detectors!) and unrealistic plans. An entrepreneurial leader and team emerged. It was a wonder to see. Refounding was happening before our eyes.

We kicked off 2017 with a meeting between Maryrose, Jeff, and me, and Maryrose laid out Current's future with a vigor I had never seen from her. It had been almost exactly one year since Current had seemed to bottom out. Jeff was relaxed this time, smiling his easygoing grin. He looked at Maryrose's page of numbers—not her projections, but her accomplishments.

"Wow," he says. "What a difference a year makes. You have done a great job."

"Yes, this team has transformed themselves," I said. "They really own this business. And I couldn't be more proud."

Maryrose offered up a sneaky smile. "Don't worry, Jeff," she said. "We got this."

And we all laughed. But the relief was palpable. This team was intent on making the future.

And so, as GE opened up more to change, the culture changed, too. We were becoming more entrepreneurial, willing to take more, smaller risks. We imagine, we act, we emerge.

You Are Not a Robot

When I had left Jeff's office in the darkest moment of Current, I had rushed to GE's Crotonville center, where I was to do my leadership talk with new managers. Each month, I spoke to recently promoted leaders about growth and culture at GE—both good and bad; about leadership lessons learned; and about how to adopt a discovery mind-set that seeks to imagine what's next and go see for yourself. As an outside-thinking, creatively driven person, besides being one of the few women at the top (I don't single out GE for this; they've done better than most), I brought a different viewpoint from other leaders.

That day, however, I was feeling particularly disappointed and upset. I am usually nervous before these discussions, even after all these years, but I was especially so on that day. I almost turned to leave, running through the excuses I could use to reschedule. But I didn't. I found my inner resolve, as always, took a deep breath, and stepped through the door to the auditorium-style room called "the pit." I was reminded that these were new managers, eager to learn and be better. Just like me.

I walked to the front of the classroom and fumbled with the computer, looking for the canned pages I had delivered a thousand times before. But then I stopped. That wouldn't do today. Something about the last couple of months just made me want to put it all out there. I was in no mood for niceties or success theater. As I looked out at their expectant faces, a silence fell over the room. They sensed almost immediately that they were in for something different.

I turned to the whiteboard behind me and started drawing a rectangular box with a much smaller checkbox inside of it, adjacent to which I wrote the sentence "I am not a robot." It was my rendering of the online "captcha" prompt that comes up when you, say, register for a newsletter or buy tickets for an event. I turned and finally started to speak:

Are you a robot?

Sure, I believe you're all humans at home. But you're here now, at work, and so I'm not so sure. And you shouldn't be either.

You ask, why? Because the machines we use shape how we think and behave. Corporations, particularly big organizations like GE, were created to function as machines. It's no accident that over time workers were referred to as cogs; unthinking, tirelessly compliant parts were the ideal employee. The very things that make you

human—your independence, your creativity, your spontaneity—
were suboptimal glitches in the system. As the management theorist
Gary Hamel says, "One doesn't have to be a Marxist to be awed
by the scale and success of early-20th-century efforts to transform
strong-willed human beings into docile employees." And now that
real robots have entered the picture, they can do all the things we did
as cogs, just much better and much faster. And they don't complain.

I suppose, then, the question really is: Just how human do you re-
main? I want you to answer that by interrogating what you believe.
Machines have no capacity for belief. So, do you believe tomorrow
can be better than today? Do you believe you have the power to
make it so? Those are the two questions that will determine your
future, and GE's.

What do such questions make you feel? Machines can't feel, either. So, do you fear that you might be inadequate to the challenge
of change that a better tomorrow implies? Or do you feel passion for
a vision you already have? I still feel both almost daily.

To be human today means living in a world in which almost
every day brings some sort of massive disturbance. Unknown un-
knowns lurking everywhere. Competitors arise out of nowhere.
Customers suddenly demand new solutions. The pace of change is
never going to be slower than today. Think about that. The pace of
change is never going to be slower than today. Change happens but
our responsibility is to shape it, adapt to it, and make it work for us.
There is no robot, no algorithm, capable of such adaptation. Yet.

There are challenges out there that threaten our survival, and
you can respond in one of two ways: either you'll open yourself up
and respond to the challenges creatively, using your imagination to
conjure something that doesn't exist today; or, you'll arrogantly assume the sufficiency of your competence—that is, the reliable processes you've always used to solve the problems you've always had.
The first move is messy, human, chaotic, forcing you to imagine a
new way forward, try things, admit mistakes, fail, learn, iterate, try

The pace of change is never going to be slower than it is today.

again. Down that path, with no guarantees, is the possibility of re-newal. The second option offers only eventual irrelevance.

I understand. You thought your competence and credentials were enough, so why rock the boat when rocking it implies new ideas and approaches that only threaten to make you less competent? You might look bad. You thought there was a formula. They basi-cally said as much in business or engineering school, right? Well, there is, and there isn't.

It would be a mistake to say that the system in place, the old OS, doesn't work. It works incredibly well. It generates and optimizes what we can measure. Unfortunately, the innovative things we ur-gently need to create, and the innovative way we need to work to make that happen, are not things and ways that can be measured in the same way.

The old metrics and new algorithms can't help us here. What we need is to imagine different, be different, do different. This is what I know as a marketer: being different gets a better price and more loyalty. This is what I know from my early studies in biology: being different paves the way for adaptation. This is what I know from my experience: taking the jobs and assignments that were unexpected or undervalued, showing up in unexpected places and getting to know people who at face value were too different—these do lead to suc-cess. It takes courage to act on instinct and not wait for ever more data to tell you what to do. It takes courage to see patterns and then use the data to validate, rather than the other way around.

That feeling you're feeling—that's fear. Fear of failure. It's easier to play it safe. Why do we need such a radical departure from what we've always done? Why not just aim to get a bit better? That doubt-ing voice in your head about all the dramatic difference I'm asking from you—that's why we're still not responding to change with the speed that's necessary. The rewards will go to those who stand up and stand out, taking what feel like unreasonable chances.

Who here feels empowered to do that—to stand up for an idea

you believe in? A few of you are raising your hands. Why not the rest of you? Who are you waiting for to tell you it's okay? Your boss? Jeff Immelt? Your mother? *Yoda?*

Don't tell me you're not empowered. There is power that is yours. Use it. Grab your own permission. No one is going to give it to you.

I don't know many of you, but I think some of you fear power. Have you thought of that? It's easier to let it be someone else's issue, someone else's decision, someone else's harebrained idea.

What if you really fear your imagination, or you fear taking a chance on it? Can you learn to conquer such fears, and take such risks? Of course you can; I did.

I was younger than all of you when I failed on a scale GE could appreciate. For the first two decades or so of my life, I did everything everybody told me. I obeyed all the rules. I got good grades, good internships. I married the perfect man, and we bought the perfect little house. I was, you might say, competent at life. It just wasn't a life I wanted to be living. If I had gone the "bit better" route, I'd still be living it.

Then, just like that, I was divorced, a single mom, with uncertain prospects. I had failed, or maybe the better way to put it is I found the nerve to be considered a failure so that I could chart my own way through unexplored territory, leaving the previously known behind. I discovered something then that opened life and work up for me—the mistakes you rectify and learn from will give you more freedom and progress and ultimately even wealth than the mediocrity you can be certain of by living and working mistake-free. You don't just live a life; you blunder your way toward creating one you love. You don't just submissively work in a company you tolerate; you agitate, sometimes rebelliously, to craft it into something great.

Of course there's a cost. Do you know where I was just before coming to this room? I was in Jeff Immelt's office. He told me that shaving my head wasn't a feasible punishment, and besides, it wouldn't

You don't just live a life; you blunder your way toward creating one you love.

really make amends for jeopardizing our bonuses. Current, the outcome of precisely the kind of imaginative leaps I'm asking you to take, will fall short of its quarterly target by $35 million, and counting. I don't need to tell you, my GE colleagues, why I initially would have preferred crying in my car now than talking to all of you.

I could give you a lot of excuses right now. I could tell you it's damn near impossible to start something like Current in an environment driven by the next quarterly report. The possibility of some innovative new business model making money is just that—a mere possibility whose chances for success are imperiled by a system that demands the certainty of short-term gains. Let me tell you, it's hard to explain to investors that if failure is not an option, then neither is success. These are the same people who scoffed at Ecomagination a dozen years ago and now demand to know why we're not even bigger in renewable energy, now that solar is growing three times faster than even the optimists projected.

But it's too easy to blame investors for organizations not taking risk and not being willing to fail. Sure, they can squeeze the life out of your future, if you let them. But they give us money so that we can grow and invest, and our obligation is to return it with a gain. The expiration date on blaming others for anything comes the moment you realize blame robs you of your agency.

Yes, working imaginatively within this reality makes it hard. Your job is operations *and* growth. Your job is to be ambidextrous, to think with both sides of your brain. Your job as emerging leaders, the kind we desperately need, requires an "and." Company out *and* market back. You have to optimize today *and* plant the seeds for tomorrow. The world is physical *and* digital. Get used to living in the in-between. The old is going away, and the new is emerging. You have to plan for multiple possible futures emerging, potentially all at once.

These are times of widening imagination gaps—where possibility goes to die. But I refuse to give up on possibility. And neither

If failure is not an
option, then neither
is success.

should you. But let's be clear, we are talking about a disciplined, action-oriented, adaptive form of problem-solving and judgment, using your critical thinking skills. It's about meeting change early. It's about being ready for change and not being surprised. It is about the ability to imagine it forward.

1. **Explore.** Discovery needs to be a continuous part of your routine. Replace an obsession with competence for curiosity. Give yourself permission to leave the familiar and seek out variation: hang out with strange people, learn provocative ideas, play with crazy tools, and visit unexpected places. Get weird. Think of life as a scavenger hunt with unimaginable rewards.

2. **Have a vision and a mission.** Tell stories about the new future you can make together with others. Get it out of your imagination and into reality. Sell it. Take action.

3. **Experiment.** Ask better questions. Create hypotheses inspired by your discoveries and test them. You won't get it right the first time. Or even the fifth time. Trial and error is the way we learn. Embrace failure, but make it fast, cheap, and survivable. At GE, going big is all we've known. The trick here is to find the right Goldilocks scale for your experiments: big enough to learn from but not so big that your bets will kill you.

4. **Share. Open up. Be transparent.** Learning to work out loud in a generous, trusting, connected way will facilitate the creation of robust feedback loops that allow you to learn and pivot with greater and greater speed and confidence.

5. **Be an emergent leader.** We're not there yet, but I can see the day in my mind's eye when nearly everyone at every level of this organization is experimenting daily, asking provocative "What if?" questions, unafraid of failure, ambidextrously attending to the company's core as they invent its future—emergent leaders running an adaptive organization that is in a constant state of reinvention.

Listen, not everyone gets to the end with a victory lap. Transformation is messy. Legacy doesn't take kindly to its obsolescence. You have to just keep working it. GE is a radically different company from the one I started with twenty-five years ago. We're more open, more entrepreneurial, and just as committed to creating the things that move, power, build, and cure the world. Clean technologies, a digital industrial company leading the fourth industrial revolution, additive manufacturing, small aviation, cell therapies, low-cost/high-tech accessible health care, these are just a few of the ways in which GE is changing the world right now.

I can't promise you a meaningful career unblemished by failure (actually, the opposite). You will struggle. What I can promise is that this kind of life, this kind of approach to leadership, will give you a more creative, a more impactful, a more purposeful career. This is business at its best.

You just have to believe two things: (1) tomorrow can be better than today, and (2) you have the power to make it so.

You are not a robot.

You're a change-maker.

You can do this.

How to Be an Emergent Leader

This book has outlined the mind-set and tactics needed to evolve as a more emergent leader—one who is ready to meet change early, navigate ambiguity, and help develop a future few can see. Here is my summary of the essential considerations for you and your team.

Ditch hierarchy. With the rise of more distributed teams and a mandate for speed and collaboration, hierarchies simply aren't effective. Organize teams around a specific mission or project, regardless of who reports to whom. Focus functional and operational reporting for critical business process and talent development.

Organize around information flows. Find ways to get data into your team projects faster. As more data becomes available, from people and machines, it gives you clues as to how to organize your teams—ideally as close to the customer as possible. For example, marketing and service teams must become customer-loyalty focused, driven to improve the customer experience quickly.

Develop a good MO. Give your team a clear brief—a Mission Objective—of what is expected, by when, and then allow them the freedom to get there and to test and fail small along the way. Increasingly, your job as a team leader or manager is to be a troubleshooter and a coach. Micromanagers aren't needed.

Seek and use feedback. Find ways to get more feedback on everything you do; ask for feedback at every interaction. It could be as simple as: Tell me one thing I didn't want to hear.

Or, Did our meeting meet your expectations? Continually get and give feedback with teams, the faster the better.

Get used to living in the in-between. Rapid, emerging change is the hallmark of our era. The old is going away and the new is emerging, at once. You will rarely have certainty and never enough data. Move forward with hypotheses and multiple scenarios, and test and learn opportunities. With faster data, you can evaluate. Know when and how to pivot your strategy and actions and still align to long-term vision.

EPILOGUE

I n late 2017, it was time for me to leave GE—this time for real, coming six months after Jeff Immelt's departure. It was the end of another era of leadership and transformation at GE. Those 16 years had felt like 112 in dog years in many ways, as we navigated through what I believe will stand as one of history's big reorderings, driven by tectonic shifts in technology and global economics. GE had certainly been reordered. In all, more than $90 billion of portfolio changes had taken place in that time. The company had become more global, more industrial, more innovative, more willing to step boldly into the new.

We had forged GE's digital path, and while still in the early stages, it was gaining traction with customers as more companies faced their digital reckoning—something that will indeed reshape most every company as they figure out how to thrive in that in-between space of physical meets digital. Most promising was GE's move into digital manufacturing, including 3-D printing metals. This could dramatically transform GE's future, playing to the company's strengths in material science and making things, and allowing GE to enter new industries like auto and aerospace parts, and even replacement parts for humans (starting with titanium hips and knees). Walk through Additive HQ in Westchester, Ohio, and you get a glimpse of the future. Collaboration, iteration, open source shape the way teams work. Jet engine parts that used to contain three hundred components are now printed as one. Teams are organized around solving a problem, delivering on missions. David Joyce, who leads Aviation and seeded additive manufacturing there, stands as an example of a leader who encouraged his teams to optimize today and also have the conviction to find, and fight for, the future. I can point to many other leaders similarly poised to shape and impact the future, if they grab the chance.

There was much to be proud of. I am proud of our work; we had impact. The culture moved faster, personal agency had taken root in parts of GE. Many people adapted to the increased pace of change. We grew businesses. GE stayed relevant and lived to see more days ahead—something that gets harder the older and bigger a company gets.

But it wasn't enough; it wasn't fast enough. The raging river of change rushed on.

With Jeff's departure, there was no victory lap, no transition worthy of the Pope, or even a celebrated CEO. Those days were gone. An activist investor bought shares in GE, amplifying pressure on short-term wins—the activist's disruptive playbook, something we might have imagined. GE's energy businesses hadn't performed well enough—some managers had failed to react faster to rapid change in service models and the growth of distributed, renewable energy. On top of this, GE tried to absorb the gargantuan acquisition of Alstom with its base of old, declining technology. The company had gaps to fill, especially to make up for the loss of GE Capital revenue and its remaining debt. Earnings targets got harder to meet. Once again, the company faced a reset moment. Investors and media critics shouted their outrage as GE's stock price declined precipitously.

Many didn't seem to understand how complex GE's transformation was. Now, GE stands as a case study of how hard it is to navigate the tension between short-term gains and long-term readiness. Investors have little patience and markets don't forgive. Lost in the dramatic reaction was that Jeff had been a courageous leader at a time when business urgently needs bold leadership. He had focused the company on industrial technology; pushed to new places; absorbed risks, setbacks, and fears of those around him. I am better because of his championship. GE was too.

John Flannery, GE's new CEO, brings his back-to-basics approach to the company, cutting costs and dramatically reducing structure. In one of our early meetings, John told me he was going to sell Current. "The team has done a great job, and I get why it's important, but it's just too small for GE." My heart broke at that; I know how the team had persevered; that distributed energy is the future. But I'm betting on Maryrose and the team to make their future; in many ways they will be better on their own. John continued to narrow GE, spinning off businesses including Healthcare, in an effort to meet investor calls for a simpler GE. GE became the last original company to fall off the Dow Jones Industrial Index—its place on the Index something we had pointed to proudly as a sign of our resiliency. You're winning until you're not. The punch to the mouth, swift and stinging.

I want to believe that there is still a place for innovative legacy companies in the world—companies whose products make the world work better and whose people find purpose in that mission. I experienced GE's impact, it is real, profound. There has to be a more sustainable model for how some companies grow—trees do not grow to the sky, nor do companies. But alas, no company is guaranteed immortality—no story, no business plan, no good intention can replace committed, constant adaptation.

This is a call for leaders who are ready for whatever emerges, courageous and committed to the power of change. You make your

You have to believe two things: (1) tomorrow can be better than today, and (2) you have the power to make it so.

own reset moments and must move swiftly to do so. Company management, boards—even investors (I'm an optimist!)—must honestly evaluate their leaders' imagination gaps, ability to move forward without all the answers, and communicate a vision, not just march on with precision.

And yes, even change-makers must change. I stayed longer than I should have. Twenty-seven years at one company today is a long time for anyone. Knowing your exit ramp is also part of the journey.

I loved GE for all its possibility—but not always its reality. The struggle to change didn't need to be so hard, and I'm not sure why I was attracted to it, except that I believe in fighting for a better future. Many talented others did too. We were committed, all in. If you see a better way, you have an obligation to pursue it. That's the change-makers rallying cry. Writing this book was a way to document the hard, messy, wonderful struggle to adapt to change, to open up and innovate more. I am grateful for the apprenticeship and support that many leaders and sparks offered to me. And for the opportunities that unlocked in me the joy of discovery and power of change. Here's how I sum it up:

- The world will never be slower or simpler than it is today. Wishing it so will not make it so.
- Change is part of everyone's job. Transformation is a never-ending journey, for your company, for your team, for you.
- The future is made by those who can go forth with courage, with adaptable, open minds, learning to discover, to agitate and instigate, and to collaborate and build, always with a bias for action.
- Story is the glue that binds us. We *need* stories to give our work and our lives meaning. Strategy is a story well told. Vision and courageous leadership never go out of style.
- Believe in possibility. Get comfortable with not knowing, with living in the in-between of what was and what will be.

Get comfortable with
not knowing, with living
in the in-between of
what was and what
will be.

It's hard. As Nobel Prize–winning economist Daniel Kahneman said (on Krista Tippett's *On Being*): "It's a very difficult principle to grasp, this idea that actually what I don't know matters enormously, and what I can't see matters enormously. The interpretation of the world imposes itself on us. We have too much confidence in our beliefs, and it really is associated with a failure of imagination."

That's it. I believe devoutly in our humanity, in our creativity, and in our need to make meaning in our lives and our work. We can't give up on imagination and possibility. Tomorrow always comes. And that's why the struggle is worth it. So now I'm off to do what I do best—to discover, imagine, struggle, and create again. I tell myself: You *can* be this. Do this. You can imagine it forward.

....
: **PERMISSION SLIP** :
....

Please excuse _____ from the way things have
                  (YOUR NAME HERE)
always been done.

Time's up on standard operating procedure.

_____ admits he/she doesn't have the answers. So
      (YOUR NAME HERE)
please excuse _____ from the expectation that they
                  (YOUR NAME HERE)
have any of it figured out.

The solution is out there. But only if you permit _____
                                                      (YOUR NAME HERE)
to try, and probably to fail and then to keep trying. The process won't be neat.

It won't fit into a crisp Power Point presentation. Instead, it will be scary and

messy and, well, weird. But that will be courageous. And awesome. And the

start of change.

Signature _____

ACKNOWLEDGMENTS

It would take volumes to thank all of the people who've helped me get here. I hope you know how much you mean to me and how honored I am to have called you colleague, teacher, and friend. GE proved to be a vital training ground for me—equal parts finishing school, business school, global immersion, and pure leadership excellence. Thank you, all.

It's times like these when the final product is not at all what I imagined, yet weirdly, much richer. The hard things turned out to be easy, and the easy to be hard. Actually, there was little easy about doing this book! Getting the tangled hairball of thoughts out of my head and into this book ranks among the hardest things I've done. That's why I want to express my gratitude here to the people who helped get the book done well.

A huge thank-you to Elyse Cheney, my literary agent. Everyone should have an agent as ferocious about quality, with as good a sense of humor and partnership as Elyse. Thanks to the Cheney Agency—Adam Eaglin, Alice Whitwham, Alex Jacobs, Claire Gillespie, and Peter Finnerty.

Thank you to Tahl Raz, my collaborator, who had the tough job of wrestling a career's worth of ideas and experiences into great shape and with the right turns of phrase. We were united in our shared interest in psychology and belief in the power of change.

Thank you to the Currency team. Editor Roger Scholl helped me experience the master craft of great editing. Thanks to publisher Tina Constable for her support, never sweating it out (at least not in front of me). And to David Drake, Campbell Wharton, Ayelet

Gruenspecht, and Megan Perritt from the sales, marketing, and publicity teams—thank you for the great efforts.

To Evan Leatherwood, thank you for being an intellectual spark—especially for the prompts on emergence. I have valued the steady streams of challenge ideas and edits from you and team SJR.

To Lorna Montalvo, Sehr Thadhani, Annette Shade, and Claire Fitzsimmons: thank you for helping to produce, organize, and amplify efforts surrounding this book. I appreciate your creativity and reality checks.

I am grateful for the limitless patience, support, and love of my family: Chris, my husband, daughters Katie and Meredith; and my parents Gene and Shelby, brother, Matt, and sister, Susan. I love you all.

INDEX

Beth Comstock is the former vice chair of GE, where for twenty-five years she led GE's efforts to accelerate new growth. She built GE's Business Innovations and GE Ventures, which develops new businesses, and oversaw the reinvention of GE Lighting. She was named GE's chief marketing officer in 2003. She served as president of integrated media at NBC Universal from 2006 to 2008, overseeing the company's digital efforts, including the early formation of Hulu. She is a corporate director of Nike. Written about and profiled extensively in the media, from the *New York Times* to *Forbes, Fortune,* and *Fast Company,* she has been named to the *Fortune* and *Forbes* lists of the world's most powerful women.

Tahl Raz is an award-winning journalist and bestselling author. Find him at tahlraz.com.